B E O W U L F

ALSO BY SEAMUS HEANEY

POETRY

Death of a Naturalist

Door into the Dark

Wintering Out

North

Field Work

Poems 1965–1975

Sweeney Astray: A Version from the Irish

Station Island

The Haw Lantern

Selected Poems 1966–1987

Seeing Things

Sweeney's Flight (with photographs by Rachel Giese)

The Spirit Level

Opened Ground: Selected Poems 1966–1996

Electric Light

District and Circle

CRITICISM

Preoccupations: Selected Prose 1968–1978

The Government of the Tongue

The Redress of Poetry

Finders Keepers: Selected Prose 1971–2001

PLAYS

The Cure at Troy: A Version of Sophocles' Philoctetes

The Burial at Thebes: A Version of Sophocles' Antigone

ALSO BY JOHN D. NILES

Beowulf: The Poem and Its Tradition

Homo Narrans: The Poetics and Anthropology of Oral Literature

Old English Enigmatic Poems and the Play of the Texts

Old English Heroic Poems and the Social Life of Texts

Beowulf and Lejre

BEOWULF

AN ILLUSTRATED EDITION

TRANSLATED BY

SEAMUS HEANEY

Illustrations edited by
John D. Niles

W. W. NORTON & COMPANY
New York • *London*

Copyright © 2008 by W. W. Norton & Company, Inc.
Copyright © 2000 by Seamus Heaney

For information about permission to reproduce selections from this book, write to
Permissions, W. W. Norton & Company, Inc., 500 Fifth Avenue,
New York, NY 10110

For information about special discounts for bulk purchases, please contact
W. W. Norton Special Sales at specialsales@wwnorton.com or 800-233-4830

Manufacturing by RR Donnelley, Crawfordsville, IN
Production manager: Anna Oler

Library of Congress Cataloging-in-Publication Data

Beowulf : an illustrated edition ; translated by Seamus Heaney ; illustrations
edited by John D. Niles. — 1st ed.
p. cm.
Includes bibliographical references.
ISBN 978-0-393-33010-6 (pbk.)
1. Epic poetry, English (Old). 2. Scandinavia—Poetry. 3. Monsters—Poetry.
4. Dragons—Poetry. I. Heaney, Seamus, 1939– II. Niles, John D.
PR1583.H434 2008
829'.3—dc22   2007027523

W. W. Norton & Company, Inc.
500 Fifth Avenue, New York, N.Y. 10110
www.wwnorton.com

W. W. Norton & Company Ltd.
Castle House, 75/76 Wells Street, London W1T 3QT

4 5 6 7 8 9 0

CONTENTS

INTRODUCTION

And now this is 'an inheritance' —
Upright, rudimentary, unshiftably planked
In the long ago, yet willable forward

Again and again and again.

BEOWULF: THE POEM

The poem called *Beowulf* was composed sometime between the middle of the seventh and the end of the tenth century of the first millennium, in the language that is to-day called Anglo-Saxon or Old English. It is a heroic narrative, more than three thousand lines long, concerning the deeds of a Scandinavian prince, also called Beowulf, and it stands as one of the foundation works of poetry in English. The fact that the English language has changed so much in the last thousand years means, however, that the poem is now generally read in translation and mostly in English courses at schools and universities. This has contributed to the impression that it was written (as Osip Mandelstam said of *The Divine Comedy*) "on official paper," which is unfortunate, since what we are dealing with is a work of the greatest imaginative vitality, a masterpiece where the structuring of the tale is as elaborate as the beautiful contrivances of its language. Its narrative elements may belong to a previous age but as a work of art it lives in its own continuous present, equal to our knowledge of reality in the present time.

The poem was written in England but the events it describes are set in Scandinavia, in a "once upon a time" that is partly historical. Its hero, Beowulf, is the biggest presence among the warriors in the land of the Geats, a territory situated in what is now southern Sweden, and early in the poem Beowulf crosses the sea to the land of the Danes in order to clear their country of a man-eating monster called Grendel. From this expedition (which involves him in a second contest with Grendel's mother) he returns in triumph and eventually rules for fifty years as king of his homeland. Then a dragon begins to terrorize the countryside and Beowulf must confront it. In a final climactic encounter, he does manage to slay the dragon, but he also meets his own death and enters the legends of his people as a warrior of high renown.

We know about the poem more or less by chance because it exists in one manuscript only. This unique copy (now in the British Library) barely survived a fire in the eighteenth century and was then transcribed and titled, retranscribed and edited, translated and adapted, interpreted and reinterpreted, until it has become canonical. For decades it has been a set book on English syllabuses at university level all over the world. The fact that many English departments require it to be studied in the original continues to generate resistance, most notably at Oxford University, where the pros and cons of the inclusion of part of it as a compulsory element in the English course have been debated regularly in recent years.

For generations of undergraduates, academic study of the poem was often just a matter of construing the meaning, getting a grip on the grammar and vocabulary of Anglo-Saxon, and being able to recognize, translate, and comment upon random extracts which were presented in the examinations. For generations of scholars too the interest had been textual and philological; then there developed a body of research into analogues and sources, a quest for stories and episodes in the folklore and legends of the Nordic peoples which would parallel or foreshadow episodes in *Beowulf*. Scholars were also preoccupied with fixing the exact time and place of the poem's composition, paying minute attention to linguistic, stylistic, and scribal details. More generally, they tried to establish the history and genealogy of the dynasties of Swedes and Geats and Danes to which the poet makes constant allusion; and they devoted themselves to a consideration of the world-view behind the poem, asking to what extent (if at all) the newly Christian understanding of the world which operates in the poet's designing mind displaces him from his imaginative at-homeness in the world of his poem—a pagan Germanic society governed by a heroic code of honour, one where the attainment of a name for warrior-prowess among the living overwhelms any concern about the soul's destiny in the afterlife.

However, when it comes to considering *Beowulf* as a work of literature, there is one publication that stands out. In 1936, the Oxford scholar and teacher J.R.R. Tolkien published an epoch-making paper entitled *"Beowulf:* The Monsters and the

Critics" which took for granted the poem's integrity and distinction as a work of art and proceeded to show in what this integrity and distinction inhered. He assumed that the poet had felt his way through the inherited material—the fabulous elements and the traditional accounts of an heroic past—and by a combination of creative intuition and conscious structuring had arrived at a unity of effect and a balanced order. He assumed, in other words, that the *Beowulf* poet was an imaginative writer rather than some kind of back-formation derived from nineteenth-century folklore and philology. Tolkien's brilliant literary treatment changed the way the poem was valued and initiated a new era—and new terms—of appreciation.

It is impossible to attain a full understanding and estimate of *Beowulf* without recourse to this immense body of commentary and elucidation. Nevertheless, readers coming to the poem for the first time are likely to be as delighted as they are discomfited by the strangeness of the names and the immediate lack of known reference points. An English speaker new to *The Iliad* or *The Odyssey* or *The Aeneid* will probably at least have heard of Troy and Helen, or of Penelope and the Cyclops, or of Dido and the golden bough. These epics may be in Greek and Latin, yet the classical heritage has entered the cultural memory enshrined in English so thoroughly that their worlds are more familiar than that of the first native epic, even though it was composed centuries after them. Achilles rings a bell, but not Scyld Scēfing. Ithaca leads the mind in a certain direction, but not Heorot. The Sibyl of Cumae will stir certain associations, but not bad Queen Modthryth. First-time readers of *Beowulf* very quickly rediscover the meaning of the term "the dark ages," and it is in the hope of dispelling some of the puzzlement they are bound to feel that I have added the marginal glosses which appear in the following pages.

Still, in spite of the sensation of being caught between a "shield-wall" of opaque references and a "word-hoard" that is old and strange, such readers are also bound to feel a certain "shock of the new." This is because the poem possesses a mythic potency. Like Shield Sheafson (as Scyld Scēfing is known in this translation), it arrives from somewhere beyond the known bourne of our experience, and having fulfilled its purpose (again like Shield), it passes once more into the beyond. In the intervening time, the poet conjures up a work as remote as Shield's funeral boat borne towards the horizon, as commanding as the horn-pronged gables of King Hrothgar's hall, as solid and dazzling as Beowulf's funeral pyre that is set ablaze at the end. These opening and closing scenes retain a haunting presence in the mind; they are set pieces but they have the life-marking power of certain dreams. They are like the pillars of the gate of horn, through which wise dreams of true art can still be said to pass.

What happens in between is what William Butler Yeats would have called a phantasmagoria. Three agons, three struggles in which the preternatural force-for-evil of the hero's enemies comes springing at him in demonic shapes. Three encounters with what the critical literature and the textbook glossaries call "the monsters." In three archetypal sites of fear: the barricaded night-house, the infested underwater current, and the reptile-haunted rocks of a wilderness. If we think of the poem in this way, its place in world art becomes clearer and more secure. We can conceive of it re-presented and transformed in performance in a *bunraku* theatre in Japan, where the puppetry and the poetry are mutually supportive, a mixture of technicolour spectacle and ritual chant. Or we can equally envisage it as an ani-mated cartoon (and there has been at least one shot at this already), full of mutat-ing graphics and minatory stereophonics. We can avoid, at any rate, the slightly cardboard effect which the word "monster" tends to introduce, and give the poem a fresh chance to sweep "in off the moors, down through the mist bands" of Anglo-Saxon England, forward into the global village of the third millennium.

Nevertheless, the dream element and overall power to haunt come at a certain readerly price. The poem abounds in passages which will leave an unprepared audi-ence bewildered. Just when the narrative seems ready to take another step ahead into the main Beowulf story, it sidesteps. For a moment it is as if we have been channel-surfed into another poem, and at two points in this translation I indicate that we are in fact participating in a poem-within-our-poem not only by the use of italics but by a slight quickening of pace and shortening of metrical rein. The passages occur in lines 883–914 and lines 1070–1158, and on each occasion a minstrel has begun to chant a poem as part of the celebration of Beowulf's achievement. In the former case, the minstrel expresses his praise by telling the story of Sigemund's victory over a dragon, which both parallels Beowulf's triumph over Grendel and prefigures his fatal encounter with the *wyrm* in his old age. In the latter—the most famous of what were once called the "digressions" in the poem, the one dealing with a fight between Danes and Frisians at the stronghold of Finn, the Frisian king—the song the minstrel sings has a less obvious bearing on the immediate situation of the hero, but its import is nevertheless central to both the historical and the imaginative world of the poem.

The "Finnsburg episode" envelops us in a society that is at once honour-bound and blood-stained, presided over by the laws of the blood-feud, where the kin of a person slain are bound to exact a price for the death, either by slaying the killer or by receiving satisfaction in the form of *wergild* (the "man-price"), a legally fixed compensation. The claustrophobic and doom-laden atmosphere of this interlude gives the reader an intense intimation of what *wyrd*, or fate, meant not only to the characters in the Finn story but to those participating in the main action of *Beowulf* itself. All conceive of themselves as hooped within the great wheel of necessity, in thrall to a code of loyalty and bravery, bound to seek glory in the eye of the warrior world. The little nations are grouped around their lord, the greater nations spoil for war and menace the little ones, a lord dies, defencelessness ensues, the enemy strikes, vengeance for the dead becomes an ethic for the living, bloodshed begets further bloodshed, the wheel turns, the generations tread and tread and tread. Which is what I meant above when I said that the import of the Finnsburg passage is central to the historical and imaginative world of the poem as a whole.

One way of reading *Beowulf* is to think of it as three agons in the hero's life, but another way would be to regard it as a poem which contemplates the destinies of three peoples by tracing their interweaving histories in the story of the central character. First we meet the Danes—variously known as the Shieldings (after Shield Sheafson, the founder of their line), the Ingwins, the Spear-Danes, the Bright-Danes, the West-Danes, and so on—a people in the full summer of their power, symbolized by the high hall built by King Hrothgar, one "meant to be a wonder of the world." The threat to this gilded order comes from within, from marshes beyond the pale, from the bottom of the haunted mere where "Cain's clan," in the shape of Grendel and his troll-dam, trawl and scavenge and bide their time. But it also comes from without, from the Heathobards, for example, whom the Danes have defeated in battle and from whom they can therefore expect retaliatory war (see 2020–69).

Beowulf actually predicts this turn of events when he goes back to his own country after saving the Danes (for the time being, at any rate) by staving off the two "reavers from hell." In the hall of his "ring-giver," Hygelac, lord of the Geats, the hero discourses about his adventures in a securely fortified cliff-top enclosure. But this security is only temporary, for it is the destiny of the Geat people to be left lordless in the end. Hygelac's alliances eventually involve him in deadly war with the Swedish king, Ongentheow, and even though he does not personally deliver the fatal stroke (two of his thanes are responsible for this—see 2484–89 and then the lengthier reprise of this incident at 2922–3003), he is known in the poem as "Ongentheow's killer." Hence it comes to pass that after the death of Beowulf, who eventually succeeds Hygelac, the Geats experience a great foreboding and the epic closes in a mood of sombre expectation. A world is passing away, the Swedes and others are massing on the borders to attack, and there is no lord or hero to rally the defence.

The Swedes, therefore, are the third nation whose history and destiny are woven into the narrative, and even though no part of the main action is set in their territory, they and their kings constantly stalk the horizon of dread within which the main protagonists pursue their conflicts and allegiances. The Swedish dimension gradually becomes an important element in the poem's emotional and imaginative geography, a geography which entails, it should be said, no very clear map-sense of the world, more an apprehension of menaced borders, of danger gathering beyond the mere and the marshes, of *mearc-stapas* "prowling the moors, huge marauders / from some other world."

Within these phantasmal boundaries, each lord's hall is an actual and a symbolic refuge. Here is heat and light, rank and ceremony, human solidarity and culture; the *duguð* share the mead-benches with the *geogoð*, the veterans with their tales of warrior kings and hero-saviours from the past rub shoulders with young braves—*þegnas, eorlas*, thanes, retainers—keen to win such renown in the future. The prospect of gaining a glorious name in the *wael-raes*, in the rush of battle-slaughter, the pride of defending one's lord and bearing heroic witness to the integrity of the bond between him and his hall-companions—a bond sealed in the *glēo* and *gidd* of peace-time feasting and ring-giving—this is what gave drive and sanction to the Germanic warrior-culture enshrined in *Beowulf*.

Heorot and Hygelac's hall are the hubs of this value system upon which the poem's action turns. But there is another, outer rim of value, a circumference of understanding within which the heroic world is occasionally viewed as from a distance and recognized for what it is, an earlier state of consciousness and culture, one which has not been altogether shed but which has now been comprehended as part of another pattern. And this circumference and pattern arise, of course, from the poet's Christianity and from his perspective as an Englishman looking back at places and legends which his ancestors knew before they made their migration from continental Europe to their new home on the island of the Britons. As a consequence of his doctrinal certitude, which is as composed as it is ardent, the poet can view the story-time of his poem with a certain historical detachment and even censure the ways of those who lived *in illo tempore*:

> *Sometimes at pagan shrines they vowed*
> *offerings to idols, swore oaths*
> *that the killer of souls might come to their aid*
> *and save the people. That was their way,*
> *their heathenish hope; deep in their hearts*
> *they remembered hell.*   (175–80)

At the same time, as a result of his inherited vernacular culture and the imaginative sympathy which distinguishes him as an artist, the poet can lend the full weight of his rhetorical power to Beowulf as he utters the first principles of the northern warrior's honour-code:

> *It is always better*
> *to avenge dear ones than to indulge in mourning.*
> *For every one of us, living in this world*
> *means waiting for our end. Let whoever can*
> *win glory before death. When a warrior is gone,*
> *that will be his best and only bulwark.*   (1384–89)

In an age when "the instability of the human subject" is constantly argued for if not presumed, there should be no problem with a poem which is woven from two such different psychic fabrics. In fact, *Beowulf* perfectly answers the early modern conception of a work of creative imagination as one in which conflicting realities find accommodation within a new order; and this reconciliation occurs, it seems to me, most poignantly and most profoundly in the poem's third section, once the dragon enters the picture and the hero in old age must gather his powers for the final climactic ordeal. From the moment Beowulf advances under the crags, into the comfortless arena bounded by the rock-wall, the reader knows he is one of those "marked by fate." The poetry is imbued with a strong intuition of *wyrd* hovering close, "unknowable but certain," and yet, because it is imagined within a consciousness which has learned to expect that the soul will find an ultimate home "among the steadfast ones," this primal human emotion has been transmuted into something less "zero at the bone," more metaphysically tempered.

A similar transposition from a plane of regard which is, as it were, helmeted and hall-bound to one which sees things in a slightly more heavenly light is discernible in the different ways the poet imagines gold. Gold is a constant element, gleaming solidly in underground vaults, on the breasts of queens or the arms and regalia of warriors on the mead-benches. It is loaded into boats as spoil, handed out in bent bars as hall gifts, buried in the earth as treasure, persisting underground as an affirmation of a people's glorious past and an elegy for it. It pervades the ethos of the poem the way sex pervades consumer culture. And yet the bullion with which Waels's son, Sigemund, weighs down the hold after an earlier dragon-slaying triumph (in the old days, long before Beowulf's time) is a more trustworthy substance than that which is secured behind the walls of Beowulf's barrow. By the end of the poem, gold has suffered a radiation from the Christian vision. It is not that it yet equals riches in the medieval sense of worldly corruption, just that its status as the ore of all value has been put in doubt. It is *lǣne*, transitory, passing from hand to hand, and its changed status is registered as a symptom of the changed world. Once the dragon is disturbed, the melancholy and sense of displacement which pervade the last movement of the poem enter the hoard as a disabling and ominous light. And the dragon himself, as a genius of the older order, is bathed in this light, so that even as he begins to stir, the reader has a premonition that the days of his empery are numbered.

Nevertheless, the dragon has a wonderful inevitability about him and a unique glamour. It is not that the other monsters are lacking in presence and aura; it is more that they remain, for all their power to terrorize, creatures of the physical world. Grendel comes alive in the reader's imagination as a kind of dog-breath in the dark, a fear of collision with some hard-boned and immensely strong android frame, a mixture of Caliban and hoplite. And while his mother too has a definite brute-bearing about her, a creature of slouch and lunge on land if seal-swift in the water, she nevertheless retains a certain non-strangeness. As antagonists of a hero being tested, Grendel and his mother possess an appropriate head-on strength. The poet may need them as figures who do the devil's work, but the poem needs them more as figures who call up and show off Beowulf's physical might and his superb gifts as a warrior. They are the right enemies for a young glory-hunter, instigators of the formal boast, worthy trophies to be carried back from the grim testing-ground— Grendel's arm is ripped off and nailed up, his head severed and paraded in Heorot. It is all consonant with the surge of youth and the compulsion to win fame "as wide as the wind's home, / as the sea around cliffs," utterly a manifestation of the Germanic heroic code.

Enter then, fifty years later, the dragon. From his dry-stone vault, from a nest where he is heaped in coils around the body-heated gold. Once he is wakened, there is something glorious in the way he manifests himself, a Fourth of July effulgence fireworking its path across the night sky; and yet, because of the centuries he has spent dormant in the tumulus, there is a foundedness as well as a lambency about him. He is at once a stratum of the earth and a streamer in the air, no painted dragon but a figure of real oneiric power, one that can easily survive the prejudice which arises at the very mention of the word "dragon." Whether in medieval art or in modern Disney cartoons, the dragon can strike us as far less horrific than he is meant to be, but in the final movement of *Beowulf*, he lodges himself in the imagination as *wyrd* rather than *wyrm*, more a destiny than a set of reptilian vertebrae.

Grendel and his mother enter Beowulf's life from the outside, accidentally, challenges which in other circumstances he might not have taken up, enemies from whom he might have been distracted or deflected. The dragon, on the other hand, is a given of his home ground, abiding in his underearth as in his understanding, waiting for the meeting, the watcher at the ford, the questioner who sits so sly, the "lion-limb," as Gerard Manley Hopkins might have called him, against whom Beowulf's body and soul must measure themselves. Dragon equals shadow-line, the psalmist's valley of the shadow of death, the embodiment of a knowledge deeply ingrained in the species which is the very knowledge of the price to be paid for physical and spiritual survival.

It has often been observed that all the scriptural references in *Beowulf* are to the Old Testament. The poet is more in sympathy with the tragic, waiting, unredeemed phase of things than with any transcendental promise. Beowulf's mood as he gets ready to fight the dragon—who could be read as a projection of Beowulf's own chthonic wisdom refined in the crucible of experience—recalls the mood of other tragic heroes: Oedipus at Colonus, Lear at his "ripeness is all" extremity, Hamlet in the last illuminations of his "prophetic soul":

> *no easy bargain*
> *would be made in that place by any man.*
>
> *The veteran king sat down on the cliff-top.*
> *He wished good luck to the Geats who had shared*

his hearth and his gold. He was sad at heart,
unsettled yet ready, sensing his death.
His fate hovered near, unknowable but certain.   *(2415–21)*

Here the poet attains a level of insight that approaches the visionary. The subjective and the inevitable are in perfect balance, what is solidly established is bathed in an element which is completely sixth-sensed, and indeed the whole slow-motion, constantly self-deferring approach to the hero's death and funeral continues to be like this. Beowulf's soul may not yet have fled "to its destined place among the steadfast ones," but there is already a beyond-the-grave aspect to him, a revenant quality about his resoluteness. This is not just metrical narrative full of anthropological interest and typical heroic-age motifs; it is poetry of a high order, in which passages of great lyric intensity—such as the "Lay of the Last Survivor" (2247–66) and, even more remarkably, the so-called "Father's Lament" (2444–62)—rise like emanations from some fissure in the bedrock of the human capacity to endure:

It was like the misery felt by an old man
who has lived to see his son's body
swing on the gallows. He begins to keen
and weep for his boy, watching the raven
gloat where he hangs: he can be of no help.
The wisdom of age is worthless to him.
Morning after morning, he wakes to remember
that his child has gone; he has no interest
in living on until another heir
is born in the hall . . .

. . . .

Alone with his longing, he lies down on his bed
and sings a lament; everything seems too large,
the steadings and the fields.

Such passages mark an ultimate stage in poetic attainment; they are the imaginative equivalent of Beowulf's spiritual state at the end, when he tells his men that "doom of battle will bear [their] lord away," in the same way that the sea-journeys so vividly described in lines 210–28 and 1903–24 are the equivalent of his exultant prime.

At these moments of lyric intensity, the keel of the poetry is deeply set in the element of sensation while the mind's lookout sways metrically and far-sightedly in the element of pure comprehension. Which is to say that the elevation of *Beowulf* is always, paradoxically, buoyantly down to earth. And nowhere is this more obviously and memorably the case than in the account of the hero's funeral with which the poem ends. Here the inexorable and the elegiac combine in a description of the funeral pyre being got ready, the body being burnt, and the barrow being constructed—a scene at once immemorial and oddly contemporary. The Geat woman who cries out in dread as the flames consume the body of her dead lord could come straight from a late-twentieth-century news report, from Rwanda or Kosovo; her keen is a nightmare glimpse into the minds of people who have survived traumatic, even monstrous events and who are now being exposed to a comfortless future. We immediately recognize her predicament and the pitch of her grief and find ourselves the better for having them expressed with such adequacy and dignity and unforgiving truth:

> On a height they kindled the hugest of all
> funeral fires; fumes of woodsmoke
> billowed darkly up, the blaze roared
> and drowned out their weeping, wind died down
> and flames wrought havoc in the hot bone-house,
> burning it to the core. They were disconsolate
> and wailed aloud for their lord's decease.
> A Geat woman too sang out in grief;
> with hair bound up, she unburdened herself
> of her worst fears, a wild litany
> of nightmare and lament: her nation invaded,
> enemies on the rampage, bodies in piles,
> slavery and abasement. Heaven swallowed the smoke.   (3143–55)

ABOUT THIS TRANSLATION

When I was an undergraduate at Queen's University, Belfast, I studied *Beowulf* and other Anglo-Saxon poems and developed not only a feel for the language but a fondness for the melancholy and fortitude that characterized the poetry. Consequently, when an invitation to translate the poem arrived from the editors of *The Norton Anthology of English Literature,* I was tempted to try my hand. While I had no great expertise in Old English, I had a strong desire to get back to the first stratum of the language and to "assay the hoard" (2509). This was during the middle years of the 1980s, when I had begun a regular teaching job at Harvard and was opening my ear to the untethered music of some contemporary American poetry. Saying yes to the *Beowulf* commission would be (I argued with myself) a kind of aural antidote, a way of ensuring that my linguistic anchor would stay lodged on the Anglo-Saxon sea-floor. So I undertook to do it.

Very soon, however, I hesitated. It was labour-intensive work, scriptorium-slow. I worked dutifully, like a sixth-former at homework. I would set myself twenty lines a day, write out my glossary of hard words in longhand, try to pick a way through the syntax, get the run of the meaning established in my head, and then hope that the lines could be turned into metrical shape and raised to the power of verse. Often, however, the whole attempt to turn it into modern English seemed to me like trying to bring down a megalith with a toy hammer. What had been so attractive in the first place, the hand-built, rock-sure feel of the thing, began to defeat me. I turned to other work, the commissioning editors did not pursue me, and the project went into abeyance.

Even so, I had an instinct that it should not be let go. An understanding I had worked out for myself concerning my own linguistic and literary origins made me reluctant to abandon the task. I had noticed, for example, that without any conscious intent on my part certain lines in the first poem in my first book conformed to the requirements of Anglo-Saxon metrics. These lines were made up of two balancing halves, each half containing two stressed syllables—"the spade sinks   into gravelly ground: / My father, digging.   I look down"—and in the case of the second line, there was alliteration linking "digging" and "down" across the caesura. Part of me, in other words, had been writing Anglo-Saxon from the start.

This was not surprising, given that the poet who had first formed my ear was Gerard Manley Hopkins. Hopkins was a chip off the Old English block, and the earliest lines I published when I was a student were as much pastiche Anglo-Saxon as they were pastiche Hopkins: "Starling thatch-watches and sudden swallow / Straight breaks to mud-nest, home-rest rafter" and so on. I have written about all this elsewhere and about the relation of my Hopkins ventriloquism to the speech patterns of Ulster—especially as these were caricatured by the poet W. R. Rodgers.

Ulster people, according to Rodgers, are "an abrupt people / who like the spiky consonants of speech / and think the soft ones cissy" and get a kick out of "anything that gives or takes attack / like Micks, Teagues, tinkers' gets, Vatican."

Joseph Brodsky once said that poets' biographies are present in the sounds they make and I suppose all I am saying is that I consider *Beowulf* to be part of my voice-right. And yet to persuade myself that I was born into its language and that its language was born into me took a while: for somebody who grew up in the political and cultural conditions of Lord Brookeborough's Northern Ireland, it could hardly have been otherwise.

Sprung from an Irish nationalist background and educated at a Northern Irish Catholic school, I had learned the Irish language and lived within a cultural and ideological frame that regarded it as the language which I should by rights have been speaking but which I had been robbed of. I have also written, for example, about the thrill I experienced when I stumbled upon the word *lachtar* in my Irish-English dictionary and found that this word, which my aunt had always used when speaking of a flock of chicks, was in fact an Irish language word, and, more than that, an Irish word associated in particular with County Derry. Yet here it was, surviving in my aunt's English speech generations after her forebears and mine had ceased to speak Irish. For a long time, therefore, the little word was—to borrow a simile from Joyce—like a rapier point of consciousness pricking me with an awareness of language-loss and cultural dispossession, and tempting me into binary thinking about language. I tended to conceive of English and Irish as adversarial tongues, as either/or conditions rather than both/ands, and this was an attitude which for a long time hampered the development of a more confident and creative way of dealing with the whole vexed question—the question, that is, of the relationship between nationality, language, history, and literary tradition in Ireland.

Luckily, I glimpsed the possibility of release from this kind of cultural determinism early on, in my first arts year at Queen's University, Belfast, when we were lectured on the history of the English language by Professor John Braidwood. Braidwood could not help informing us, for example, that the word "whiskey" is the same word as the Irish and Scots Gaelic word *uisce*, meaning water, and that the River Usk in Britain is therefore to some extent the River Uisce (or Whiskey); and so in my mind the stream was suddenly turned into a kind of linguistic river of rivers issuing from a pristine Celto-British Land of Cockaigne, a riverrun of Finnegans Wakespeak pouring out of the cleft rock of some pre-political, prelapsarian, ur-philological Big Rock Candy Mountain—and all of this had a wonderfully sweetening effect upon me. The Irish/English duality, the Celtic/Saxon antithesis were momentarily collapsed, and in the resulting etymological eddy a gleam of recognition flashed through the synapses and I glimpsed an elsewhere of potential which seemed at the same time to be a somewhere being remembered. The place on the language map where the Usk and the *uisce* and the whiskey coincided was definitely a place where the spirit might find a loophole, an escape route from what John Montague has called "the partitioned intellect," away into some unpartitioned linguistic country, a region where one's language would not be a simple badge of ethnicity or a matter of cultural preference or official imposition, but an entry into further language. And I eventually came upon one of these loopholes in *Beowulf* itself.

What happened was that I found in the glossary to C. L. Wrenn's edition of the poem the Old English word meaning "to suffer," the word *þolian*; and although at first it looked completely strange with its thorn symbol instead of the familiar *th*, I gradually realized that it was not strange at all, for it was the word that older and less educated people would have used in the country where I grew up. "They'll just have to learn to thole," my aunt would say about some family who had suffered an unforeseen bereavement. And now suddenly here was "thole" in theofficial textual world, mediated through the apparatus of a scholarly edition, a little bleeper to remind me that my aunt's language was not just a self-enclosed family possession but an historical heritage, one that involved the journey *þolian* had made north into Scotland and then across into Ulster with the planters and then across from the planters to the locals who had originally spoken Irish and then farther across again when the Scots Irish emigrated to the American South in the eighteenth century. When I read in John Crowe Ransom the line "Sweet ladies, long may ye bloom, and toughly I hope ye may thole," my heart lifted again, the world widened, something was furthered. The far-flungness of the word, the phenomenological pleasure of finding it variously transformed by Ransom's modernity and *Beowulf*'s venerability made me feel vaguely something for which again I only found the words years later. What I was experiencing as I kept meeting up with *thole* on its multicultural odyssey was the feeling which Osip Mandelstam once defined as a "nostalgia for world culture." And this was a nostalgia I didn't even know I suffered until I experienced its fulfilment in this little epiphany. It was as if, on the analogy of baptism by desire, I had undergone something like illumination by philology. And even though I did not know it at the time, I had by then reached the point where I was ready to translate *Beowulf*. *Þolian* had opened my right-of-way.

So, in a sense, the decision to accept Norton's invitation was taken thirty-five years before the invitation was actually issued. But between one's sense of readiness to take on a subject and the actual inscription of the first lines, there is always a problematical hiatus. To put it another way: from the point of view of the writer, words in a poem need what the Polish poet Anna Swir once called "the equivalent of a biological right to life." The erotics of composition are essential to the process, some pre-reflective excitation and orientation, some sense that your own little verse-craft can dock safe and sound at the big quay of the language. And this is as true for translators as it is for poets attempting original work.

It is one thing to find lexical meanings for the words and to have some feel for how the metre might go, but it is quite another thing to find the tuning fork that will give you the note and pitch for the overall music of the work. Without some melody sensed or promised, it is simply impossible for a poet to establish the translator's right-of-way into and through a text. I was therefore lucky to hear this enabling note almost straight away, a familiar local voice, one that had belonged to relatives of my father's, people whom I had once described in a poem as "big voiced Scullions."

I called them "big voiced" because when the men of the family spoke, the words they uttered came across with a weighty distinctness, phonetic units as separate and defined as delph platters displayed on a dresser shelf. A simple sentence such as "We cut the corn to-day" took on immense dignity when one of the Scullions spoke it. They had a kind of Native American solemnity of utterance, as if they were announcing verdicts rather than making small talk. And when I came to ask myself how I wanted *Beowulf* to sound in my version, I realized I wanted it to be speakable by one of those relatives. I therefore tried to frame the famous opening lines in cadences that would have suited their voices, but that still echoed with the sound and sense of the Anglo-Saxon:

Hwæt wē Gār-Dena   in geār-dagum
þēod-cyninga   þrym gefrūnon,
hū ðā æþelingas   ellen fremedon.

Conventional renderings of *hwæt*, the first word of the poem, tend towards the archaic literary, with "lo" and "hark" and "behold" and "attend" and—more colloquially—"listen" being some of the solutions offered previously. But in Hiberno-English Scullionspeak, the particle "so" came naturally to the rescue, because in that idiom "so" operates as an expression which obliterates all previous discourse and narrative, and at the same time functions as an exclamation calling for immediate attention. So, "so" it was:

So. The Spear-Danes in days gone by
and the kings who ruled them had courage and greatness.
We have heard of those princes' heroic campaigns.

I came to the task of translating *Beowulf* with a prejudice in favour of forthright delivery. I remembered the voice of the poem as being attractively direct, even though the diction was ornate and the narrative method at times oblique. What I had always loved was a kind of foursquareness about the utterance, a feeling of living inside a constantly indicative mood, in the presence of an understanding that assumes you share an awareness of the perilous nature of life and are yet capable of seeing it steadily and, when necessary, sternly. There is an undeluded quality about the *Beowulf* poet's sense of the world which gives his lines immense emotional credibility and allows him to make general observations about life which are far too grounded in experience and reticence to be called "moralizing." These so-called "gnomic" parts of the poem have the cadence and force of earned wisdom, and their combination of cogency and verity was again something that I could remember from the speech I heard as a youngster in the Scullion kitchen. When I translate lines 24–25 as "Behaviour that's admired / is the path to power among people everywhere," I am attending as much to the grain of my original vernacular as to the content of the Anglo-Saxon lines. But then the evidence suggests that this middle ground between oral tradition and the demands of written practice was also the ground occupied by the *Beowulf* poet. The style of the poem is hospitable to the kind of formulaic phrases which are the stock-in-trade of oral bards, and yet it is marked too by the self-consciousness of an artist convinced that "we must labour to be beautiful."

In one area, my own labours have been less than thorough-going. I have not followed the strict metrical rules that bound the Anglo-Saxon *scop*. I have been guided by the fundamental pattern of four stresses to the line, but I allow myself several transgressions. For example, I don't always employ alliteration, and sometimes I alliterate only in one half of the line. When these breaches occur, it is because I prefer to let the natural "sound of sense" prevail over the demands of the convention: I have been reluctant to force an artificial shape or an unusual word choice just for the sake of correctness.

In general, the alliteration varies from the shadowy to the substantial, from the properly to the improperly distributed. Substantial and proper are such lines as

> The fórtunes of wár   fávoured Hróthgar   (64)
> the híghest in the land,   would lénd advíce   (172)
> and fínd friéndship   in the Fáther's embráce   (188).

Here the caesura is definite, there are two stresses in each half of the line, and the first stressed syllable of the second half alliterates with the first or the second or both of the stressed syllables in the first half. The main deviation from this is one which other translators have allowed themselves—the freedom, that is, to alliterate on the fourth stressed syllable, a practice which breaks the rule but which nevertheless does bind the line together:

> We have héard of those prínces'   heróic campáigns   (3)
> and he cróssed óver   into the Lórd's kéeping   (27).

In the course of the translation, such deviations, distortions, syncopations, and extensions do occur; what I was after first and foremost was a narrative line that sounded as if it meant business, and I was prepared to sacrifice other things in pursuit of this directness of utterance.

The appositional nature of the Old English syntax, for example, is somewhat slighted here, as is the *Beowulf* poet's resourcefulness with synonyms and (to a lesser extent) his genius for compound-making, kennings, and all sorts of variation. Usually—as at line 1209, where I render *ȳða ful* as "frothing wave-vat," and line 1523, where *beado-lēoma* becomes "battle-torch"—I try to match the poet's analogy-seeking habit at its most original; and I use all the common coinages for the lord of the nation, variously referred to as "ring-giver," "treasure-giver," "his people's shield" or "shepherd" or "helmet." I have been less faithful, however, to the way the poet rings the changes when it comes to compounds meaning a sword or a spear or a battle or any bloody encounter with foes. Old English abounds in vigorous and evocative and specifically poetic words for these things, but I have tended to follow modern usage and in the main have called a sword a sword.

There was one area, however, where a certain strangeness in the diction came naturally. In those instances where a local Ulster word seemed either poetically or historically right, I felt free to use it. For example, at lines 324 and 2988 I use the word "graith" for "harness" and at 3026 "hoked" for "rooted about" because the local term seemed in each case to have special body and force. Then, for reasons of historical suggestiveness, I have in several instances used the word "bawn" to refer to Hrothgar's hall. In Elizabethan English, bawn (from the Irish *bó-dhún*, a fort for cattle) referred specifically to the fortified dwellings which the English planters built in Ireland to keep the dispossessed natives at bay, so it seemed the proper term to apply to the embattled keep where Hrothgar waits and watches. Indeed, every time I read the lovely interlude that tells of the minstrel singing in Heorot just before the first attacks of Grendel, I cannot help thinking of Edmund Spenser in Kilcolman Castle, reading the early cantos of *The Faerie Queene* to Sir Walter Raleigh, just before the Irish burned the castle and drove Spenser out of Munster back to the Elizabethan court. Putting a bawn into *Beowulf* seems one way for an Irish poet to come to terms with that complex history of conquest and colony, absorption and resistance, integrity and antagonism, a history which has to be clearly acknowledged by all concerned in order to render it ever more "willable forward / Again and again and again."

S.H.

ACKNOWLEDGEMENTS

The proposal that I should translate *Beowulf* came in the early 1980s from the editors of *The Norton Anthology of English Literature*, so my first thanks go to M. H. Abrams and Jon Stallworthy, who encouraged the late John Benedict to commission some preliminary passages. Then, when I got going in earnest, Norton appointed Professor Alfred David to keep a learned eye on what I was making of the original, and without his annotations on the first draft and his many queries and suggested alternatives as the manuscript advanced towards completion, this translation would have been a weaker and a wobblier thing. Al's responses were informed by scholarship and by a lifetime's experience of teaching the poem, so they were invaluable. Nevertheless, I was often reluctant to follow his advice and persisted many times in what we both knew were erroneous ways, so he is not to be held responsible for any failures here in the construing of the original or for the different directions in which it is occasionally skewed.

I am also grateful to W. W. Norton & Company for allowing the translation to be published by Faber and Faber in London and Farrar, Straus and Giroux in New York.

At Faber's, I benefited greatly from Christopher Reid's editorial pencil on the first draft and Paul Keegan's on the second. I also had important encouragement and instruction in the latter stages of the work from colleagues at Harvard, who now include by happy coincidence the present General Editor of *The Norton Anthology*, Professor Stephen Greenblatt. I remember with special pleasure a medievalists' seminar where I finally recanted on the use of the word "gilly" in the presence of Professors Larry Benson, Dan Donoghue, Joseph Harris, and Derek Pearsall. Professor John D. Niles happened to attend that seminar and I was lucky to enjoy another, too brief discussion with him in Berkeley, worrying about word choices and wondering about the prejudice in favour of Anglo-Saxon over Latinate diction in translations of the poem.

Helen Vendler's reading helped, as ever, in many points of detail, and I received other particular and important comments from Professor Mary Clayton and Peter Sacks.

Extracts from the first hundred lines of the translation appeared in *The Haw Lantern* (1987) and *Causley at 70* (1987). Excerpts from the more recent work were published in *Agni, The Sunday Times, The Threepenny Review, The Times Literary Supplement*; also in *A Parcel of Poems: For Ted Hughes on His Sixty-fifth Birthday* and *The Literary Man, Essays Presented to Donald W. Hannah*. Lines 88–98 were printed in January 1999 by Bow & Arrow Press as a tribute to Professor William Alfred, himself a translator of the poem and, while he lived, one of the great teachers of it. Bits of the introduction first appeared in *The Sunday Times* and in an article entitled "Further Language" (*Studies in the Literary Imagination*, vol. XXX, no. 2). The epigraph to the introduction is from my poem "The Settle Bed" (*Seeing Things*, 1991). The broken lines on p. 151 indicate lacunae in the original text.

S.H.

A NOTE ON NAMES

Old English, like Modern German, contained many compound words, most of which have been lost in Modern English. Most of the names in *Beowulf* are compounds. Hrothgar is a combination of words meaning "glory" and "spear"; the name of his older brother, Heorogar, comes from "army" and "spear"; Hrothgar's sons Hrethric and Hrothmund contain the first elements of their father's name combined, respectively, with *ric* (kingdom, empire, Modern German *Reich*) and *mund* (hand, protection). As in the case of the Danish dynasty, family names often alliterate. Masculine names of the warrior class have military associations. The importance of family and the demands of alliteration frequently lead to the designation of characters by formulas identifying them in terms of relationships. Thus Beowulf is referred to as "son of Ecgtheow" or "kinsman of Hygelac" (his uncle and lord).

The Old English spellings of names are mostly preserved in the translation. A few rules of pronunciation are worth keeping in mind. Initial *H* before *r* was sounded, and so Hrothgar's name alliterates with that of his brother Heorogar. The combination *cg* has the value of *dg* in words like "edge." The first element in the name of Beowulf's father "Ecgtheow" is the same word as "edge," and, by the figure of speech called synecdoche (a part of something stands for the whole), *ecg* stands for *sword* and Ecgtheow means "sword-servant."

Alfred David

BEOWULF

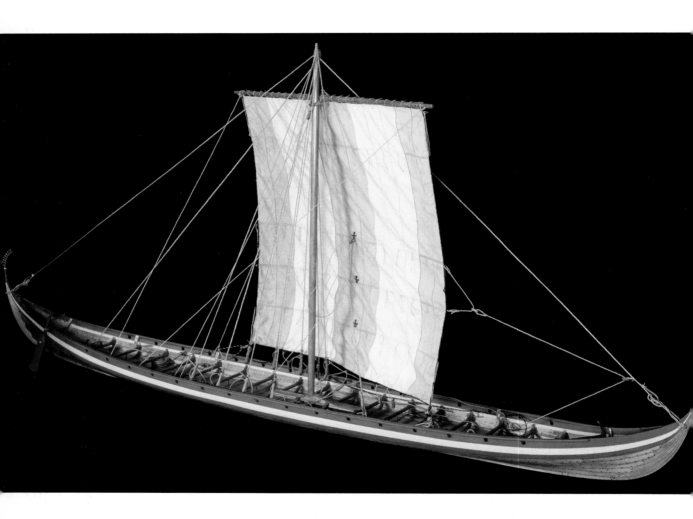

So. The Spear-Danes in days gone by
and the kings who ruled them had courage and greatness.
We have heard of those princes' heroic campaigns.

There was Shield Sheafson, scourge of many tribes,
a wrecker of mead-benches, rampaging among foes.
This terror of the hall-troops had come far.
A foundling to start with, he would flourish later on
as his powers waxed and his worth was proved.
In the end each clan on the outlying coasts
10 beyond the whale-road had to yield to him
and begin to pay tribute. That was one good king.

Afterwards a boy-child was born to Shield,
a cub in the yard, a comfort sent
by God to that nation. He knew what they had tholed,
the long times and troubles they'd come through
without a leader; so the Lord of Life,
the glorious Almighty, made this man renowned.
Shield had fathered a famous son:
Beow's name was known through the north.
20 And a young prince must be prudent like that,
giving freely while his father lives
so that afterwards in age when fighting starts

Model of Viking Age warship whose buried timbers were partially recovered at Ladby, on the island of Funen, Denmark. Despite some anachronism involved in this idea, the poet may have thought in terms of ships like this when speaking of tribute having been brought to Shield from "beyond the whale-road." Ninth or early tenth century.

steadfast companions will stand by him
and hold the line. Behaviour that's admired
is the path to power among people everywhere.

Shield was still thriving when his time came

Shield's funeral

and he crossed over into the Lord's keeping.
His warrior band did what he bade them
when he laid down the law among the Danes:
30   they shouldered him out to the sea's flood,
the chief they revered who had long ruled them.
A ring-whorled prow rode in the harbour,
ice-clad, outbound, a craft for a prince.
They stretched their beloved lord in his boat,
laid out by the mast, amidships,
the great ring-giver. Far-fetched treasures
were piled upon him, and precious gear.
I never heard before of a ship so well furbished
with battle tackle, bladed weapons
40   and coats of mail. The massed treasure
was loaded on top of him: it would travel far
on out into the ocean's sway.
They decked his body no less bountifully
with offerings than those first ones did
who cast him away when he was a child
and launched him alone out over the waves.
And they set a gold standard up
high above his head and let him drift
to wind and tide, bewailing him
50   and mourning their loss. No man can tell,
no wise man in hall or weathered veteran
knows for certain who salvaged that load.

Then it fell to Beow to keep the forts.

In 1986–1988, at Gammel Lejre near Roskilde on the island of Zealand, Denmark, were discovered the post-holes of a great hall built ca. A.D. 890. Further excavations in 2004–2005 revealed this to be the third of three halls built in succession at Lejre, which was famed during the Middle Ages as the former seat of power of the Shielding (or Skjöldung) kings. The earliest hall was built ca. 550.

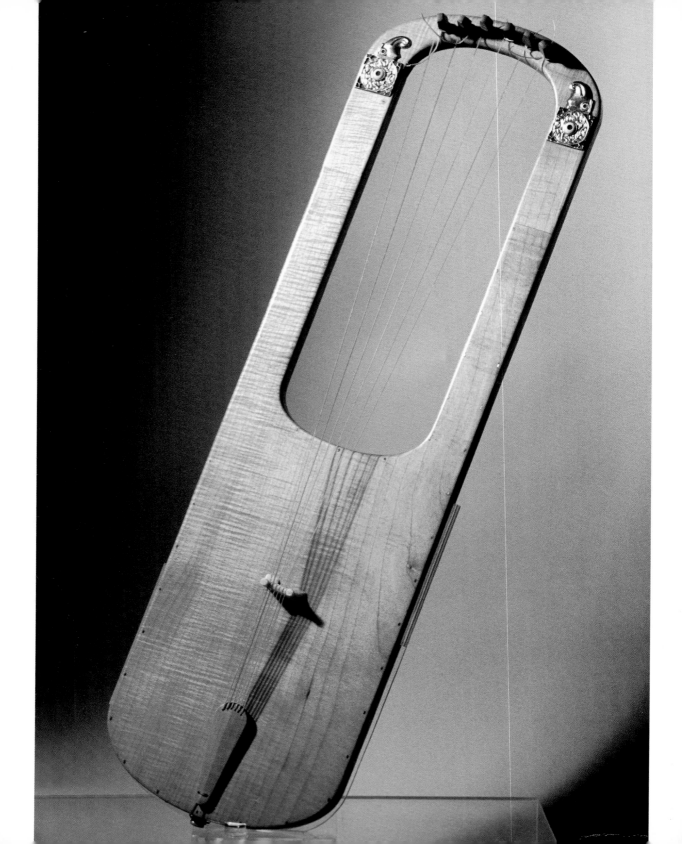

He was well regarded and ruled the Danes
for a long time after his father took leave
of his life on earth. And then his heir,
the great Halfdane, held sway
for as long as he lived, their elder and warlord.
He was four times a father, this fighter prince:
60   one by one they entered the world,
Heorogar, Hrothgar, the good Halga
and a daughter, I have heard, who was Onela's queen,
a balm in bed to the battle-scarred Swede.

*Shield's heirs: his son
Beow succeeded by
Halfdane, Halfdane by
Hrothgar*

The fortunes of war favoured Hrothgar.
Friends and kinsmen flocked to his ranks,
young followers, a force that grew
to be a mighty army. So his mind turned
to hall-building: he handed down orders
for men to work on a great mead-hall
70   meant to be a wonder of the world forever;
it would be his throne-room and there he would dispense
his God-given goods to young and old—
but not the common land or people's lives.
Far and wide through the world, I have heard,
orders for work to adorn that wallstead
were sent to many peoples. And soon it stood there,
finished and ready, in full view,
the hall of halls. Heorot was the name
he had settled on it, whose utterance was law.
80   Nor did he renege, but doled out rings
and torques at the table. The hall towered,
its gables wide and high and awaiting
a barbarous burning. That doom abided,
but in time it would come: the killer instinct
unleashed among in-laws, the blood-lust rampant.

*King Hrothgar builds
Heorot Hall*

Replica of lyre from Mound 1 at Sutton Hoo, Suffolk. Lyres have occasionally been found in high-status pagan graves of the late Germanic Iron Age. People of this era clearly enjoyed music and song, as they are shown doing at the beginning of Beowulf *when a court singer celebrates the Creation. This lyre had six strings and was made of beech wood. Seventh century.*

Then a powerful demon, a prowler through the dark, *Heorot is threatened*
nursed a hard grievance. It harrowed him
to hear the din of the loud banquet
every day in the hall, the harp being struck
90 and the clear song of a skilled poet
telling with mastery of man's beginnings,
how the Almighty had made the earth
a gleaming plain girdled with waters;
in His splendour He set the sun and the moon
to be earth's lamplight, lanterns for men,
and filled the broad lap of the world
with branches and leaves; and quickened life
in every other thing that moved.

So times were pleasant for the people there *Grendel, a monster descended from "Cain's clan," begins to prowl*
100 until finally one, a fiend out of hell,
began to work his evil in the world.
Grendel was the name of this grim demon
haunting the marches, marauding round the heath
and the desolate fens; he had dwelt for a time
in misery among the banished monsters,
Cain's clan, whom the Creator had outlawed
and condemned as outcasts. For the killing of Abel
the Eternal Lord had exacted a price:
Cain got no good from committing that murder
110 because the Almighty made him anathema
and out of the curse of his exile there sprang
ogres and elves and evil phantoms
and the giants too who strove with God
time and again until He gave them their reward.

So, after nightfall, Grendel set out *Grendel attacks Heorot*
for the lofty house, to see how the Ring-Danes

Portrait of a cannibalistic giant, from an Anglo-Saxon illustrated version of Wonders of the East *(London, British Library Cotton Tiberius B.v, fol. 81b detail). While no traveler would want to meet up with this creature, the satanic malice that the* Beowulf *poet ascribes to Grendel is absent here. Compare, however, a different illustration from the same manuscript reproduced on page 46. Late eleventh century.*

9

were settling into it after their drink,
and there he came upon them, a company of the best
asleep from their feasting, insensible to pain
120   and human sorrow. Suddenly then
the God-cursed brute was creating havoc:
greedy and grim, he grabbed thirty men
from their resting places and rushed to his lair,
flushed up and inflamed from the raid,
blundering back with the butchered corpses.

Then as dawn brightened and the day broke
Grendel's powers of destruction were plain:
their wassail was over, they wept to heaven
and mourned under morning. Their mighty prince,
130   the storied leader, sat stricken and helpless,
humiliated by the loss of his guard,
bewildered and stunned, staring aghast
at the demon's trail, in deep distress.
He was numb with grief, but got no respite
for one night later merciless Grendel
struck again with more gruesome murders.
Malignant by nature, he never showed remorse.
It was easy then to meet with a man
shifting himself to a safer distance
140   to bed in the bothies, for who could be blind
to the evidence of his eyes, the obviousness
of that hall-watcher's hate? Whoever escaped
kept a weather-eye open and moved away.

So Grendel ruled in defiance of right,
one against all, until the greatest house

*King Hrothgar's
distress and
helplessness*

in the world stood empty, a deserted wallstead.
For twelve winters, seasons of woe,

One uncanny element in the Danish episodes of Beowulf *is that Grendel cannot approach Hrothgar's throne, which is apparently protected by God (lines 168–69). Thrones of this period were probably small, portable seats rather than towering structures. This carved stool, recovered from a boat burial at Feddersen Wierde, northern Germany, may be an example. Fifth century.*

the lord of the Shieldings suffered under
his load of sorrow; and so, before long,
150   the news was known over the whole world.
Sad lays were sung about the beset king,
the vicious raids and ravages of Grendel,
his long and unrelenting feud,
nothing but war; how he would never
parley or make peace with any Dane
nor stop his death-dealing nor pay the death-price.
No counsellor could ever expect
fair reparation from those rabid hands.
All were endangered; young and old
160   were hunted down by that dark death-shadow
who lurked and swooped in the long nights
on the misty moors; nobody knows
where these reavers from hell roam on their errands.

So Grendel waged his lonely war,
inflicting constant cruelties on the people,
atrocious hurt. He took over Heorot,
haunted the glittering hall after dark,
but the throne itself, the treasure-seat,
he was kept from approaching; he was the Lord's outcast.

170   These were hard times, heart-breaking
for the prince of the Shieldings; powerful counsellors,
the highest in the land, would lend advice,
plotting how best the bold defenders
might resist and beat off sudden attacks.
Sometimes at pagan shrines they vowed
offerings to idols, swore oaths
that the killer of souls might come to their aid
and save the people. That was their way,

The Danes, hard-pressed, turn for help to heathen gods

In their desperation, the Danes offer sacrifices at pagan shrines, a practice the poet sternly condemns. This small gold figurine from Slipshavn Skov, on the island of Funen, Denmark, is thought to have been a pagan idol. A figure that may represent a deity is depicted as naked except for a neck ring. The original is 6.7 cm (2³/₄ inches) in height. Ca. fifth century.

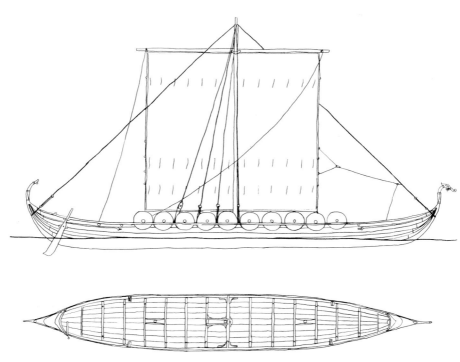

their heathenish hope; deep in their hearts
180   they remembered hell. The Almighty Judge
of good deeds and bad, the Lord God,
Head of the Heavens and High King of the World,
was unknown to them. Oh, cursed is he
who in time of trouble has to thrust his soul
in the fire's embrace, forfeiting help;
he has nowhere to turn. But blessed is he
who after death can approach the Lord
and find friendship in the Father's embrace.

So that troubled time continued, woe
190   that never stopped, steady affliction
for Halfdane's son, too hard an ordeal.
There was panic after dark, people endured
raids in the night, riven by the terror.

When he heard about Grendel, Hygelac's thane
was on home ground, over in Geatland.
There was no one else like him alive.
In his day, he was the mightiest man on earth,
high-born and powerful. He ordered a boat
that would ply the waves. He announced his plan:
200   to sail the swan's road and search out that king,
the famous prince who needed defenders.
Nobody tried to keep him from going,
no elder denied him, dear as he was to them.
Instead, they inspected omens and spurred
his ambition to go, whilst he moved about
like the leader he was, enlisting men,
the best he could find; with fourteen others
the warrior boarded the boat as captain,
a canny pilot along coast and currents.

Time went by, the boat was on water,

in close under the cliffs.

Men climbed eagerly up the gangplank,

sand churned in surf, warriors loaded

a cargo of weapons, shining war-gear

in the vessel's hold, then heaved out,

away with a will in their wood-wreathed ship.

Over the waves, with the wind behind her

and foam at her neck, she flew like a bird

until her curved prow had covered the distance

220 and on the following day, at the due hour,

those seafarers sighted land,

sunlit cliffs, sheer crags

and looming headlands, the landfall they sought.

It was the end of their voyage and the Geats vaulted

over the side, out on to the sand,

and moored their ship. There was a clash of mail

and a thresh of gear. They thanked God

for that easy crossing on a calm sea.

When the watchman on the wall, the Shieldings' lookout

230 whose job it was to guard the sea-cliffs,

saw shields glittering on the gangplank

and battle-equipment being unloaded

he had to find out who and what

the arrivals were. So he rode to the shore,

this horseman of Hrothgar's, and challenged them

in formal terms, flourishing his spear:

"What kind of men are you who arrive

rigged out for combat in coats of mail,

sailing here over the sea-lanes

240 in your steep-hulled boat? I have been stationed

The hero and his troop sail from the land of the Geats

The Danish coast-guard challenges the outsiders

As a gesture asserting his authority, the watchman who guards the Danish coast shakes his spear overhead when addressing the strangers who have landed. Spears were the basic weapon of war for men of this era. This silver-inlaid spearhead, recovered from a bog at Vimose, on the island of Funen, Denmark, must have belonged to a person of high rank. Early third century.

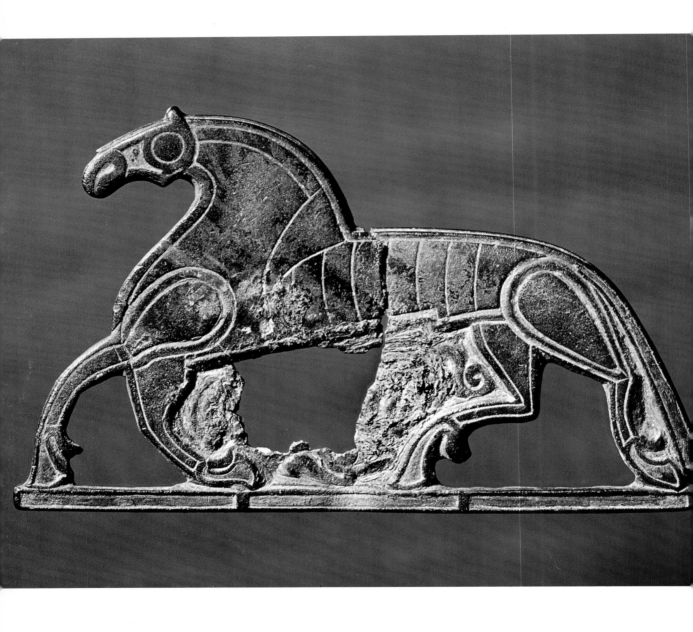

as lookout on this coast for a long time.
My job is to watch the waves for raiders,
any danger to the Danish shore.
Never before has a force under arms
disembarked so openly—not bothering to ask
if the sentries allowed them safe passage
or the clan had consented. Nor have I seen
a mightier man-at-arms on this earth
than the one standing here: unless I am mistaken,
250   he is truly noble. This is no mere
hanger-on in a hero's armour.
So now, before you fare inland
as interlopers, I have to be informed
about who you are and where you hail from.
Outsiders from across the water,
I say it again: the sooner you tell
where you come from and why, the better."

The leader of the troop unlocked his word-hoard;
the distinguished one delivered this answer:

*The Geat hero
announces himself and
explains his mission*

260   "We belong by birth to the Geat people
and owe allegiance to Lord Hygelac.
In his day, my father was a famous man,
a noble warrior-lord named Ecgtheow.
He outlasted many a long winter
and went on his way. All over the world
men wise in counsel continue to remember him.
We come in good faith to find your lord
and nation's shield, the son of Halfdane.
Give us the right advice and direction.
270   We have arrived here on a great errand
to the lord of the Danes, and I believe therefore
there should be nothing hidden or withheld between us.

Fine horses were signs of wealth and status during the Germanic Iron Age, just as they are today. They are sometimes depicted in stylized form in the metalwork of this period, as in this example from Veggerslev, Jutland, Denmark. The Danish coast-guard in Beowulf *is mounted, and his horse lends him prestige as well as the ability to respond quickly to danger. Ca. eighth century.*

So tell us if what we have heard is true
about this threat, whatever it is,
this danger abroad in the dark nights,
this corpse-maker mongering death
in the Shieldings' country. I come to proffer
my wholehearted help and counsel.
I can show the wise Hrothgar a way
280 to defeat his enemy and find respite—
if any respite is to reach him, ever.
I can calm the turmoil and terror in his mind.
Otherwise, he must endure woes
and live with grief for as long as his hall
stands at the horizon, on its high ground."

*The coast-guard allows
the Geats to pass*

Undaunted, sitting astride his horse,
the coast-guard answered, "Anyone with gumption
and a sharp mind will take the measure
of two things: what's said and what's done.
290 I believe what you have told me: that you are a troop
loyal to our king. So come ahead
with your arms and your gear, and I will guide you.
What's more, I'll order my own comrades
on their word of honour to watch your boat
down there on the strand—keep her safe
in her fresh tar, until the time comes
for her curved prow to preen on the waves
and bear this hero back to Geatland.
May one so valiant and venturesome
300 come unharmed through the clash of battle."

So they went on their way. The ship rode the water,
broad-beamed, bound by its hawser
and anchored fast. Boar-shapes flashed

*The arms worn by Beowulf's men identify them as members of the aristocratic warrior class. "Boar-shapes
flashed" on their helmets, the poet states. This image of a boar from Benty Grange, Derbyshire, surmounted a
helmet as an emblem of ferocity in war. Though modeled in part on Roman parade helmets, Germanic helmets
had a distinctive style. Late seventh or early eighth century.*

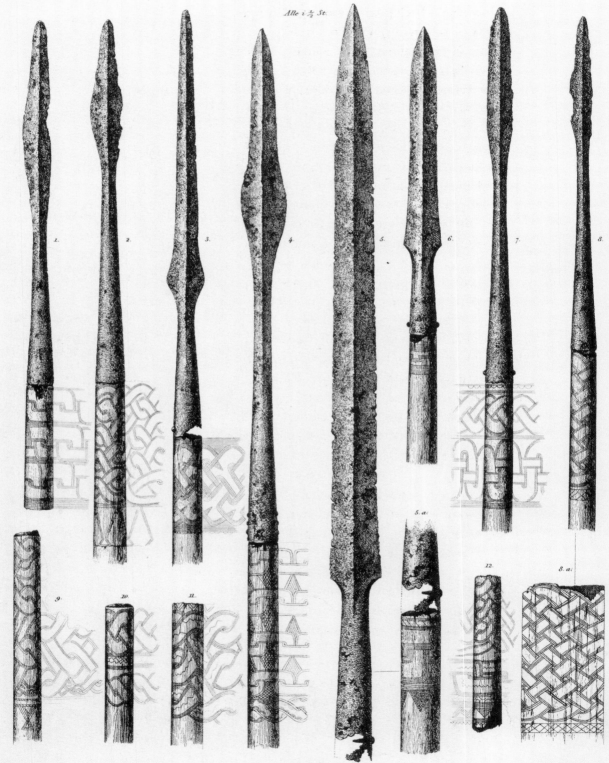

Alle i ½ St.

1. 2. 3. 4. 5. 6. 7. 8.

9. 10. 11. 5. a. 12. 8. a.

J. Magn. Petersen del. & sc.

above their cheek-guards, the brightly forged
work of goldsmiths, watching over
those stern-faced men. They marched in step,
hurrying on till the timbered hall
rose before them, radiant with gold.
Nobody on earth knew of another
310 building like it. Majesty lodged there,
its light shone over many lands.
So their gallant escort guided them
to that dazzling stronghold and indicated
the shortest way to it; then the noble warrior
wheeled on his horse and spoke these words:
"It is time for me to go. May the Almighty
Father keep you and in His kindness
watch over your exploits. I'm away to the sea,
back on alert against enemy raiders."

320 It was a paved track, a path that kept them
in marching order. Their mail-shirts glinted,
hard and hand-linked; the high-gloss iron
of their armour rang. So they duly arrived
in their grim war-graith and gear at the hall,
and, weary from the sea, stacked wide shields
of the toughest hardwood against the wall,
then collapsed on the benches; battle-dress
and weapons clashed. They collected their spears
in a seafarers' stook, a stand of greyish
330 tapering ash. And the troops themselves
were as good as their weapons.

                Then a proud warrior
questioned the men concerning their origins:
"Where do you come from, carrying these
decorated shields and shirts of mail,

They arrive at Heorot

The Geatish warriors visiting Heorot are not permitted to carry their ordinary weapons into the hall, which was a sanctuary. Instead, they stack their shields and spears outside the door. These spears with decorated shafts were recovered from Kragehul bog, Funen, Denmark, where they were deposited as a votive offering. Third century.

these cheek-hinged helmets and javelins?
I am Hrothgar's herald and officer.
I have never seen so impressive or large
an assembly of strangers. Stoutness of heart,
bravery not banishment, must have brought you to Hrothgar."

340   The man whose name was known for courage,
the Geat leader, resolute in his helmet,
answered in return: "We are retainers
from Hygelac's band. Beowulf is my name.
If your lord and master, the most renowned
son of Halfdane, will hear me out
and graciously allow me to greet him in person,
I am ready and willing to report my errand."

Beowulf announces his name

Wulfgar replied, a Wendel chief
renowned as a warrior, well known for his wisdom

Formalities are observed

350   and the temper of his mind: "I will take this message,
in accordance with your wish, to our noble king,
our dear lord, friend of the Danes,
the giver of rings. I will go and ask him
about your coming here, then hurry back
with whatever reply it pleases him to give."

With that he turned to where Hrothgar sat,
an old man among retainers;
the valiant follower stood four-square
in front of his king: he knew the courtesies.
360   Wulfgar addressed his dear lord:
"People from Geatland have put ashore.
They have sailed far over the wide sea.
They call the chief in charge of their band

King Hrothgar promises to reward Beowulf handsomely if the hero succeeds in killing Grendel. This collection of precious objects, known as the Lejre hoard, was discovered in 1850 not far from the village of Lejre, on the island of Zealand. Though of later date than the time when the poem is set, it would have been a suitable reward for someone's exceptional service. Early Viking period.

by the name of Beowulf. They beg, my lord,
an audience with you, exchange of words
and formal greeting. Most gracious Hrothgar,
do not refuse them, but grant them a reply.
From their arms and appointment, they appear well born
and worthy of respect, especially the one
370   who has led them this far: he is formidable indeed."

Hrothgar, protector of Shieldings, replied:

Hrothgar recognizes Beowulf's name and approves his arrival

"I used to know him when he was a young boy.
His father before him was called Ecgtheow.
Hrethel the Geat gave Ecgtheow
his daughter in marriage. This man is their son,
here to follow up an old friendship.
A crew of seamen who sailed for me once
with a gift-cargo across to Geatland
returned with marvellous tales about him:
380   a thane, they declared, with the strength of thirty
in the grip of each hand. Now Holy God
has, in His goodness, guided him here
to the West-Danes, to defend us from Grendel.
This is my hope; and for his heroism
I will recompense him with a rich treasure.
Go immediately, bid him and the Geats
he has in attendance to assemble and enter.
Say, moreover, when you speak to them,
they are welcome to Denmark."
                 At the door of the hall,
390   Wulfgar duly delivered the message:
"My lord, the conquering king of the Danes,
bids me announce that he knows your ancestry;
also that he welcomes you here to Heorot
and salutes your arrival from across the sea.

Shields, like spears, must have been commonplace items during the Germanic Iron Age, but few have survived because of the perishable nature of the wood of which they were chiefly made. An exception is this shield from Thorsbjerg bog, Schleswig, Germany. An iron boss protected the bearer's hand, while an iron band reinforced the outer rim. Third century.

You are free now to move forward
to meet Hrothgar, in helmets and armour,
but shields must stay here and spears be stacked
until the outcome of the audience is clear."

The hero arose, surrounded closely
400 by his powerful thanes. A party remained
under orders to keep watch on the arms;
the rest proceeded, led by their prince
under Heorot's roof. And standing on the hearth
in webbed links that the smith had woven,
the fine-forged mesh of his gleaming mail-shirt,
resolute in his helmet, Beowulf spoke:
"Greetings to Hrothgar. I am Hygelac's kinsman,
one of his hall-troop. When I was younger,
I had great triumphs. Then news of Grendel,
410 hard to ignore, reached me at home:
sailors brought stories of the plight you suffer
in this legendary hall, how it lies deserted,
empty and useless once the evening light
hides itself under heaven's dome.
So every elder and experienced councilman
among my people supported my resolve
to come here to you, King Hrothgar,
because all knew of my awesome strength.
They had seen me boltered in the blood of enemies
420 when I battled and bound five beasts,
raided a troll-nest and in the night-sea
slaughtered sea-brutes. I have suffered extremes
and avenged the Geats (their enemies brought it
upon themselves, I devastated them).
Now I mean to be a match for Grendel,
settle the outcome in single combat.

Beowulf enters Heorot. He gives an account of his heroic exploits

He declares he will fight Grendel

Beowulf takes great pride in his byrnie, or coat of mail, which (as he states in line 453) was made by Weland the master smith. The equivalent figure in Old Norse tradition, Völundr, was king of the elves. This carving from a small ivory box known as the Franks Casket shows Weland at his forge, being visited by two women. A detail of the carving shows the decapitated torso of one of his enemies lying below. Ca. eighth century.

And so, my request, O king of Bright-Danes,
dear prince of the Shieldings, friend of the people
and their ring of defence, my one request
430   is that you won't refuse me, who have come this far,
the privilege of purifying Heorot,
with my own men to help me, and nobody else.
I have heard moreover that the monster scorns
in his reckless way to use weapons;
therefore, to heighten Hygelac's fame
and gladden his heart, I hereby renounce
sword and the shelter of the broad shield,
the heavy war-board: hand-to-hand
is how it will be, a life-and-death
440   fight with the fiend. Whichever one death fells
must deem it a just judgement by God.
If Grendel wins, it will be a gruesome day;
he will glut himself on the Geats in the war-hall,
swoop without fear on that flower of manhood
as on others before. Then my face won't be there
to be covered in death: he will carry me away
as he goes to ground, gorged and bloodied;
he will run gloating with my raw corpse
and feed on it alone, in a cruel frenzy,
450   fouling his moor-nest. No need then
to lament for long or lay out my body:
if the battle takes me, send back
this breast-webbing that Weland fashioned
and Hrethel gave me, to Lord Hygelac.
Fate goes ever as fate must."

Hrothgar, the helmet of Shieldings, spoke:
"Beowulf, my friend, you have travelled here
to favour us with help and to fight for us.

Hrothgar recollects a
friendship and tells of
Grendel's raids

There was a feud one time, begun by your father.

460 With his own hands he had killed Heatholaf,
who was a Wulfing; so war was looming
and his people, in fear of it, forced him to leave.
He came away then over rolling waves
to the South-Danes here, the sons of honour.
I was then in the first flush of kingship,
establishing my sway over all the rich strongholds
of this heroic land. Heorogar,
my older brother and the better man,
also a son of Halfdane's, had died.

470 Finally I healed the feud by paying:
I shipped a treasure-trove to the Wulfings
and Ecgtheow acknowledged me with oaths of allegiance.

"It bothers me to have to burden anyone
with all the grief Grendel has caused
and the havoc he has wreaked upon us in Heorot,
our humiliations. My household-guard
are on the wane, fate sweeps them away
into Grendel's clutches—

but God can easily
halt these raids and harrowing attacks!

480 "Time and again, when the goblets passed
and seasoned fighters got flushed with beer
they would pledge themselves to protect Heorot
and wait for Grendel with whetted swords.
But when dawn broke and day crept in
over each empty, blood-spattered bench,
the floor of the mead-hall where they had feasted
would be slick with slaughter. And so they died,
faithful retainers, and my following dwindled.

As a person of immense wealth, Hrothgar would not have served drink to his guests in ordinary vessels. This glass vessel recovered from a grave at Himlingøje, on the island of Zealand, Denmark, exemplifies the fine wares that were sometimes imported to Scandinavia during the Roman Iron Age, whether as a result of trade or rewards or plunder. Third century.

"Now take your place at the table, relish
the triumph of heroes to your heart's content."

Then a bench was cleared in that banquet hall
so the Geats could have room to be together
and the party sat, proud in their bearing,
strong and stalwart. An attendant stood by
with a decorated pitcher, pouring bright
helpings of mead. And the minstrel sang,
filling Heorot with his head-clearing voice,
gladdening that great rally of Geats and Danes.

A feast in Heorot

From where he crouched at the king's feet,
Unferth, a son of Ecglaf's, spoke
contrary words. Beowulf's coming,
his sea-braving, made him sick with envy:
he could not brook or abide the fact
that anyone else alive under heaven
might enjoy greater regard than he did:
"Are you the Beowulf who took on Breca
in a swimming match on the open sea,
risking the water just to prove that you could win?
It was sheer vanity made you venture out
on the main deep. And no matter who tried,
friend or foe, to deflect the pair of you,
neither would back down: the sea-test obsessed you.
You waded in, embracing water,
taking its measure, mastering currents,
riding on the swell. The ocean swayed,
winter went wild in the waves, but you vied
for seven nights; and then he outswam you,
came ashore the stronger contender.
He was cast up safe and sound one morning

*Unferth strikes a
discordant note*

*Unferth's version of a
swimming contest*

490

500

510

---

*Beowulf proves his credentials for the Grendel fight by recounting the details of an earlier exploit when he and
a prince named Breca vied with one another in a contest on the high seas. This stylized head of a sea-beast,
recovered from the River Schelde in Belgium, suggests the nature of the monsters that harried him, in his
account of these events. Ca. fourth–sixth century.*

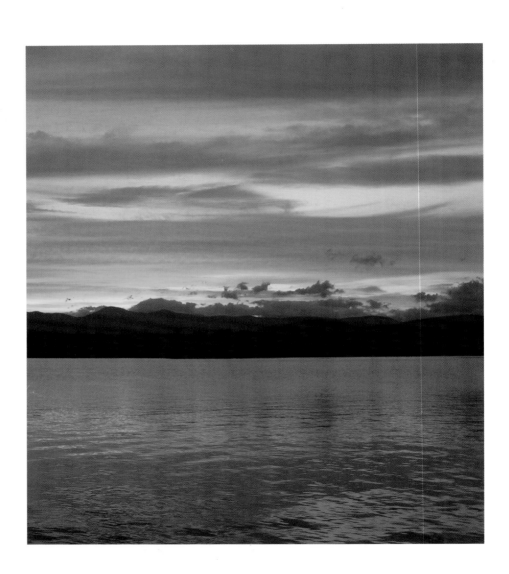

520 among the Heathoreams, then made his way
to where he belonged in Bronding country,
home again, sure of his ground
in strongroom and bawn. So Breca made good
his boast upon you and was proved right.
No matter, therefore, how you may have fared
in every bout and battle until now,
this time you'll be worsted; no one has ever
outlasted an entire night against Grendel."

Beowulf, Ecgtheow's son, replied:

Beowulf corrects
Unferth

530 "Well, friend Unferth, you have had your say
about Breca and me. But it was mostly beer
that was doing the talking. The truth is this:
when the going was heavy in those high waves,
I was the strongest swimmer of all.
We'd been children together and we grew up
daring ourselves to outdo each other,
boasting and urging each other to risk
our lives on the sea. And so it turned out.
Each of us swam holding a sword,
540 a naked, hard-proofed blade for protection
against the whale-beasts. But Breca could never
move out farther or faster from me
than I could manage to move from him.
Shoulder to shoulder, we struggled on
for five nights, until the long flow
and pitch of the waves, the perishing cold,
night falling and winds from the north
drove us apart. The deep boiled up
and its wallowing sent the sea-brutes wild.
550 My armour helped me to hold out;
my hard-ringed chain-mail, hand-forged and linked,

---

*After the young Beowulf emerged victorious from his fight against sea-monsters, "Light came from the east, /
. . . and the waves / went quiet," we are told (lines 569–71). In Beowulf, as in many cultures, the coming of
light has beneficent associations. Though taken in Maine rather than Scandinavia, this photograph is meant
to represent calm waters after a storm.*

a fine, close-fitting filigree of gold,
kept me safe when some ocean creature
pulled me to the bottom. Pinioned fast
and swathed in its grip, I was granted one
final chance: my sword plunged
and the ordeal was over. Through my own hands,
the fury of battle had finished off the sea-beast.

*Beowulf tells of his
ordeal in the sea*

"Time and again, foul things attacked me,
560   lurking and stalking, but I lashed out,
gave as good as I got with my sword.
My flesh was not for feasting on,
there would be no monsters gnawing and gloating
over their banquet at the bottom of the sea.
Instead, in the morning, mangled and sleeping
the sleep of the sword, they slopped and floated
like the ocean's leavings. From now on
sailors would be safe, the deep-sea raids
were over for good. Light came from the east,
570   bright guarantee of God, and the waves
went quiet; I could see headlands
and buffeted cliffs. Often, for undaunted courage,
fate spares the man it has not already marked.
However it occurred, my sword had killed
nine sea-monsters. Such night-dangers
and hard ordeals I have never heard of
nor of a man more desolate in surging waves.
But worn out as I was, I survived,
came through with my life. The ocean lifted
580   and laid me ashore, I landed safe
on the coast of Finland.
                  Now I cannot recall
any fight you entered, Unferth,

Queen Wealhtheow comes forth "adorned in her gold," as befits a woman of her rank (lines 612–14). This fine Germanic-style necklace from Desborough, Northamptonshire, is not only beautifully made, it also provides a parallel to the quasi-Christian character of the pagan Danish court of Beowulf, *for included among its pendants is a decorative cross. Seventh century.*

that bears comparison. I don't boast when I say
that neither you nor Breca were ever much
celebrated for swordsmanship
or for facing danger on the field of battle.
You killed your own kith and kin,
so for all your cleverness and quick tongue,
you will suffer damnation in the depths of hell.

590 The fact is, Unferth, if you were truly
as keen or courageous as you claim to be
Grendel would never have got away with
such unchecked atrocity, attacks on your king,
havoc in Heorot and horrors everywhere.
But he knows he need never be in dread
of your blade making a mizzle of his blood
or of vengeance arriving ever from this quarter—
from the Victory-Shieldings, the shoulderers of the spear.
He knows he can trample down you Danes
600 to his heart's content, humiliate and murder
without fear of reprisal. But he will find me different.
I will show him how Geats shape to kill
in the heat of battle. Then whoever wants to
may go bravely to mead, when morning light,
scarfed in sun-dazzle, shines forth from the south
and brings another daybreak to the world."

Then the grey-haired treasure-giver was glad;
far-famed in battle, the prince of Bright-Danes
and keeper of his people counted on Beowulf,
610 on the warrior's steadfastness and his word.
So the laughter started, the din got louder
and the crowd was happy. Wealhtheow came in,
Hrothgar's queen, observing the courtesies.
Adorned in her gold, she graciously saluted

Unferth rebuked. Beowulf reaffirms his determination to defeat Grendel

Wealhtheow, Hrothgar's queen, graces the banquet

Like the glass vessel from Himlingøje depicted on page 32, these Frankish-style glass claw beakers found in a great pagan burial mound at Taplow, Buckinghamshire, exemplify the finest luxury goods of their day. Funnel shaped, with hollow globular projections open to the interior, they were evidently meant to accompany a person of high rank into the next world. Late sixth century.

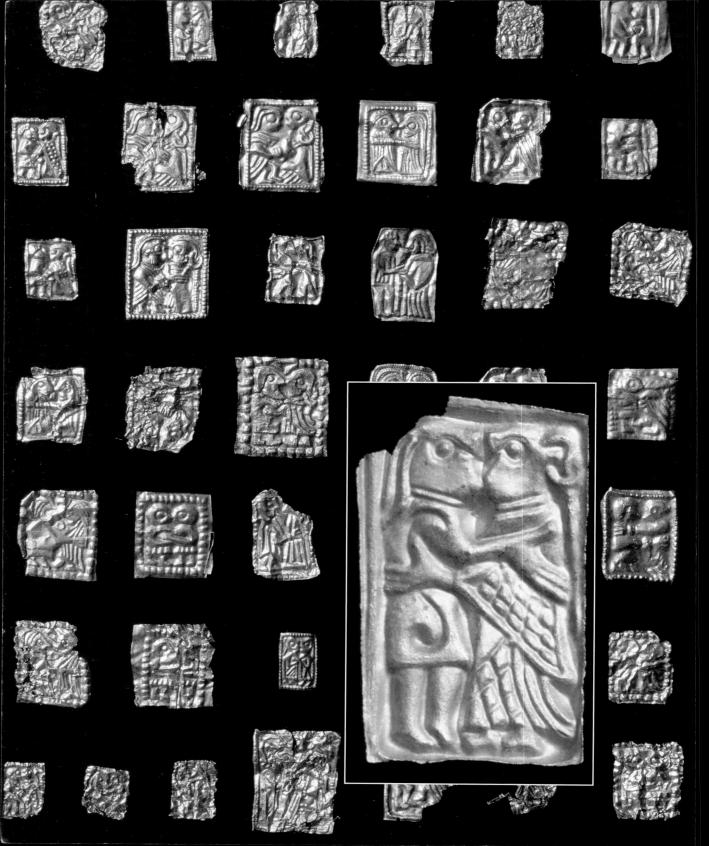

the men in hall, then handed the cup
first to Hrothgar, their homeland's guardian,
urging him to drink deep and enjoy it
because he was dear to them. And he drank it down
like the warlord he was, with festive cheer.
620   So the Helming woman went on her rounds,
queenly and dignified, decked out in rings,
offering the goblet to all ranks,
treating the household and the assembled troop
until it was Beowulf's turn to take it from her hand.
With measured words she welcomed the Geat
and thanked God for granting her wish
that a deliverer she could believe in would arrive
to ease their afflictions. He accepted the cup,
a daunting man, dangerous in action
630   and eager for it always. He addressed Wealhtheow;
Beowulf, son of Ecgtheow, said:

"I had a fixed purpose when I put to sea.

Beowulf's formal boast

As I sat in the boat with my band of men,
I meant to perform to the uttermost
what your people wanted or perish in the attempt,
in the fiend's clutches. And I shall fulfil that purpose,
prove myself with a proud deed
or meet my death here in the mead-hall."

This formal boast by Beowulf the Geat
640   pleased the lady well and she went to sit
by Hrothgar, regal and arrayed with gold.

Then it was like old times in the echoing hall,

*Hrothgar leaves
Heorot in Beowulf's
keeping*

proud talk and the people happy,
loud and excited; until soon enough

Tiny gold-foil plaques embossed with stylized images of couples have been found at a number of Iron Age set-tlements. These examples, from Lundeborg on the island of Funen, may have been thought to promote the fer-tility of ruling families, such as the Danish royal couple of Beowulf. *Sixth–seventh century. Inset: Miniature gold plaque from Helgö, Uppland, Sweden. Sixth–seventh century.*

Halfdane's heir had to be away
to his night's rest. He realized
that the demon was going to descend on the hall,
that he had plotted all day, from dawn-light
until darkness gathered again over the world
650   and stealthy night-shapes came stealing forth
under the cloud-murk. The company stood
as the two leaders took leave of each other:
Hrothgar wished Beowulf health and good luck,
named him hall-warden and announced as follows:
"Never, since my hand could hold a shield
have I entrusted or given control
of the Danes' hall to anyone but you.
Ward and guard it, for it is the greatest of houses.
Be on your mettle now, keep in mind your fame,
660   beware of the enemy. There's nothing you wish for
that won't be yours if you win through alive."

Hrothgar departed then with his house-guard.
The lord of the Shieldings, their shelter in war,
left the mead-hall to lie with Wealhtheow,
his queen and bedmate. The King of Glory
(as people learned) had posted a lookout
who was a match for Grendel, a guard against monsters,
special protection to the Danish prince.
And the Geat placed complete trust
670   in his strength of limb and the Lord's favour.
He began to remove his iron breast-mail,
took off the helmet and handed his attendant
the patterned sword, a smith's masterpiece,
ordering him to keep the equipment guarded.
And before he bedded down, Beowulf,
that prince of goodness, proudly asserted:

Beowulf renounces the use of weapons

While the fertile fields at Lejre, Denmark, typically look benign by day (see page 4), the wooded hills to the west of the village can take on an ominous aspect when night falls. Grendel visited the hall Heorot only when "night-shapes came stealing forth / under the cloud-murk." The Beowulf *poet's grand tale of terror may have its origins in simpler legends localized in this part of Denmark.*

"When it comes to fighting, I count myself
as dangerous any day as Grendel.
So it won't be a cutting edge I'll wield
680   to mow him down, easily as I might.
He has no idea of the arts of war,
of shield or sword-play, although he does possess
a wild strength. No weapons, therefore,
for either this night: unarmed he shall face me
if face me he dares. And may the Divine Lord
in His wisdom grant the glory of victory
to whichever side He sees fit."

Then down the brave man lay with his bolster
under his head and his whole company
690   of sea-rovers at rest beside him.
None of them expected he would ever see
his homeland again or get back
to his native place and the people who reared him.
They knew too well the way it was before,
how often the Danes had fallen prey
to death in the mead-hall. But the Lord was weaving
a victory on His war-loom for the Weather-Geats.
Through the strength of one they all prevailed;
they would crush their enemy and come through
700   in triumph and gladness. The truth is clear:
Almighty God rules over mankind
and always has.
                Then out of the night
came the shadow-stalker, stealthy and swift;
the hall-guards were slack, asleep at their posts,
all except one; it was widely understood
that as long as God disallowed it,
the fiend could not bear them to his shadow-bourne.

*The Geats await
Grendel's attack*

Portrait of a demon at hell mouth, from an Anglo-Saxon illuminated manuscript of Wonders of the East. *The demon's eyes are painted a brilliant red as if giving off flames. Similarly, Grendel represents evil incarnate, and "a baleful light, / flame more than light, flared from his eyes" (lines 726–27). London, British Library Cotton Tiberius B.v, fol. 87b. Late eleventh century.*

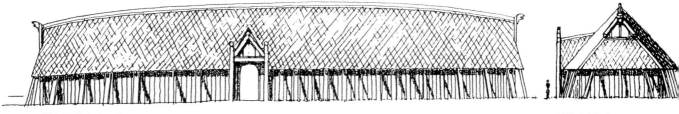

FACADE MOD NORD

VESTGAVL

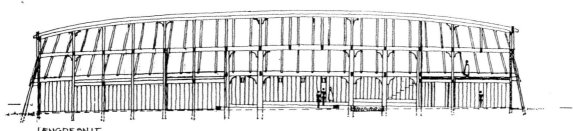

LÆNGDESNIT

One man, however, was in fighting mood,
awake and on edge, spoiling for action.

710 In off the moors, down through the mist bands *Grendel strikes*
God-cursed Grendel came greedily loping.
The bane of the race of men roamed forth,
hunting for a prey in the high hall.
Under the cloud-murk he moved towards it
until it shone above him, a sheer keep
of fortified gold. Nor was that the first time
he had scouted the grounds of Hrothgar's dwelling—
although never in his life, before or since,
did he find harder fortune or hall-defenders.
720 Spurned and joyless, he journeyed on ahead
and arrived at the bawn. The iron-braced door
turned on its hinge when his hands touched it.
Then his rage boiled over, he ripped open
the mouth of the building, maddening for blood,
pacing the length of the patterned floor
with his loathsome tread, while a baleful light,
flame more than light, flared from his eyes.
He saw many men in the mansion, sleeping,
a ranked company of kinsmen and warriors
730 quartered together. And his glee was demonic,
picturing the mayhem: before morning
he would rip life from limb and devour them,
feed on their flesh; but his fate that night
was due to change, his days of ravening
had come to an end.
           Mighty and canny, *A Geat warrior
perishes*
Hygelac's kinsman was keenly watching
for the first move the monster would make.
Nor did the creature keep him waiting

---

*The Viking Age hall at Lejre measured 48.3 meters (or about 158 feet) in length and 11.5 meters (or about 38
feet) in breadth at its midpoint. Its height can only be estimated, but with stout posts and strong beams, the
hall could have boasted a very large interior space. The* Beowulf *poet and his audience may have visualized
Heorot in terms like these.*

but struck suddenly and started in;
740 he grabbed and mauled a man on his bench,
bit into his bone-lappings, bolted down his blood
and gorged on him in lumps, leaving the body
utterly lifeless, eaten up
hand and foot. Venturing closer,
his talon was raised to attack Beowulf
where he lay on the bed; he was bearing in
with open claw when the alert hero's
comeback and armlock forestalled him utterly.
The captain of evil discovered himself
750 in a handgrip harder than anything
he had ever encountered in any man
on the face of the earth. Every bone in his body
quailed and recoiled, but he could not escape.
He was desperate to flee to his den and hide
with the devil's litter, for in all his days
he had never been clamped or cornered like this.
Then Hygelac's trusty retainer recalled
his bedtime speech, sprang to his feet
and got a firm hold. Fingers were bursting,
760 the monster back-tracking, the man overpowering.
The dread of the land was desperate to escape,
to take a roundabout road and flee
to his lair in the fens. The latching power
in his fingers weakened; it was the worst trip
the terror-monger had taken to Heorot.
And now the timbers trembled and sang,
a hall-session that harrowed every Dane
inside the stockade: stumbling in fury,
the two contenders crashed through the building.
770 The hall clattered and hammered, but somehow
survived the onslaught and kept standing:

Although the timbers of Heorot "trembled and sang" as Beowulf grappled with Grendel, the hall stood firm. The great buildings of this period, like the great ships, were constructed of sturdy timbers joined by carpenters who were masters of their craft. This photo shows a late Viking Age smith's tool chest from Mästermyr, Gotland, together with associated tools and other objects. Eleventh century.

it was handsomely structured, a sturdy frame
braced with the best of blacksmith's work
inside and out. The story goes
that as the pair struggled, mead-benches were smashed
and sprung off the floor, gold fittings and all.
Before then, no Shielding elder would believe
there was any power or person upon earth
capable of wrecking their horn-rigged hall
780   unless the burning embrace of a fire
engulf it in flame. Then an extraordinary
wail arose, and bewildering fear
came over the Danes. Everyone felt it
who heard that cry as it echoed off the wall,
a God-cursed scream and strain of catastrophe,
the howl of the loser, the lament of the hell-serf
keening his wound. He was overwhelmed,
manacled tight by the man who of all men
was foremost and strongest in the days of this life.

790   But the earl-troop's leader was not inclined
to allow his caller to depart alive:
he did not consider that life of much account
to anyone anywhere. Time and again,
Beowulf's warriors worked to defend
their lord's life, laying about them
as best they could with their ancestral blades.
Stalwart in action, they kept striking out
on every side, seeking to cut
straight to the soul. When they joined the struggle
800   there was something they could not have known at the time,
that no blade on earth, no blacksmith's art
could ever damage their demon opponent.

*Beowulf's thanes
defend him*

Heorot, we are told, was "braced with the best of blacksmith's work / inside and out." The poet's description is probably based on reality. This collection of bolts, nails, and other hardware was recovered during excavations at the Viking Age settlement at Lejre, Denmark, where a great hall once towered. The remains of a smithy were discovered close by the hall.

He had conjured the harm from the cutting edge
of every weapon. But his going away
out of this world and the days of his life
would be agony to him, and his alien spirit
would travel far into fiends' keeping.

Then he who had harrowed the hearts of men
with pain and affliction in former times

810 and had given offence also to God
found that his bodily powers failed him.
Hygelac's kinsman kept him helplessly
locked in a handgrip. As long as either lived,
he was hateful to the other. The monster's whole
body was in pain, a tremendous wound
appeared on his shoulder. Sinews split
and the bone-lappings burst. Beowulf was granted
the glory of winning; Grendel was driven
under the fen-banks, fatally hurt,

820 to his desolate lair. His days were numbered,
the end of his life was coming over him,
he knew it for certain; and one bloody clash
had fulfilled the dearest wishes of the Danes.
The man who had lately landed among them,
proud and sure, had purged the hall,
kept it from harm; he was happy with his nightwork
and the courage he had shown. The Geat captain
had boldly fulfilled his boast to the Danes:
he had healed and relieved a huge distress,

830 unremitting humiliations,
the hard fate they'd been forced to undergo,
no small affliction. Clear proof of this
could be seen in the hand the hero displayed
high up near the roof: the whole of Grendel's

The morning after Grendel's defeat, the monster's footprints are tracked across the moors as far as a pool "of bloodshot water [that] wallowed and surged" (line 846). Perhaps no illustration can do justice to this scene, but this photo is meant to be suggestive of it. The picture was actually taken at a serene spot in Ireland; its colors were subsequently distorted.

shoulder and arm, his awesome grasp.

Then morning came and many a warrior
gathered, as I've heard, around the gift-hall,
clan-chiefs flocking from far and near
down wide-ranging roads, wondering greatly

The morning after: relief and rejoicings

840   at the monster's footprints. His fatal departure
was regretted by no-one who witnessed his trail,
the ignominious marks of his flight
where he'd skulked away, exhausted in spirit
and beaten in battle, bloodying the path,
hauling his doom to the demons' mere.
The bloodshot water wallowed and surged,
there were loathsome upthrows and overturnings
of waves and gore and wound-slurry.
With his death upon him, he had dived deep
850   into his marsh-den, drowned out his life
and his heathen soul: hell claimed him there.

Then away they rode, the old retainers
with many a young man following after,
a troop on horseback, in high spirits
on their bay steeds. Beowulf's doings
were praised over and over again.
Nowhere, they said, north or south
between the two seas or under the tall sky
on the broad earth was there anyone better
860   to raise a shield or to rule a kingdom.
Yet there was no laying of blame on their lord,
the noble Hrothgar; he was a good king.

At times the war-band broke into a gallop,
letting their chestnut horses race

On their way back from Grendel's mere, the men race their horses. Scandinavian horses of the Germanic and Viking eras were smaller than their modern counterparts. Horses of this older type are bred and maintained at the Historical-Archaeological Research Centre located at Lejre, Denmark, where on occasion they are ridden by "Iron Age" riders.

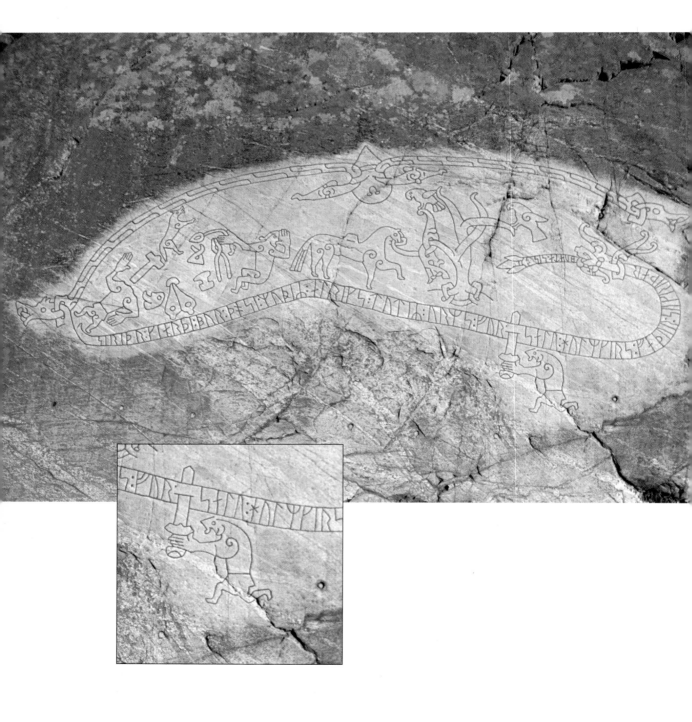

wherever they found the going good
on those well-known tracks. Meanwhile, a thane
of the king's household, a carrier of tales,
a traditional singer deeply schooled
in the lore of the past, linked a new theme
870   to a strict metre. The man started
to recite with skill, rehearsing Beowulf's
triumphs and feats in well-fashioned lines,
entwining his words.

*Hrothgar's minstrel
sings about Beowulf*

               He told what he'd heard
repeated in songs about Sigemund's exploits,
all of those many feats and marvels,
the struggles and wanderings of Waels's son,
things unknown to anyone
except to Fitela, feuds and foul doings
confided by uncle to nephew when he felt
880   the urge to speak of them: always they had been
partners in the fight, friends in need.
They killed giants, their conquering swords
had brought them down.

*The tale of Sigemund,
the dragon-slayer.
Appropriate for
Beowulf, who has
defeated Grendel*

               After his death
Sigemund's glory   grew and grew
because of his courage   when he killed the dragon,
the guardian of the hoard.   Under grey stone
he had dared to enter   all by himself
to face the worst   without Fitela.
But it came to pass   that his sword plunged
890   *right through   those radiant scales*
and drove into the wall.   The dragon died of it.
His daring had given him   total possession
of the treasure hoard,   his to dispose of
however he liked.   He loaded a boat:

After his victory over Grendel, Beowulf is compared implicitly to the legendary hero Sigemund, who in turn corresponds to Sigurd, the famous dragon-slayer of Old Norse heroic tradition. Carved into a large stone at Ramsund, in Södermanland, southern Sweden, are scenes from the life of Sigurd, who is shown impaling a dragon on his sword. The dragon's body is a ribbon of runes.

Waels's son   weighted her hold
with dazzling spoils.   The hot dragon melted.

Sigemund's name   was known everywhere.
He was utterly valiant   and venturesome,
a fence round his fighters   and flourished therefore
900 *after King Heremod's   prowess declined*
and his campaigns slowed down.   The king was betrayed,
ambushed in Jutland,   overpowered
and done away with.   The waves of his grief
had beaten him down,   made him a burden,
a source of anxiety   to his own nobles:
that expedition   was often condemned
in those earlier times   by experienced men,
men who relied   on his lordship for redress,
who presumed that the part   of a prince was to thrive
910 *on his father's throne   and defend the nation,*
the Shielding land   where they lived and belonged,
its holdings and strongholds.   Such was Beowulf
in the affection of his friends   and of everyone alive.
But evil entered   into Heremod.

*King Heremod
remembered and
contrasted with
Beowulf*

Meanwhile, the Danes kept racing their mounts
down sandy lanes. The light of day
broke and kept brightening. Bands of retainers
galloped in excitement to the gabled hall
to see the marvel; and the king himself,
920 guardian of the ring-hoard, goodness in person,
walked in majesty from the women's quarters
with a numerous train, attended by his queen
and her crowd of maidens, across to the mead-hall.

When Hrothgar arrived at the hall, he spoke,

Hrothgar stands "under the steep eaves" of Heorot to gaze upon Grendel's arm and claw. This computer-generated drawing of the Viking Age hall at Lejre, Zealand, is superimposed on a photograph of the landscape where the hall once stood. The drawing is based on architecturally precise calculations based on the size, depth, angle, and relative placement of the postholes. At far left is an ancient burial mound, "Mysselhøj."

standing on the steps, under the steep eaves,
gazing at the roofwork and Grendel's talon:
"First and foremost, let the Almighty Father
be thanked for this sight. I suffered a long
harrowing by Grendel. But the Heavenly Shepherd

930 can work His wonders always and everywhere.
Not long since, it seemed I would never
be granted the slightest solace or relief
from any of my burdens: the best of houses
glittered and reeked and ran with blood.
This one worry outweighed all others—
a constant distress to counsellors entrusted
with defending the people's forts from assault
by monsters and demons. But now a man,
with the Lord's assistance, has accomplished something .

940 none of us could manage before now
for all our efforts. Whoever she was
who brought forth this flower of manhood,
if she is still alive, that woman can say
that in her labour the Lord of Ages
bestowed a grace on her. So now, Beowulf,
I adopt you in my heart as a dear son.
Nourish and maintain this new connection,
you noblest of men; there'll be nothing you'll want for,
no worldly goods that won't be yours.

950 I have often honoured smaller achievements,
recognized warriors not nearly as worthy,
lavished rewards on the less deserving.
But you have made yourself immortal
by your glorious action. May the God of Ages
continue to keep and requite you well."

Beowulf, son of Ecgtheow, spoke:

Beowulf may never have been taught the mysteries of the Redemption, but he is aware that punishment awaits the damned (line 978). In its lower panel, this illustration depicts hell as a place where eternal torture can be expected at the hands of sadistic jailers. Angels and the enthroned Lord are shown above, with Saint Peter. London, British Library Stowe 944 (the Winchester Liber Vitae), fol. 7a. Early eleventh century.

King Hrothgar gives thanks for the relief of Heorot and adopts Beowulf "in his heart"

63

"We have gone through with a glorious endeavour
and been much favoured in this fight we dared
against the unknown. Nevertheless,
960   if you could have seen the monster himself
where he lay beaten, I would have been better pleased.
My plan was to pounce, pin him down
in a tight grip and grapple him to death—
have him panting for life, powerless and clasped
in my bare hands, his body in thrall.
But I couldn't stop him from slipping my hold.
The Lord allowed it, my lock on him
wasn't strong enough, he struggled fiercely
and broke and ran. Yet he bought his freedom
970   at a high price, for he left his hand
and arm and shoulder to show he had been here,
a cold comfort for having come among us.
And now he won't be long for this world.
He has done his worst but the wound will end him.
He is hasped and hooped and hirpling with pain,
limping and looped in it. Like a man outlawed
for wickedness, he must await
the mighty judgement of God in majesty."

There was less tampering and big talk then
980   from Unferth the boaster, less of his blather
as the hall-thanes eyed the awful proof
of the hero's prowess, the splayed hand
up under the eaves. Every nail,
claw-scale and spur, every spike
and welt on the hand of that heathen brute
was like barbed steel. Everybody said
there was no honed iron hard enough
to pierce him through, no time-proofed blade

In preparation for the banquet that takes place in Heorot on the day after the hero's victory over Grendel, the hall is adorned with gold-threaded hangings. This gold-threaded braid from Snartemo, in Vest-Agder, Norway, would also have caught people's eyes. The original braid is below, a modern reconstruction above. Migration Age.

that could cut his brutal, blood-caked claw.

990 Then the order was given for all hands
to help to refurbish Heorot immediately:
men and women thronging the wine-hall,
getting it ready. Gold thread shone
in the wall-hangings, woven scenes
that attracted and held the eye's attention.
But iron-braced as the inside of it had been,
that bright room lay in ruins now.
The very doors had been dragged from their hinges.
Only the roof remained unscathed
1000 by the time the guilt-fouled fiend turned tail
in despair of his life. But death is not easily
escaped from by anyone:
all of us with souls, earth-dwellers
and children of men, must make our way
to a destination already ordained
where the body, after the banqueting,
sleeps on its deathbed.

The damaged hall
repaired

                       Then the due time arrived
for Halfdane's son to proceed to the hall.
The king himself would sit down to feast.
1010 No group ever gathered in greater numbers
or better order around their ring-giver.
The benches filled with famous men
who fell to with relish; round upon round
of mead was passed; those powerful kinsmen,
Hrothgar and Hrothulf, were in high spirits
in the raftered hall. Inside Heorot
there was nothing but friendship. The Shielding nation
was not yet familiar with feud and betrayal.

A victory feast

The helmet that King Hrothgar presents to Beowulf is said to be surmounted by an embossed ridge (Old English wala; see lines 1029–33). Though perhaps meant more for display than for actual warfare, this helmet from Vendel grave 12, Uppland, Sweden, shows how such a ridge would have protected the wearer from a sword-stroke directed from above. Seventh century.

Then Halfdane's son presented Beowulf

*Victory gifts presented
to Beowulf*

1020   with a gold standard as a victory gift,
an embroidered banner; also breast-mail
and a helmet; and a sword carried high,
that was both precious object and token of honour.
So Beowulf drank his drink, at ease;
it was hardly a shame to be showered with such gifts
in front of the hall-troops. There haven't been many
moments, I am sure, when men exchanged
four such treasures at so friendly a sitting.
An embossed ridge, a band lapped with wire

1030   arched over the helmet: head-protection
to keep the keen-ground cutting edge
from damaging it when danger threatened
and the man was battling behind his shield.
Next the king ordered eight horses
with gold bridles to be brought through the yard
into the hall. The harness of one
included a saddle of sumptuous design,
the battle-seat where the son of Halfdane
rode when he wished to join the sword-play:

1040   wherever the killing and carnage were the worst,
he would be to the fore, fighting hard.
Then the Danish prince, descendant of Ing,
handed over both the arms and the horses,
urging Beowulf to use them well.
And so their leader, the lord and guard
of coffer and strongroom, with customary grace
bestowed upon Beowulf both sets of gifts.
A fair witness can see how well each one behaved.

The chieftain went on to reward the others:

*The other Geats are
rewarded*

1050   each man on the bench who had sailed with Beowulf

---

*Viking Age torque found near Lejre, Denmark. When Hrothgar rewards each of Beowulf's men for having
helped to defeat Grendel, one can imagine him offering gifts of this kind. Gold and silver torques—whether in
the form of armbands or necklaces—were prestigious items of exchange and display throughout the ancient
North. This particular one has seen better days.*

and risked the voyage received a bounty,
some treasured possession. And compensation,
a price in gold, was settled for the Geat
Grendel had cruelly killed earlier—
as he would have killed more, had not mindful God
and one man's daring prevented that doom.
Past and present, God's will prevails.
Hence, understanding is always best
and a prudent mind. Whoever remains
1060   for long here in this earthly life
will enjoy and endure more than enough.

They sang then and played to please the hero,
words and music for their warrior prince,
harp tunes and tales of adventure:
there were high times on the hall benches
and the king's poet performed his part
with the saga of Finn and his sons, unfolding
the tale of the fierce attack in Friesland
where Hnaef, king of the Danes, met death.

*Another performance
by the minstrel*

1070   *Hildeburh*

                  had little cause

to credit the Jutes:

                  son and brother,

she lost them both

                on the battlefield.

She, bereft

             and blameless, they

foredoomed, cut down

              and spear-gored. She,

the woman in shock,

               waylaid by grief,

*Hildeburh, a Danish
princess married to the
Frisian King Finn,
loses her son
(unnamed here) and
her brother Hnaef in a
fight at Finn's hall*

---

*In the song about Finn and Hengest, Finn, king of the Frisians, tries to settle the violence that has broken out
at his hall by distributing treasures with an even hand to his own men and his Danish in-laws. Gold rings
such as these, which were part of a hoard unearthed at Lillesø, near Gudme on the island of Funen, Denmark,
could have served his purpose. Ca. fifth century.*

Hoc's daughter—
　　　　　how could she not
lament her fate
　　　　　when morning came
and the light broke
　　　　　on her murdered dears?
And so farewell
　　　　　delight on earth,
1080　war carried away
　　　　　Finn's troop of thanes,
all but a few.
　　　　　How then could Finn
hold the line
　　　　　or fight on
to the end with Hengest,
　　　　　how save
the rump of his force
　　　　　from that enemy chief?
So a truce was offered
　　　　　as follows: first
separate quarters
　　　　　to be cleared for the Danes,
hall and throne
　　　　　to be shared with the Frisians.
Then, second:
　　　　　every day
at the dole-out of gifts
　　　　　Finn, son of Focwald,
1090　should honour the Danes,
　　　　　bestow with an even
hand to Hengest
　　　　　and Hengest's men
the wrought-gold rings,

The Danish attack is bloody but indecisive. Hnaef is killed, Hengest takes charge and makes a truce with Finn and the Frisians

> bounty to match
>
> the measure he gave
>
>   his own Frisians—
>
> to keep morale
>
>   in the beer-hall high.
>
> Both sides then
>
>   sealed their agreement.
>
> With oaths to Hengest
>
>   Finn swore
>
> openly, solemnly,
>
>   that the battle survivors
>
> would be guaranteed
>
>   honour and status.
>
> No infringement
>
>   by word or deed,
>
> no provocation
>
>   would be permitted.
>
> Their own ring-giver
>
>   after all
>
> was dead and gone,
>
>   they were leaderless,
>
> in forced allegiance
>
>   to his murderer.
>
> So if any Frisian
>
>   stirred up bad blood
>
> with insinuations
>
>   or taunts about this,
>
> the blade of the sword
>
>   would arbitrate it.
>
> A funeral pyre
>
>   was then prepared,
>
> effulgent gold
>
>   brought out from the hoard.

1100 *(line marker)*

The Danish survivors to be quartered and given parity of treatment with the Frisians and their allies, the Jutes

The bodies of the slain burnt on the pyre

73

The pride and prince
                    of the Shieldings lay
1110   awaiting the flame.
                    Everywhere
there were blood-plastered
                    coats of mail.
The pyre was heaped
                    with boar-shaped helmets
forged in gold,
                    with the gashed corpses
of well-born Danes—
                    many had fallen.
Then Hildeburh
                    ordered her own
son's body
                    be burnt with Hnaef's,
the flesh on his bones
                    to sputter and blaze
beside his uncle's.
                    The woman wailed
and sang keens,
                    the warrior went up.
1120   Carcass flame
                    swirled and fumed,
they stood round the burial
                    mound and howled
as heads melted,
                    crusted gashes
spattered and ran
                    bloody matter.
The glutton element
                    flamed and consumed
the dead of both sides.

To provoke blood vengeance for Hnaef, a Danish warrior places a sword on Hengest's lap—perhaps the same blade that had belonged to his dead leader. Swords in Beowulf are often said to shine with wavy patterns—an apparent reference to the variegated sheen of pattern-welded blades. These blades, though corroded, show the effects of pattern-welding. Viking Age.

Their great days were gone.
Warriors scattered
            to homes and forts
all over Friesland,
            fewer now, feeling
loss of friends.
            Hengest stayed,
lived out that whole
            resentful, blood-sullen
1130 winter with Finn,
            homesick and helpless.
No ring-whorled prow
            could up then
and away on the sea.
            Wind and water
raged with storms,
            wave and shingle
were shackled in ice
            until another year
appeared in the yard
            as it does to this day,
the seasons constant,
            the wonder of light
coming over us.
            Then winter was gone,
earth's lap grew lovely,
            longing woke
in the cooped-up exile
            for a voyage home—
1140 but more for vengeance,
            some way of bringing
things to a head:
            his sword arm hankered

The Danes, homesick and resentful, spend a winter in exile

Spring comes

Hengest's followers bide their time over the winter, keeping an uneasy truce with their Frisian hosts as long as ice locks the shores. This photo shows a winter landscape at the "Iron Age" village at the Historical-Archaeological Experimental Centre, Lejre, Zealand. A modern reconstruction, the village is situated among some hills located less than a mile west of the excavated hall sites.

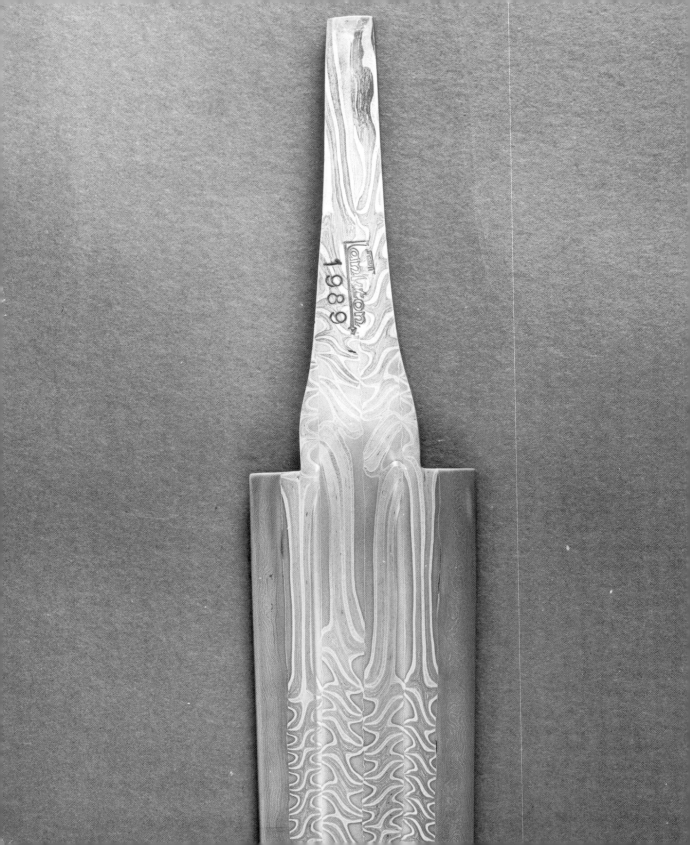

to greet the Jutes.
                      So he did not balk
once Hunlafing
                      placed on his lap
Dazzle-the-Duel,
                      the best sword of all,
whose edges Jutes
                      knew only too well.
Thus blood was spilled,
                      the gallant Finn
slain in his home
                      after Guthlaf and Oslaf
back from their voyage
                      made old accusation:
the brutal ambush,
                      the fate they had suffered,
1150   all blamed on Finn.
                      The wildness in them
had to brim over.
                      The hall ran red
with blood of enemies.
                      Finn was cut down,
the queen brought away
                      and everything
the Shieldings could find
                      inside Finn's walls—
the Frisian king's
                      gold collars and gemstones—
swept off to the ship.
                      Over sea-lanes then
back to Daneland
                      the warrior troop
bore that lady home.

This pattern-welded blade was forged by the American swordsmith Scott Langton in 1989. To manufacture such a blade, the maker welds together a number of rods made of hard steel (for the edge) and of more pliable wrought iron (for the core). The core rods are twisted so as to produce a premeditated pattern or "grain." Compare the Viking Age blades depicted on page 74.

The poem was over,
the poet had performed, a pleasant murmur
1160   started on the benches, stewards did the rounds
with wine in splendid jugs, and Wealhtheow came to sit
in her gold crown between two good men,
uncle and nephew, each one of whom
still trusted the other; and the forthright Unferth,
admired by all for his mind and courage
although under a cloud for killing his brothers,
reclined near the king.
              The queen spoke:
"Enjoy this drink, my most generous lord;
raise up your goblet, entertain the Geats
1170   duly and gently, discourse with them,
be open-handed, happy and fond.
Relish their company, but recollect as well
all of the boons that have been bestowed on you.
The bright court of Heorot has been cleansed
and now the word is that you want to adopt
this warrior as a son. So, while you may,
bask in your fortune, and then bequeath
kingdom and nation to your kith and kin,
before your decease. I am certain of Hrothulf.
1180   He is noble and will use the young ones well.
He will not let you down. Should you die before him,
he will treat our children truly and fairly.
He will honour, I am sure, our two sons,
repay them in kind when he recollects
all the good things we gave him once,
the favour and respect he found in his childhood."

She turned then to the bench where her boys sat,
Hrethric and Hrothmund, with other nobles' sons,

Top: When Queen Wealhtheow comes forth to greet her guests, she moves "under a gold bēag*," a word that can denote almost any kind of round ornament; Heaney translates the phrase "in her gold crown." This gold ornament from Strårup, Jutland, is of unknown function but may have been a diadem. Roman or early Germanic Iron Age. Bottom: Gold bracteate used as a pendant. It is stamped with runes and images of a (mythological?) horse and a head. Fifth–sixth century.*

all the youth together; and that good man,
1190   Beowulf the Geat, sat between the brothers.

The cup was carried to him, kind words
spoken in welcome and a wealth of wrought gold
graciously bestowed: two arm bangles,
a mail-shirt and rings, and the most resplendent
torque of gold I ever heard tell of
anywhere on earth or under heaven.

Gifts presented, including a torque: Beowulf will present it in due course to King Hygelac, who will die wearing it

There was no hoard like it since Hama snatched
the Brosings' neck-chain and bore it away
with its gems and settings to his shining fort,
1200   away from Eormenric's wiles and hatred,
and thereby ensured his eternal reward.
Hygelac the Geat, grandson of Swerting,
wore this neck-ring on his last raid;
at bay under his banner, he defended the booty,
treasure he had won. Fate swept him away
because of his proud need to provoke
a feud with the Frisians. He fell beneath his shield,
in the same gem-crusted, kingly gear
he had worn when he crossed the frothing wave-vat.
1210   So the dead king fell into Frankish hands.
They took his breast-mail, also his neck-torque,
and punier warriors plundered the slain
when the carnage ended; Geat corpses
covered the field.

Applause filled the hall.
Then Wealhtheow pronounced in the presence of the company:
"Take delight in this torque, dear Beowulf,
wear it for luck and wear also this mail

Wealhtheow rewards Beowulf with a necklace or torque that the poet compares to the necklace of the Brosings. In Old Norse tradition, this treasure was owned by the goddess Frejya. This large, superbly decorated gold necklace, shown in detail below, is from Färjestaden, on the island of Öland, Sweden. It is suggestive of the kind of treasure the poet may have had in mind. Fifth–sixth century.

from our people's armoury: may you prosper in them!
Be acclaimed for strength, for kindly guidance

1220   to these two boys, and your bounty will be sure.
You have won renown: you are known to all men
far and near, now and forever.
Your sway is wide as the wind's home,
as the sea around cliffs. And so, my prince,
I wish you a lifetime's luck and blessings
to enjoy this treasure. Treat my sons
with tender care, be strong and kind.
Here each comrade is true to the other,
loyal to lord, loving in spirit.

1230   The thanes have one purpose, the people are ready:
having drunk and pledged, the ranks do as I bid."

She moved then to her place. Men were drinking wine   *Bedtime in Heorot*
at that rare feast; how could they know fate,
the grim shape of things to come,
the threat looming over many thanes
as night approached and King Hrothgar prepared
to retire to his quarters? Retainers in great numbers
were posted on guard as so often in the past.
Benches were pushed back, bedding gear and bolsters

1240   spread across the floor, and one man
lay down to his rest, already marked for death.
At their heads they placed their polished timber
battle-shields; and on the bench above them,
each man's kit was kept to hand:
a towering war-helmet, webbed mail-shirt
and great-shafted spear. It was their habit
always and everywhere to be ready for action,
at home or in the camp, in whatever case
and at whatever time the need arose

The foundations of the earliest hall built at Lejre, Denmark, have been radiocarbon dated to the mid-sixth cen-
tury—the approximate time when Beowulf *is set. The hall was used for perhaps a hundred years. This*
computer-generated image represents an artist's impression of what that hall might have looked like when sil-
houetted against the evening sky, with a fire blazing within.

1250 to rally round their lord. They were a right people.

*Another threat is
lurking in the night*

They went to sleep. And one paid dearly
for his night's ease, as had happened to them often,
ever since Grendel occupied the gold-hall,
committing evil until the end came,
death after his crimes. Then it became clear,
obvious to everyone once the fight was over,
that an avenger lurked and was still alive,
grimly biding time. Grendel's mother,
monstrous hell-bride, brooded on her wrongs.
1260 She had been forced down into fearful waters,
the cold depths, after Cain had killed
his father's son, felled his own
brother with a sword. Branded an outlaw,
marked by having murdered, he moved into the wilds,
shunned company and joy. And from Cain there sprang
misbegotten spirits, among them Grendel,
the banished and accursed, due to come to grips
with that watcher in Heorot waiting to do battle.
The monster wrenched and wrestled with him
1270 but Beowulf was mindful of his mighty strength,
the wondrous gifts God had showered on him:
He relied for help on the Lord of All,
on His care and favour. So he overcame the foe,
brought down the hell-brute. Broken and bowed,
outcast from all sweetness, the enemy of mankind
made for his death-den. But now his mother
had sallied forth on a savage journey,
grief-racked and ravenous, desperate for revenge.

She came to Heorot. There, inside the hall,
1280 Danes lay asleep, earls who would soon endure

*Grendel's mother
attacks*

---

*Since Grendel's mother is never described in any detail, she is almost impossible to visualize. Fantastic crea-
tures of all kinds, however, abound in her neighborhood, as they do in the decorative arts of early medieval
Europe. This gold ornament from Galsted, Denmark, depicts a pair of beasts flanking a humanlike head. Late
Germanic Iron Age.*

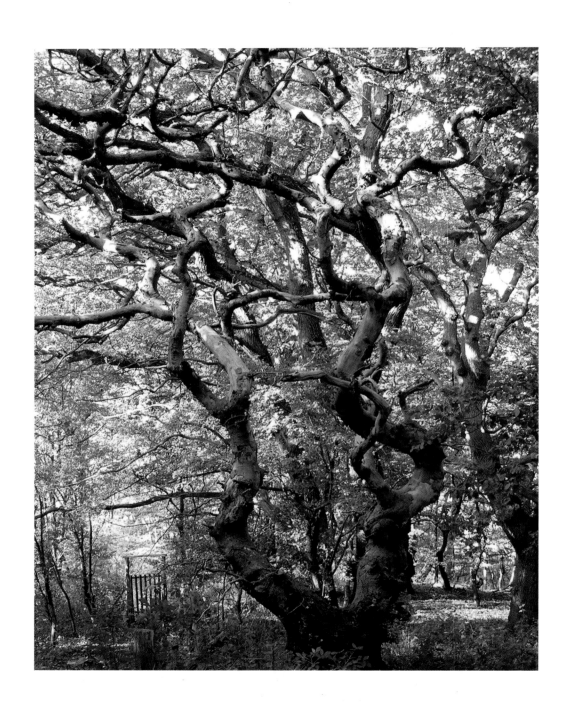

a great reversal, once Grendel's mother
attacked and entered. Her onslaught was less
only by as much as an amazon warrior's
strength is less than an armed man's
when the hefted sword, its hammered edge
and gleaming blade slathered in blood,
razes the sturdy boar-ridge off a helmet.
Then in the hall, hard-honed swords
were grabbed from the bench, many a broad shield
1290   lifted and braced; there was little thought of helmets
or woven mail when they woke in terror.

The hell-dam was in panic, desperate to get out,
in mortal terror the moment she was found.
She had pounced and taken one of the retainers
in a tight hold, then headed for the fen.
To Hrothgar, this man was the most beloved
of the friends he trusted between the two seas.
She had done away with a great warrior,
ambushed him at rest.
                      Beowulf was elsewhere.
1300   Earlier, after the award of the treasure,
the Geat had been given another lodging.
There was uproar in Heorot. She had snatched their trophy,
Grendel's bloodied hand. It was a fresh blow
to the afflicted bawn. The bargain was hard,
both parties having to pay
with the lives of friends. And the old lord,
the grey-haired warrior, was heartsore and weary
when he heard the news: his highest-placed adviser,
his dearest companion, was dead and gone.

Oak tree near Langesø, Zealand. A mile or so west of the hall sites at Lejre is a hummocky region known to Ice Age geologists as a dead ice landscape. It consists chiefly of hillocks interspersed by pools. Densely wooded in parts, it is a natural haven for wildlife. Grendel's mother dwells in some such terrain, with its terrors greatly magnified by the poet's art.

1310   Beowulf was quickly brought to the chamber:
the winner of fights, the arch-warrior,
came first-footing in with his fellow troops
to where the king in his wisdom waited,
still wondering whether Almighty God
would ever turn the tide of his misfortunes.
So Beowulf entered with his band in attendance
and the wooden floor-boards banged and rang
as he advanced, hurrying to address
the prince of the Ingwins, asking if he'd rested

1320   since the urgent summons had come as a surprise.

Then Hrothgar, the Shieldings' helmet, spoke:
"Rest? What is rest? Sorrow has returned.
Alas for the Danes! Aeschere is dead.
He was Yrmenlaf's elder brother
and a soul-mate to me, a true mentor,
my right-hand man when the ranks clashed
and our boar-crests had to take a battering
in the line of action. Aeschere was everything
the world admires in a wise man and a friend.

1330   Then this roaming killer came in a fury
and slaughtered him in Heorot. Where she is hiding,
glutting on the corpse and glorying in her escape,
I cannot tell; she has taken up the feud
because of last night, when you killed Grendel,
wrestled and racked him in ruinous combat
since for too long he had terrorized us
with his depredations. He died in battle,
paid with his life; and now this powerful
other one arrives, this force for evil

1340   driven to avenge her kinsman's death.
Or so it seems to thanes in their grief,

Hrothgar laments the death of his counsellor. He knows Grendel's mother must avenge her son

Alders growing in a pool near Knapsø, near Lejre on the island of Zealand. The demonic pool where Grendel and his mother make their home has no existence outside the world of fantasy. Still, this pool, located in the midst of the dead ice landscape west of Lejre, provides a conceivable analogue to the poet's mere, with its "maze of tree-roots mirrored in its surface" (line 1364).

in the anguish every thane endures
at the loss of a ring-giver, now that the hand
that bestowed so richly has been stilled in death.

"I have heard it said by my people in hall, *The country people's tales about the monsters*
counsellors who live in the upland country,
that they have seen two such creatures
prowling the moors, huge marauders
from some other world. One of these things,
1350   as far as anyone ever can discern,
looks like a woman; the other, warped
in the shape of a man, moves beyond the pale
bigger than any man, an unnatural birth
called Grendel by country people
in former days. They are fatherless creatures,
and their whole ancestry is hidden in a past
of demons and ghosts. They dwell apart
among wolves on the hills, on windswept crags
and treacherous keshes, where cold streams
1360   pour down the mountain and disappear
under mist and moorland.

                    A few miles from here *The haunted mere*
a frost-stiffened wood waits and keeps watch
above a mere; the overhanging bank
is a maze of tree-roots mirrored in its surface.
At night there, something uncanny happens:
the water burns. And the mere bottom
has never been sounded by the sons of men.
On its bank, the heather-stepper halts:
the hart in flight from pursuing hounds
1370   will turn to face them with firm-set horns
and die in the wood rather than dive
beneath its surface. That is no good place.

Left: A hart pursued by hounds, the poet says, will give up its life rather than plunge into Grendel's mere. This stylized image of a stag, excavated from Mound 1 at Sutton Hoo, surmounted a remarkable emblem of royalty. Seventh century. Top right: This rune-inscribed, carved wooden footstool was found at Feddersen Wierde, northern Germany, like the throne on page 10. Fifth century. Bottom right: On the underside of the Feddersen Wierde footstool is carved a vivid image of a stag attacked by a hound.

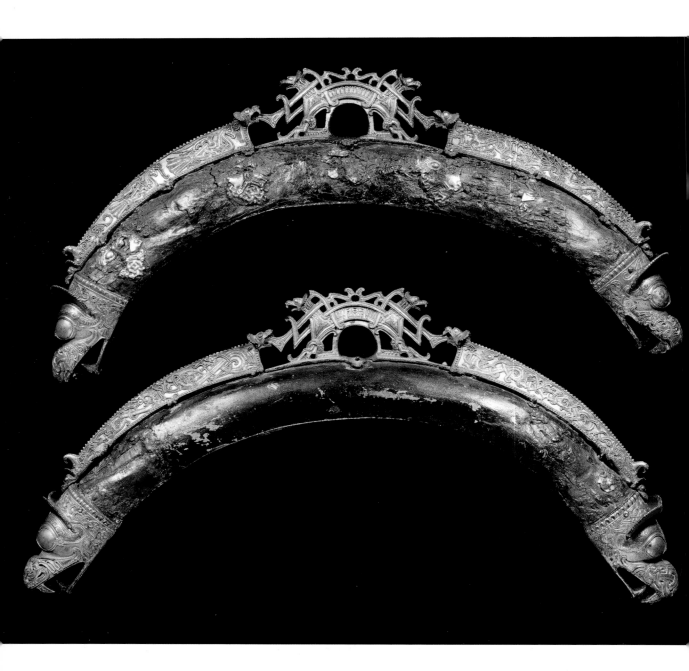

When wind blows up and stormy weather
makes clouds scud and the skies weep,
out of its depths a dirty surge
is pitched towards the heavens. Now help depends
again on you and on you alone.
The gap of danger where the demon waits
is still unknown to you. Seek it if you dare.
1380 I will compensate you for settling the feud
as I did the last time with lavish wealth,
coffers of coiled gold, if you come back."

Beowulf, son of Ecgtheow, spoke:
"Wise sir, do not grieve. It is always better
to avenge dear ones than to indulge in mourning.
For every one of us, living in this world
means waiting for our end. Let whoever can
win glory before death. When a warrior is gone,
that will be his best and only bulwark.
1390 So arise, my lord, and let us immediately
set forth on the trail of this troll-dam.
I guarantee you: she will not get away,
not to dens under ground nor upland groves
nor the ocean floor. She'll have nowhere to flee to.
Endure your troubles to-day. Bear up
and be the man I expect you to be."

*Beowulf bolsters
Hrothgar's courage.
He proclaims the
heroic code that guides
their lives*

With that the old lord sprang to his feet
and praised God for Beowulf's pledge.
Then a bit and halter were brought for his horse
1400 with the plaited mane. The wise king mounted
the royal saddle and rode out in style
with a force of shield-bearers. The forest paths
were marked all over with the monster's tracks,

*The expedition to
the mere*

*Pair of richly decorated saddlebows from Søllested, on the island of Funen, Denmark. Hrothgar takes the lead
on horseback as the men set out for Grendel's mere. His horse would naturally have been fitted with a precious
saddle. These saddlebows, with their beast-head terminals, are among the most impressive equestrian orna-
ments known from the prehistoric period in Denmark. Viking Age.*

her trail on the ground wherever she had gone
across the dark moors, dragging away
the body of that thane, Hrothgar's best
counsellor and overseer of the country.
So the noble prince proceeded undismayed
up fells and screes, along narrow footpaths
1410   and ways where they were forced into single file,
ledges on cliffs above lairs of water-monsters.
He went in front with a few men,
good judges of the lie of the land,
and suddenly discovered the dismal wood,
mountain trees growing out at an angle
above grey stones: the bloodshot water
surged underneath. It was a sore blow
to all of the Danes, friends of the Shieldings,
a hurt to each and every one
1420   of that noble company when they came upon
Aeschere's head at the foot of the cliff.

Everybody gazed as the hot gore
kept wallowing up and an urgent war-horn
repeated its notes: the whole party
sat down to watch. The water was infested
with all kinds of reptiles. There were writhing sea-dragons
and monsters slouching on slopes by the cliff,
serpents and wild things such as those that often
surface at dawn to roam the sail-road
1430   and doom the voyage. Down they plunged,
lashing in anger at the loud call
of the battle-bugle. An arrow from the bow
of the Geat chief got one of them
as he surged to the surface: the seasoned shaft
stuck deep in his flank and his freedom in the water

On their way to the mere, the men walk "along narrow footpaths / and ways where they were forced into single file." No landscape on earth matches the uncanny features of Grendel's mere. Still, a single-file pathway like this one, which leads over Langesø into woods west of Lejre, might present a forbidding aspect on certain days.

got less and less. It was his last swim.
He was swiftly overwhelmed in the shallows,
prodded by barbed boar-spears,
cornered, beaten, pulled up on the bank,
1440   a strange lake-birth, a loathsome catch
men gazed at in awe.

                    Beowulf got ready,   *Beowulf arms for the*
donned his war-gear, indifferent to death;   *underwater fight*
his mighty, hand-forged, fine-webbed mail
would soon meet with the menace underwater.
It would keep the bone-cage of his body safe:
no enemy's clasp could crush him in it,
no vicious armlock choke his life out.
To guard his head he had a glittering helmet
that was due to be muddied on the mere bottom
1450   and blurred in the upswirl. It was of beaten gold,
princely headgear hooped and hasped
by a weapon-smith who had worked wonders
in days gone by and adorned it with boar-shapes;
since then it had resisted every sword.
And another item lent by Unferth
at that moment of need was of no small importance:
the brehon handed him a hilted weapon,
a rare and ancient sword named Hrunting.
The iron blade with its ill-boding patterns
1460   had been tempered in blood. It had never failed
the hand of anyone who hefted it in battle,
anyone who had fought and faced the worst
in the gap of danger. This was not the first time
it had been called to perform heroic feats.

When he lent that blade to the better swordsman,
Unferth, the strong-built son of Ecglaf,

The waters of Grendel's mere are infested with serpents and sea-dragons. One of these creatures is shot with an arrow, then speared and dragged ashore. This carved figurehead from Oseberg, in Vestfold, Norway, represents a serpent of the kind once thought to harry mariners on the high seas. Beowulf shows no distress at the prospect of tangling with such creatures. Ca. 800–850.

99

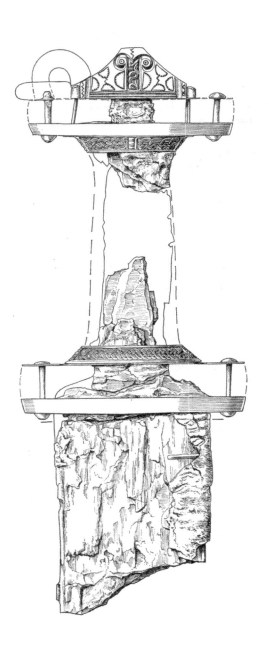

could hardly have remembered the ranting speech
he had made in his cups. He was not man enough
to face the turmoil of a fight under water
1470   and the risk to his life. So there he lost
fame and repute. It was different for the other
rigged out in his gear, ready to do battle.

Beowulf, son of Ecgtheow, spoke: *Beowulf takes his leave*
"Wisest of kings, now that I have come
to the point of action, I ask you to recall
what we said earlier: that you, son of Halfdane
and gold-friend to retainers, that you, if I should fall
and suffer death while serving your cause,
would act like a father to me afterwards.
1480   If this combat kills me, take care
of my young company, my comrades in arms.
And be sure also, my beloved Hrothgar,
to send Hygelac the treasures I received.
Let the lord of the Geats gaze on that gold,
let Hrethel's son take note of it and see
that I found a ring-giver of rare magnificence
and enjoyed the good of his generosity.
And Unferth is to have what I inherited:
to that far-famed man I bequeath my own
1490   sharp-honed, wave-sheened wonderblade.
With Hrunting I shall gain glory or die."

After these words, the prince of the Weather-Geats
was impatient to be away and plunged suddenly:
without more ado, he dived into the heaving
depths of the lake. It was the best part of a day
before he could see the solid bottom.

Left: This sword found in a barrow at Coombe, Kent, is a fine example of an Anglo-Saxon ring-hilted sword of the pagan era. Before Beowulf dives into Grendel's mere, he arms himself with a "rare and ancient sword" that Unferth loans him. Ca. seventh century. Right: Drawing of the sword's hilt, showing where the ring was once attached.

101

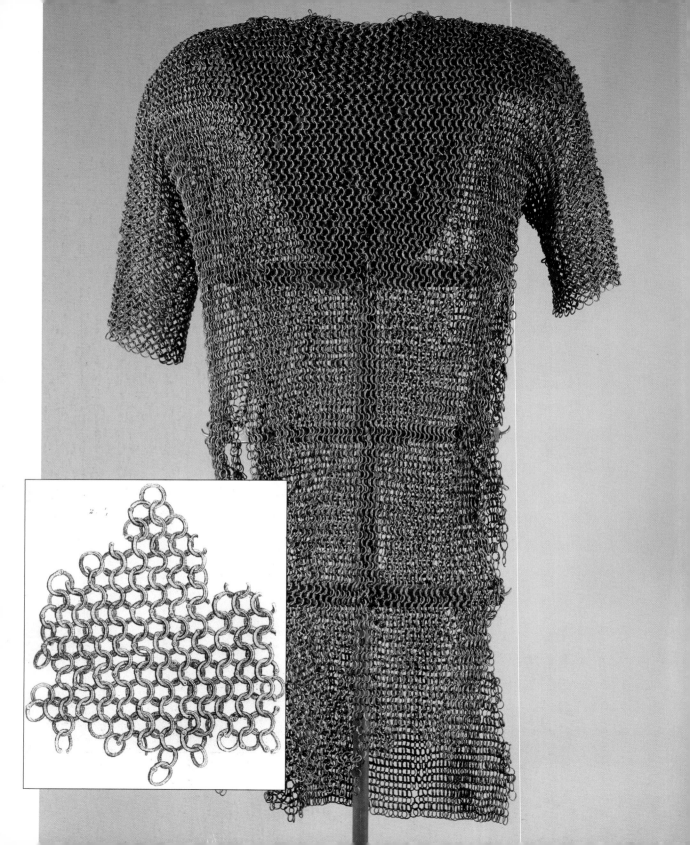

Quickly the one who haunted those waters,
who had scavenged and gone her gluttonous rounds
for a hundred seasons, sensed a human
1500   observing her outlandish lair from above.
So she lunged and clutched and managed to catch him
in her brutal grip; but his body, for all that,
remained unscathed: the mesh of the chain-mail
saved him on the outside. Her savage talons
failed to rip the web of his warshirt.
Then once she touched bottom, that wolfish swimmer
carried the ring-mailed prince to her court
so that for all his courage he could never use
the weapons he carried; and a bewildering horde
1510   came at him from the depths, droves of sea-beasts
who attacked with tusks and tore at his chain-mail
in a ghastly onslaught. The gallant man
could see he had entered some hellish turn-hole
and yet the water did not work against him
because the hall-roofing held off
the force of the current; then he saw firelight,
a gleam and flare-up, a glimmer of brightness.

The hero observed that swamp-thing from hell,
the tarn-hag in all her terrible strength,
1520   then heaved his war-sword and swung his arm:
the decorated blade came down ringing
and singing on her head. But he soon found
his battle-torch extinguished: the shining blade
refused to bite. It spared her and failed
the man in his need. It had gone through many
hand-to-hand fights, had hewed the armour
and helmets of the doomed, but here at last
the fabulous powers of that heirloom failed.

Beowulf is captured by Grendel's mother

His sword fails to do damage

Byrnie, or chain-mail shirt, recovered from a bog at Vimose, on the island of Funen, Denmark, where it had been deposited in the early third century A.D. It consists of about twenty thousand iron rings individually joined together. Without such protection (the poet makes clear), Beowulf would have perished at the bottom of Grendel's mere. Inset: Detail of the Vimose byrnie.

Hygelac's kinsman kept thinking about

1530 his name and fame: he never lost heart.

Then, in a fury, he flung his sword away.

The keen, inlaid, worm-loop-patterned steel

was hurled to the ground: he would have to rely

on the might of his arm. So must a man do

who intends to gain enduring glory

in a combat. Life doesn't cost him a thought.

Then the prince of War-Geats, warming to this fight

with Grendel's mother, gripped her shoulder

and laid about him in a battle frenzy:

1540 he pitched his killer opponent to the floor

but she rose quickly and retaliated,

grappled him tightly in her grim embrace.

The sure-footed fighter felt daunted,

the strongest of warriors stumbled and fell.

So she pounced upon him and pulled out

a broad, whetted knife: now she would avenge

her only child. But the mesh of chain-mail

on Beowulf's shoulder shielded his life,

turned the edge and tip of the blade.

1550 The son of Ecgtheow would have surely perished

and the Geats lost their warrior under the wide earth

had the strong links and locks of his war-gear

not helped to save him: holy God

decided the victory. It was easy for the Lord,

the Ruler of Heaven, to redress the balance

once Beowulf got back up on his feet.

Then he saw a blade that boded well,

a sword in her armoury, an ancient heirloom

from the days of the giants, an ideal weapon,

1560 one that any warrior would envy,

He fights back with his bare hands

Beowulf discovers a mighty sword and slays his opponent

Unlike her son, Grendel's mother does not scorn to use weapons. When she has the hero down, she drives a "broad, whetted knife" against his chest. This dagger found in the River Danube near Belgrade would have looked exotic to the people of the Beowulf *poet's day, and so they might have thought of it as suiting the Grendel-kin, who seem like a throwback to an earlier age. Roman Iron Age.*

105

but so huge and heavy of itself
only Beowulf could wield it in a battle.
So the Shieldings' hero, hard-pressed and enraged,
took a firm hold of the hilt and swung
the blade in an arc, a resolute blow
that bit deep into her neck-bone
and severed it entirely, toppling the doomed
house of her flesh; she fell to the floor.
The sword dripped blood, the swordsman was elated.

1570   A light appeared and the place brightened
the way the sky does when heaven's candle
is shining clearly. He inspected the vault:
with sword held high, its hilt raised
to guard and threaten, Hygelac's thane
scouted by the wall in Grendel's wake.
Now the weapon was to prove its worth.
The warrior determined to take revenge
for every gross act Grendel had committed—
and not only for that one occasion
1580   when he'd come to slaughter the sleeping troops,
fifteen of Hrothgar's house-guards
surprised on their benches and ruthlessly devoured,
and as many again carried away,
a brutal plunder. Beowulf in his fury
now settled that score: he saw the monster
in his resting place, war-weary and wrecked,
a lifeless corpse, a casualty
of the battle in Heorot. The body gaped
at the stroke dealt to it after death:
1590   Beowulf cut the corpse's head off.

Immediately the counsellors keeping a lookout

*He proceeds to behead
Grendel's corpse*

The hero's victory over Grendel's mother is decided by God. Moreover, it is accompanied by a blaze of light that illuminates the scene "the way the sky does when heaven's candle / is shining clearly." This image taken in southwest Wisconsin, on a day without monsters, can serve as one of many possible counterparts to the poet's vision. An ancient Indian effigy mound is to the right.

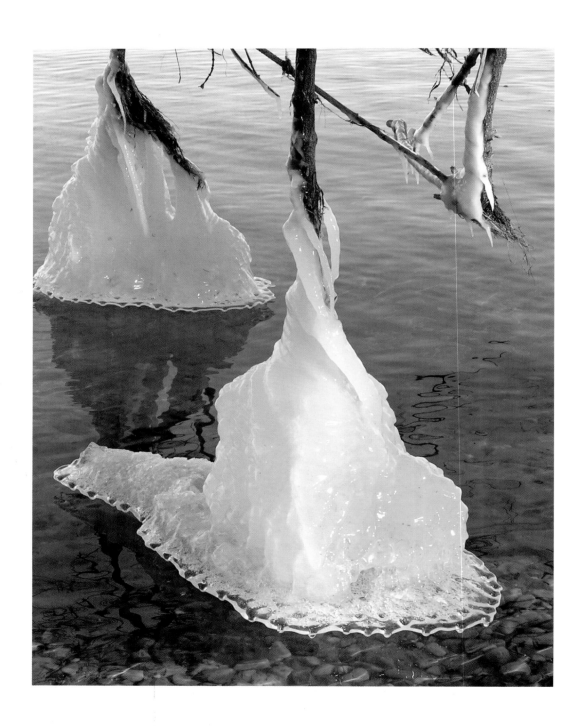

with Hrothgar, watching the lake water,
saw a heave-up and surge of waves
and blood in the backwash. They bowed grey heads,
spoke in their sage, experienced way
about the good warrior, how they never again
expected to see that prince returning
in triumph to their king. It was clear to many
that the wolf of the deep had destroyed him forever.

Forebodings of those on the shore

1600   The ninth hour of the day arrived.
The brave Shieldings abandoned the cliff-top
and the king went home; but sick at heart,
staring at the mere, the strangers held on.
They wished, without hope, to behold their lord,
Beowulf himself.
           Meanwhile, the sword

The sword blade melts

began to wilt into gory icicles,
to slather and thaw. It was a wonderful thing,
the way it all melted as ice melts
when the Father eases the fetters off the frost
1610   and unravels the water-ropes. He who wields power
over time and tide: He is the true Lord.

The Geat captain saw treasure in abundance
but carried no spoils from those quarters
except for the head and the inlaid hilt
embossed with jewels; its blade had melted
and the scrollwork on it burnt, so scalding was the blood
of the poisonous fiend who had perished there.
Then away he swam, the one who had survived
the fall of his enemies, flailing to the surface.
1620   The wide water, the waves and pools
were no longer infested once the wandering fiend

Beowulf returns with the sword's hilt and Grendel's head

A second miraculous event accompanies the victory over Grendel's mother. The blade of the giant-wrought sword that the hero has wielded begins to melt away like ice in springtime, leaving only the hilt behind. The shores of northern lakes (such as this lake in southern Wisconsin) sometimes present arresting scenes when ice has melted and refrozen in unusual formations, as the poet may have noticed.

let go of her life and this unreliable world.
The seafarers' leader made for land,
resolutely swimming, delighted with his prize,
the mighty load he was lugging to the surface.
His thanes advanced in a troop to meet him,
thanking God and taking great delight
in seeing their prince back safe and sound.
Quickly the hero's helmet and mail-shirt
1630   were loosed and unlaced. The lake settled,
clouds darkened above the bloodshot depths.

With high hearts they headed away
along footpaths and trails through the fields,
roads that they knew, each of them wrestling
with the head they were carrying from the lakeside cliff,
men kingly in their courage and capable
of difficult work. It was a task for four
to hoist Grendel's head on a spear
and bear it under strain to the bright hall.
1640   But soon enough they neared the place,
fourteen Geats in fine fettle,
striding across the outlying ground
in a delighted throng around their leader.

In he came then, the thane's commander,
the arch-warrior, to address Hrothgar:
his courage was proven, his glory was secure.
Grendel's head was hauled by the hair,
dragged across the floor where the people were drinking,
a horror for both queen and company to behold.
1650   They stared in awe. It was an astonishing sight.

Beowulf, son of Ecgtheow, spoke:

He displays Grendel's head in Heorot

When the hero emerges in triumph from the monsters' pool, his men greet him joyfully. The pool subsides, with its eerie "bloodshot depths." This photo of alders reflected in a stagnant pool was taken near Knapsø, in the dead ice landscape west of Lejre, in an area that has since been bulldozed to be converted into a golf course. Compare the image of the same pond on page 90.

111

"So, son of Halfdane, prince of the Shieldings,
we are glad to bring this booty from the lake.
It is a token of triumph and we tender it to you.
I barely survived the battle under water.
It was hard-fought, a desperate affair
that could have gone badly; if God had not helped me,
the outcome would have been quick and fatal.
Although Hrunting is hard-edged,
1660   I could never bring it to bear in battle.
But the Lord of Men allowed me to behold—
for He often helps the unbefriended—
an ancient sword shining on the wall,
a weapon made for giants, there for the wielding.
Then my moment came in the combat and I struck
the dwellers in that den. Next thing the damascened
sword blade melted; it bloated and it burned
in their rushing blood. I have wrested the hilt
from the enemies' hand, avenged the evil
1670   done to the Danes; it is what was due.
And this I pledge, O prince of the Shieldings:
you can sleep secure with your company of troops
in Heorot Hall. Never need you fear
for a single thane of your sept or nation,
young warriors or old, that laying waste of life
that you and your people endured of yore."

Then the gold hilt was handed over
to the old lord, a relic from long ago
for the venerable ruler. That rare smithwork
1680   was passed on to the prince of the Danes
when those devils perished; once death removed
that murdering, guilt-steeped, God-cursed fiend,
eliminating his unholy life

Beowulf presents to Hrothgar the rune-inscribed sword-hilt he has brought back with him from the mere—a "relic from long ago" fashioned by giants. This beautifully decorated sword-hilt from Ultuna, Sweden, was made by men, not giants. With its zoomorphic interlace design, it calls to mind the consummate craft of metalworkers of the late Germanic Iron Age.

113

and his mother's as well, it was willed to that king
who of all the lavish gift-lords of the north
was the best regarded between the two seas.

Hrothgar spoke; he examined the hilt,
that relic of old times. It was engraved all over
and showed how war first came into the world
and the flood destroyed the tribe of giants.
They suffered a terrible severance from the Lord;
the Almighty made the waters rise,
drowned them in the deluge for retribution.
In pure gold inlay on the sword-guards
there were rune-markings correctly incised,
stating and recording for whom the sword
had been first made and ornamented
with its scrollworked hilt. Then everyone hushed
as the son of Halfdane spoke this wisdom.

Hrothgar's address to
Beowulf

"A protector of his people, pledged to uphold
truth and justice and to respect tradition,
is entitled to affirm that this man
was born to distinction. Beowulf, my friend,
your fame has gone far and wide,
you are known everywhere. In all things you are even-tempered,
prudent and resolute. So I stand firm by the promise of friendship
we exchanged before. Forever you will be
your people's mainstay and your own warriors'
helping hand.
             Heremod was different,
the way he behaved to Ecgwala's sons.
His rise in the world brought little joy
to the Danish people, only death and destruction.

He contrasts Beowulf
with King Heremod

1690

1700

1710

Left: This sword from Chessel Down, on the Isle of Wight, was sheathed in a rune-inscribed scabbard. Top right: Drawing of runes on the Chessel Down scabbard mouthpiece. Bottom right: The pommel of this sword from Guilton, Kent, is incised with runelike marks. It is unlikely that the reason they are hard to read is that they were inscribed in the age of giants, like the runes mentioned in Beowulf.

115

He vented his rage on men he caroused with,
killed his own comrades, a pariah king
who cut himself off from his own kind,
even though Almighty God had made him
eminent and powerful and marked him from the start
for a happy life. But a change happened,
he grew bloodthirsty, gave no more rings
1720   to honour the Danes. He suffered in the end
for having plagued his people for so long:
his life lost happiness.

                So learn from this
and understand true values. I who tell you
have wintered into wisdom.

                    It is a great wonder

Hrothgar's discourse on the dangers of power

how Almighty God in His magnificence
favours our race with rank and scope
and the gift of wisdom; His sway is wide.
Sometimes He allows the mind of a man
of distinguished birth to follow its bent,
1730   grants him fulfilment and felicity on earth
and forts to command in his own country.
He permits him to lord it in many lands
until the man in his unthinkingness
forgets that it will ever end for him.
He indulges his desires; illness and old age
mean nothing to him; his mind is untroubled
by envy or malice or the thought of enemies
with their hate-honed swords. The whole world
conforms to his will, he is kept from the worst
1740   until an element of overweening
enters him and takes hold
while the soul's guard, its sentry, drowses,
grown too distracted. A killer stalks him,

One of the oddities of Beowulf *is that in lines 1700–1784, one of the most forceful sermons of the early Middle Ages is put into the mouth of a pagan. Although Hrothgar knows nothing of Christ, he has an unclouded knowledge of God and of His workings. This image of God crowned in majesty is from an eleventh-century Anglo-Saxon illuminated manuscript now in Trinity College, Cambridge (MS B 104, fol. 16b).*

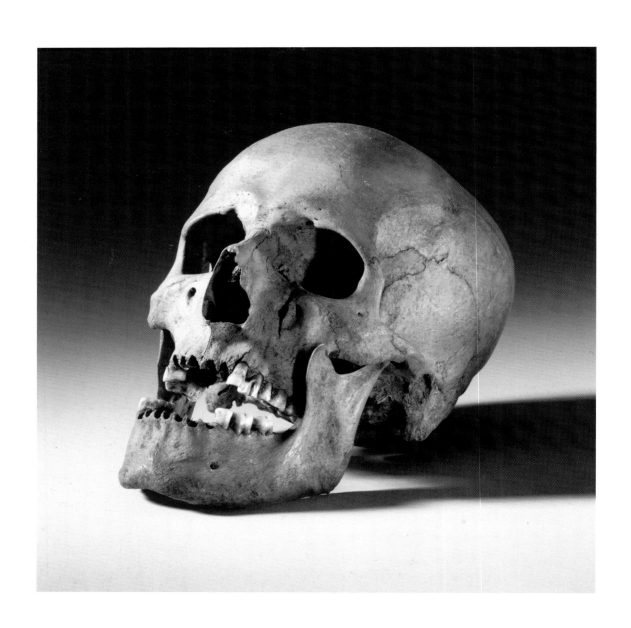

an archer who draws a deadly bow.
And then the man is hit in the heart,
the arrow flies beneath his defences,
the devious promptings of the demon start.
His old possessions seem paltry to him now.
He covets and resents; dishonours custom
1750 and bestows no gold; and because of good things
that the Heavenly Powers gave him in the past
he ignores the shape of things to come.
Then finally the end arrives
when the body he was lent collapses and falls
prey to its death; ancestral possessions
and the goods he hoarded are inherited by another
who lets them go with a liberal hand.

"O flower of warriors, beware of that trap.
Choose, dear Beowulf, the better part,
1760 eternal rewards. Do not give way to pride.
For a brief while your strength is in bloom
but it fades quickly; and soon there will follow
illness or the sword to lay you low,
or a sudden fire or surge of water
or jabbing blade or javelin from the air
or repellent age. Your piercing eye
will dim and darken; and death will arrive,
dear warrior, to sweep you away.

Beowulf is exhorted to be mindful of the fragility of life

"Just so I ruled the Ring-Danes' country
1770 for fifty years, defended them in wartime
with spear and sword against constant assaults
by many tribes: I came to believe
my enemies had faded from the face of the earth.
Still, what happened was a hard reversal

No life is immune to danger: Hrothgar's experience proves it

At the moment of Beowulf's greatest triumph, Hrothgar reminds him that sooner or later, one or another death will await him, perhaps from "jabbing blade or javelin." This human skull from Uglemosen, on the island of Lolland, Denmark, brings this message home. The skull is pierced by a hole under the left eye—the result of a lance wound, evidently. Early Germanic Iron Age.

119

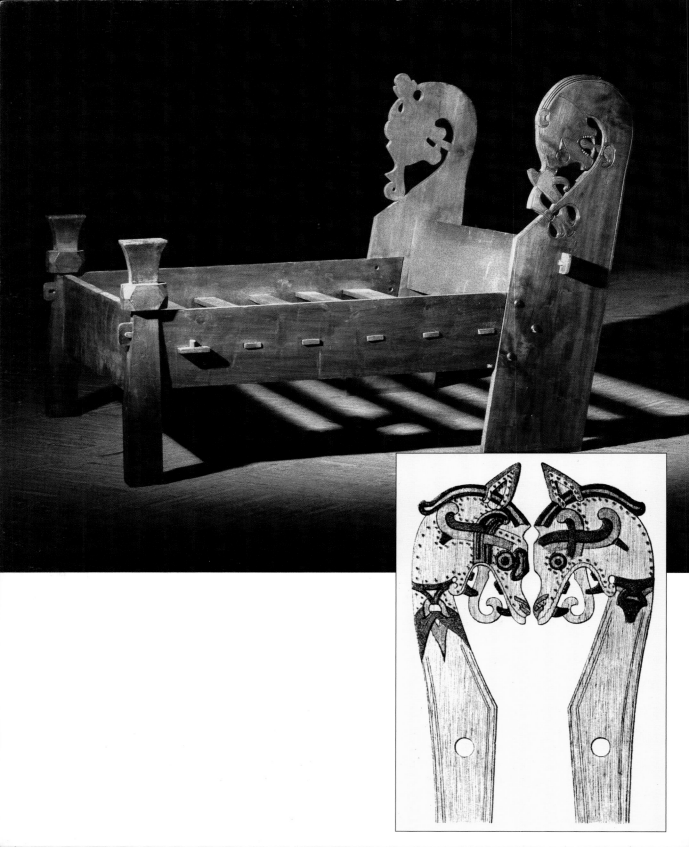

from bliss to grief. Grendel struck
after lying in wait. He laid waste to the land
and from that moment my mind was in dread
of his depredations. So I praise God
in His heavenly glory that I lived to behold
1780   this head dripping blood and that after such harrowing
I can look upon it in triumph at last.
Take your place, then, with pride and pleasure
and move to the feast. To-morrow morning
our treasure will be shared and showered upon you."

The Geat was elated and gladly obeyed
the old man's bidding; he sat on the bench.
And soon all was restored, the same as before.
Happiness came back, the hall was thronged,
and a banquet set forth; black night fell
1790   and covered them in darkness.
                       Then the company rose
for the old campaigner: the grey-haired prince
was ready for bed. And a need for rest
came over the brave shield-bearing Geat.
He was a weary seafarer, far from home,
so immediately a house-guard guided him out,
one whose office entailed looking after
whatever a thane on the road in those days
might need or require. It was noble courtesy.

That great heart rested. The hall towered,
1800   gold-shingled and gabled, and the guest slept in it
until the black raven with raucous glee
announced heaven's joy, and a hurry of brightness
overran the shadows. Warriors rose quickly,
impatient to be off: their own country

A feast. The warriors rest

Top: Exhausted after his fight in the depths of the mere, Beowulf retires to separate sleeping quarters. The Danish king and queen, too, have spent each night in a separate longhouse, it seems. One can imagine the royal couple sleeping in a handsome bed like this reconstructed one from Oseberg, in Vestfold, Norway. Ca. 800–850. Bottom: Reconstructed carved double-sided headboard from Gokstad, in Vestfold, Norway. Ca. 900.

121

was beckoning the nobles; and the bold voyager
longed to be aboard his distant boat.
Then that stalwart fighter ordered Hrunting
to be brought to Unferth, and bade Unferth
take the sword and thanked him for lending it.
1810   He said he had found it a friend in battle
and a powerful help; he put no blame
on the blade's cutting edge. He was a considerate man.

And there the warriors stood in their war-gear,
eager to go, while their honoured lord
approached the platform where the other sat.
The undaunted hero addressed Hrothgar.
Beowulf, son of Ecgtheow, spoke:
"Now we who crossed the wide sea
have to inform you that we feel a desire
1820   to return to Hygelac. Here we have been welcomed
and thoroughly entertained. You have treated us well.
If there is any favour on earth I can perform
beyond deeds of arms I have done already,
anything that would merit your affections more,
I shall act, my lord, with alacrity.
If ever I hear from across the ocean
that people on your borders are threatening battle
as attackers have done from time to time,
I shall land with a thousand thanes at my back
1830   to help your cause. Hygelac may be young
to rule a nation, but this much I know
about the king of the Geats: he will come to my aid
and want to support me by word and action
in your hour of need, when honour dictates
that I raise a hedge of spears around you.
Then if Hrethric should think about travelling

*Beowulf and his band
prepare to depart*

*In keeping with his character as a man of action, Beowulf prefers not to prolong his stay in Denmark. He says
farewell to his host and promises him renewed assistance from across the sea if needed in the future. This photo
of headlands and clouds (taken in the west of Scotland) is suggestive of the eternal lure and beauty of the sea
for people of venturesome spirit.*

123

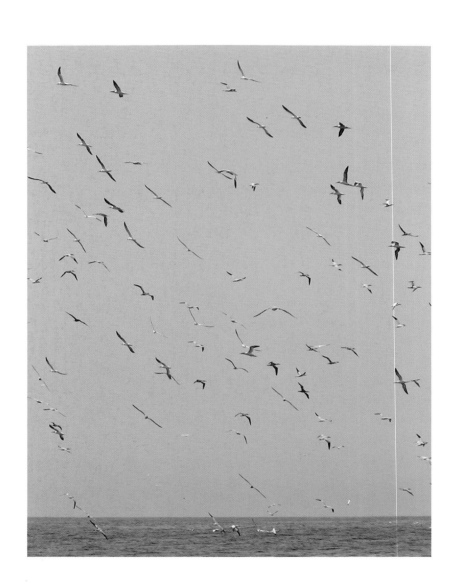

as a king's son to the court of the Geats,
he will find many friends. Foreign places
yield more to one who is himself worth meeting."

1840 Hrothgar spoke and answered him:

*Hrothgar declares that
Beowulf is fit to be
king of the Geats*

"The Lord in His wisdom sent you those words
and they came from the heart. I have never heard
so young a man make truer observations.
You are strong in body and mature in mind,
impressive in speech. If it should come to pass
that Hrethel's descendant dies beneath a spear,
if deadly battle or the sword blade or disease
fells the prince who guards your people
and you are still alive, then I firmly believe
the seafaring Geats won't find a man
worthier of acclaim as their king and defender
than you, if only you would undertake
the lordship of your homeland. My liking for you
deepens with time, dear Beowulf.
What you have done is to draw two peoples,
the Geat nation and us neighbouring Danes,
into shared peace and a pact of friendship
in spite of hatreds we have harboured in the past.
For as long as I rule this far-flung land
treasures will change hands and each side will treat
the other with gifts; across the gannet's bath,
over the broad sea, whorled prows will bring
presents and tokens. I know your people
are beyond reproach in every respect,
steadfast in the old way with friend or foe."

Then the earls' defender furnished the hero
with twelve treasures and told him to set out,

*Gifts presented,
farewells taken*

---

*Gannets soaring and diving off the North Atlantic coast. Hrothgar speaks of the sea as "the gannet's bath."
Some other kennings (or two-tiered metaphorical terms) for the sea in Old English poetry are "the courtyard
of winds," "the cup of waves," "the whale's bridle path," and "the bridle-path of the sail"—that is, of the ship,
viewed as a sea-steed. The hero's ship moves in poetry, not just in water.*

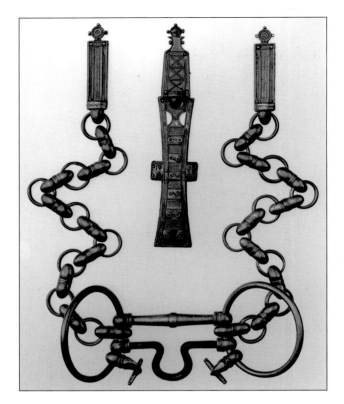

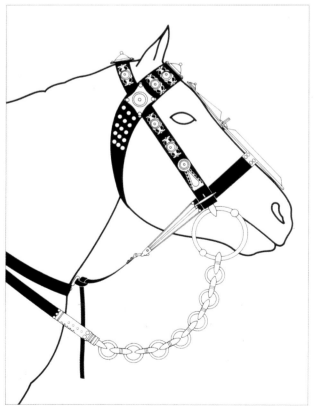

sail with those gifts safely home
to the people he loved, but to return promptly.
1870 And so the good and grey-haired Dane,
that high-born king, kissed Beowulf
and embraced his neck, then broke down
in sudden tears. Two forebodings
disturbed him in his wisdom, but one was stronger:
nevermore would they meet each other
face to face. And such was his affection
that he could not help being overcome:
his fondness for the man was so deep-founded,
it warmed his heart and wound the heartstrings
1880 tight in his breast.
           The embrace ended
and Beowulf, glorious in his gold regalia,
stepped the green earth. Straining at anchor
and ready for boarding, his boat awaited him.
So they went on their journey, and Hrothgar's generosity
was praised repeatedly. He was a peerless king
until old age sapped his strength and did him
mortal harm, as it has done so many.

Down to the waves then, dressed in the web
of their chain-mail and warshirts the young men marched

*The Geats march back
to the shore*

1890 in high spirits. The coast-guard spied them,
thanes setting forth, the same as before.
His salute this time from the top of the cliff
was far from unmannerly; he galloped to meet them
and as they took ship in their shining gear,
he said how welcome they would be in Geatland.
Then the broad hull was beached on the sand
to be cargoed with treasure, horses and war-gear.
The curved prow motioned; the mast stood high

*Top: The same coast-guard who had challenged the Geats upon their arrival in Denmark now rides down from
the bluffs to help send them off. His horse both provides mobility and embodies his authority. These equestrian
trappings were found in a bog at Vimose, on the island of Funen, Denmark. Early third century. Bottom:
Drawing showing the use of such equestrian trappings.*

above Hrothgar's riches in the loaded hold.

1900 The guard who had watched the boat was given
a sword with gold fittings and in future days
that present would make him a respected man
at his place on the mead-bench.

                            Then the keel plunged
and shook in the sea; and they sailed from Denmark.

Right away the mast was rigged with its sea-shawl;
sail-ropes were tightened, timbers drummed
and stiff winds kept the wave-crosser
skimming ahead; as she heaved forward,
her foamy neck was fleet and buoyant,
1910 a lapped prow loping over currents,
until finally the Geats caught sight of coastline
and familiar cliffs. The keel reared up,
wind lifted it home, it hit on the land.

They sail from Denmark

The harbour guard came hurrying out
to the rolling water: he had watched the offing
long and hard, on the lookout for those friends.
With the anchor cables, he moored their craft
right where it had beached, in case a backwash
might catch the hull and carry it away.
1920 Then he ordered the prince's treasure-trove
to be carried ashore. It was a short step
from there to where Hrethel's son and heir,
Hygelac the gold-giver, makes his home
on a secure cliff, in the company of retainers.

They arrive at Hygelac's stronghold

The building was magnificent, the king majestic,
ensconced in his hall; and although Hygd, his queen,

At the Viking Ship Museum, Denmark, carpenters using traditional tools and materials have built a number of full-scale replicas of Viking Age ships. The Helge Ask, a replica of the light warship known as Skuldelev 5 (see page 14), is one of these. Fully seaworthy, it has been used for trials of the square sail and the outboard steering oar used in Viking times.

was young, a few short years at court,
her mind was thoughtful and her manners sure.
Haereth's daughter behaved generously

Queen Hygd
introduced. The story
of Queen Modthryth,
Hygd's opposite, is
told by the poet

1930   and stinted nothing when she distributed
bounty to the Geats.

                    Great Queen Modthryth
perpetrated terrible wrongs.
If any retainer ever made bold
to look her in the face, if an eye not her lord's
stared at her directly during daylight,
the outcome was sealed: he was kept bound
in hand-tightened shackles, racked, tortured
until doom was pronounced—death by the sword,
slash of blade, blood-gush and death qualms

1940   in an evil display. Even a queen
outstanding in beauty must not overstep like that.
A queen should weave peace, not punish the innocent
with loss of life for imagined insults.
But Hemming's kinsman put a halt to her ways
and drinkers round the table had another tale:
she was less of a bane to people's lives,
less cruel-minded, after she was married
to the brave Offa, a bride arrayed
in her gold finery, given away

1950   by a caring father, ferried to her young prince
over dim seas. In days to come
she would grace the throne and grow famous
for her good deeds and conduct of life,
her high devotion to the hero king
who was the best king, it has been said,
between the two seas or anywhere else
on the face of the earth. Offa was honoured
far and wide for his generous ways,

"The building was magnificent," the poet says of King Hygelac's hall (line 1925). This house built in 1941 at the Viking-era fortress at Trelleborg, on the island of Zealand, gives an impression of such a building. It is a full-scale replica of one of thirty-one such longhouses built at Trelleborg in the late tenth century. Certain of its architectural details (such as the porch) may not be reconstructed accurately, however.

his fighting spirit and his far-seeing
1960   defence of his homeland; from him there sprang Eomer,
Garmund's grandson, kinsman of Hemming,
his warriors' mainstay and master of the field.

Heroic Beowulf and his band of men
crossed the wide strand, striding along
the sandy foreshore; the sun shone,
the world's candle warmed them from the south
as they hastened to where, as they had heard,
the young king, Ongentheow's killer
and his people's protector, was dispensing rings
1970   inside his bawn. Beowulf's return
was reported to Hygelac as soon as possible,
news that the captain was now in the enclosure,
his battle-brother back from the fray
alive and well, walking to the hall.
Room was quickly made, on the king's orders,
and the troops filed across the cleared floor.

*Beowulf and his troop
are welcomed in
Hygelac's hall*

After Hygelac had offered greetings
to his loyal thane in lofty speech,
he and his kinsman, that hale survivor,
1980   sat face to face. Haereth's daughter
moved about with the mead-jug in her hand,
taking care of the company, filling the cups
that warriors held out. Then Hygelac began
to put courteous questions to his old comrade
in the high hall. He hankered to know
every tale the Sea-Geats had to tell.

"How did you fare on your foreign voyage,
dear Beowulf, when you abruptly decided

*Hygelac questions
Beowulf*

Interior of the Trelleborg longhouse. Trelleborg is thought to have been one of four fortresses built by King Harald Gormsson (d. ca. 985) as part of his successful campaign to win control over all Denmark. Each of the thirty-one houses at Trelleborg was about 30 meters (or about 98 feet) long, built of stout beams, with a dirt floor, a central hearth, and raised platforms that could have been used as beds.

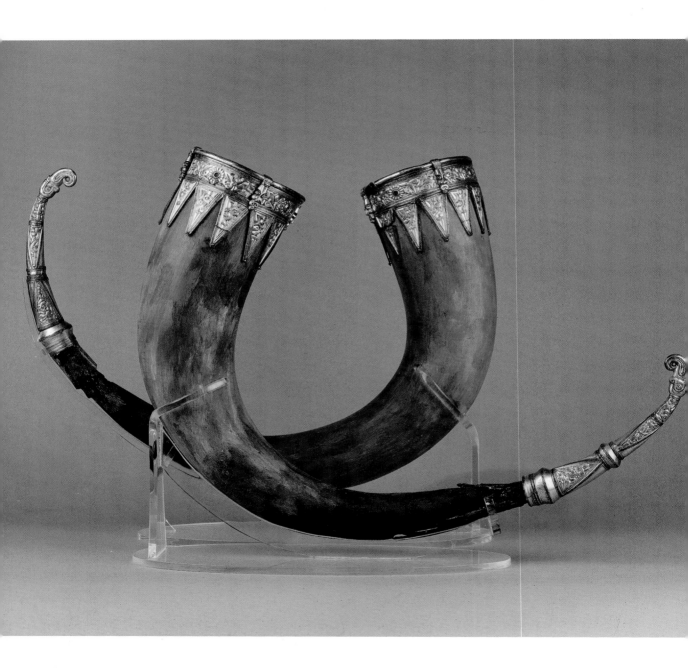

to sail away across the salt water
1990 and fight at Heorot? Did you help Hrothgar
much in the end? Could you ease the prince
of his well-known troubles? Your undertaking
cast my spirits down, I dreaded the outcome
of your expedition and pleaded with you
long and hard to leave the killer be,
let the South-Danes settle their own
blood-feud with Grendel. So God be thanked
I am granted this sight of you, safe and sound."

Beowulf, son of Ecgtheow, spoke:

Beowulf tells what
happened in the land
of the Danes

2000 "What happened, Lord Hygelac, is hardly a secret
any more among men in this world—
myself and Grendel coming to grips
on the very spot where he visited destruction
on the Victory-Shieldings and violated
life and limb, losses I avenged
so no earthly offspring of Grendel's
need ever boast of that bout before dawn,
no matter how long the last of his evil
family survives.
                    When I first landed
2010 I hastened to the ring-hall and saluted Hrothgar.
Once he discovered why I had come
the son of Halfdane sent me immediately
to sit with his own sons on the bench.
It was a happy gathering. In my whole life
I have never seen mead enjoyed more
in any hall on earth. Sometimes the queen
herself appeared, peace-pledge between nations,
to hearten the young ones and hand out
a torque to a warrior, then take her place.

While King Hygelac questions Beowulf about how he fared in Denmark, Queen Hygd pours drinks. These two grandiose drinking horns were buried in a pagan funeral mound at Taplow, Buckinghamshire. Only the silver-gilt fittings are original. The horns came from an aurochs, a huge ox that was hunted to extinction in northern Europe sometime before the poet's day. Late sixth century.

2020   Sometimes Hrothgar's daughter distributed
ale to older ranks, in order on the benches:
I heard the company call her Freawaru
as she made her rounds, presenting men
with the gem-studded bowl, young bride-to-be
to the gracious Ingeld, in her gold-trimmed attire.
The friend of the Shieldings favours her betrothal:
the guardian of the kingdom sees good in it
and hopes this woman will heal old wounds
and grievous feuds.

                 But generally the spear
2030   is prompt to retaliate when a prince is killed,
no matter how admirable the bride may be.

He foresees the grim
consequence of a
proposed marriage

"Think how the Heathobards will be bound to feel,
their lord, Ingeld, and his loyal thanes,
when he walks in with that woman to the feast:
Danes are at the table, being entertained,
honoured guests in glittering regalia,
burnished ring-mail that was their hosts' birthright,
looted when the Heathobards could no longer wield
their weapons in the shield-clash, when they went down
2040   with their beloved comrades and forfeited their lives.
Then an old spearman will speak while they are drinking,
having glimpsed some heirloom that brings alive
memories of the massacre; his mood will darken
and heart-stricken, in the stress of his emotion,
he will begin to test a young man's temper
and stir up trouble, starting like this:
'Now, my friend, don't you recognize
your father's sword, his favourite weapon,
the one he wore when he went out in his war-mask
2050   to face the Danes on that final day?

When the Danes
appear at Freawaru's
wedding, their hosts,
the Heathobards, will
be stirred to avenge an
old defeat

*While recounting his adventures, Beowulf remarks that the Danish princess Freawaru served drink to the men
in Heorot. Though engaged to be married to Ingeld, chieftain of the Heathobards, Freawaru was still living at
home. Given her father's wealth and status, it is not overly fanciful to imagine her wearing exotic jewelry, such
as this pair of eagle brooches from Visigothic Spain. Early sixth century.*

After Wethergeld died and his men were doomed
the Shieldings quickly claimed the field,
and now here's a son of one or other
of those same killers coming through our hall
overbearing us, mouthing boasts,
and rigged in armour that by right is yours.'
And so he keeps on, recalling and accusing,
working things up with bitter words
until one of the lady's retainers lies

2060   spattered in blood, split open
on his father's account. The killer knows
the lie of the land and escapes with his life.
Then on both sides the oath-bound lords
will break the peace, a passionate hate
will build up in Ingeld and love for his bride
will falter in him as the feud rankles.
I therefore suspect the good faith of the Heathobards,
the truth of their friendship and the trustworthiness
of their alliance with the Danes.

                 But now, my lord,

*The tale of the fight
with Grendel resumed*

2070   I shall carry on with my account of Grendel,
the whole story of everything that happened
in the hand-to-hand fight.

                After heaven's gem
had gone mildly to earth, that maddened spirit,
the terror of those twilights, came to attack us
where we stood guard, still safe inside the hall.
There deadly violence came down on Handscio
and he fell as fate ordained, the first to perish,
rigged out for the combat. A comrade from our ranks
had come to grief in Grendel's maw:

2080   he ate up the entire body.
There was blood on his teeth, he was bloated and furious,

---

*Beowulf tells Hygelac of the violence that he fears will erupt after Princess Freawaru arrives in Ingeld's hall
with her Danish retainers. Ingeld's father had been killed by the Danes, and such an event is seldom forgotten.
This woodcut by the Danish artist Sigurd Vasegaard (made for an edition of the* History of the Danes *by
Saxo Grammaticus) captures the mood of such a scene.*

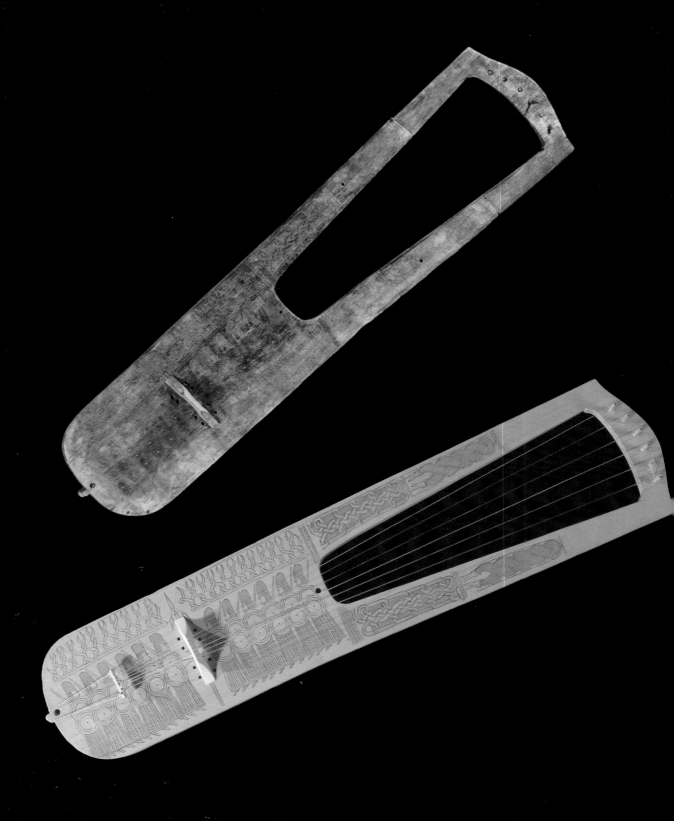

all roused up, yet still unready
to leave the hall empty-handed;
renowned for his might, he matched himself against me,
wildly reaching. He had this roomy pouch,
a strange accoutrement, intricately strung
and hung at the ready, a rare patchwork
of devilishly fitted dragon-skins.
I had done him no wrong, yet the raging demon
wanted to cram me and many another
2090   into this bag—but it was not to be
once I got to my feet in a blind fury.
It would take too long to tell how I repaid
the terror of the land for every life he took
and so won credit for you, my king,
and for all your people. And although he got away
to enjoy life's sweetness for a while longer,
his right hand stayed behind him in Heorot,
evidence of his miserable overthrow
2100   as he dived into murk on the mere bottom.

"I got lavish rewards from the lord of the Danes
for my part in the battle, beaten gold
and much else, once morning came
and we took our places at the banquet table.
There was singing and excitement: an old reciter,
a carrier of stories, recalled the early days.
At times some hero made the timbered harp
tremble with sweetness, or related true
and tragic happenings; at times the king
2110   gave the proper turn to some fantastic tale,
or a battle-scarred veteran, bowed with age,
would begin to remember the martial deeds

*Beowulf recalls the
feast in Heorot*

---

*Top: Beowulf recalls those times in Heorot when a musician "made the timbered harp / tremble with sweet-
ness." This six-stringed lyre from Trossingen, Germany, survives very nearly intact. Its shape conforms fairly
closely to that of the reconstructed lyre from Sutton Hoo (page 6). Ca. A.D. 600. Bottom: Modern replica of the
Trossingen lyre, showing its inscribed frieze of warriors.*

of his youth and prime and be overcome
as the past welled up in his wintry heart.

"We were happy there the whole day long
and enjoyed our time until another night
descended upon us. Then suddenly
the vehement mother avenged her son
and wreaked destruction. Death had robbed her,

2120   Geats had slain Grendel, so his ghastly dam
struck back and with bare-faced defiance
laid a man low. Thus life departed
from the sage Aeschere, an elder wise in counsel.
But afterwards, on the morning following,
the Danes could not burn the dead body
nor lay the remains of the man they loved
on his funeral pyre. She had fled with the corpse
and taken refuge beneath torrents on the mountain.
It was a hard blow for Hrothgar to bear,

2130   harder than any he had undergone before.
And so the heartsore king beseeched me
in your royal name to take my chances
underwater, to win glory
and prove my worth. He promised me rewards.
Hence, as is well known, I went to my encounter
with the terror-monger at the bottom of the tarn.
For a while it was hand-to-hand between us,
then blood went curling along the currents
and I beheaded Grendel's mother in the hall

2140   with a mighty sword. I barely managed
to escape with my life; my time had not yet come.
But Halfdane's heir, the shelter of those earls,
again endowed me with gifts in abundance.

*He tells about
Grendel's mother*

---

*This image of an oak tree overhanging Knapsø, west of Lejre, calls to mind the strange landscape associated
with Grendel's mere. When recounting his adventures, Beowulf makes little attempt to evoke the horrors of
that scenery. This is typical of the poet's narrative technique. An event may be mentioned (or a scene recalled)
twice or three times, but never in the same terms as before.*

"Thus the king acted with due custom.
I was paid and recompensed completely,
given full measure and the freedom to choose
from Hrothgar's treasures by Hrothgar himself.
These, King Hygelac, I am happy to present
to you as gifts. It is still upon your grace
2150   that all favour depends. I have few kinsmen
who are close, my king, except for your kind self."
Then he ordered the boar-framed standard to be brought,
the battle-topping helmet, the mail-shirt grey as hoar-frost
and the precious war-sword; and proceeded with his speech.

*Beowulf presents
Hygelac with the
treasures he has won*

"When Hrothgar presented this war-gear to me
he instructed me, my lord, to give you some account
of why it signifies his special favour.
He said it had belonged to his older brother,
King Heorogar, who had long kept it,
2160   but that Heorogar had never bequeathed it
to his son Heoroweard, that worthy scion,
loyal as he was.
               Enjoy it well."

I heard four horses were handed over next.
Beowulf bestowed four bay steeds
to go with the armour, swift gallopers,
all alike. So ought a kinsman act,
instead of plotting and planning in secret
to bring people to grief, or conspiring to arrange
the death of comrades. The warrior king
2170   was uncle to Beowulf and honoured by his nephew:
each was concerned for the other's good.

I heard he presented Hygd with a gorget,

---

*Beowulf remarks that he was "given . . . the freedom to choose / from Hrothgar's treasures" for a suitable
reward. Having many good options, he might have picked out a treasure like this one. Pieces of polished gar-
net are fitted into individually shaped gold chambers, in the cloisonné technique that is characteristic of fine
jewelry of the pagan Germanic period. This splendid disc pendant is from Faversham, Kent. Seventh century.*

the priceless torque that the prince's daughter,
Wealhtheow, had given him; and three horses,
supple creatures, brilliantly saddled.
The bright necklace would be luminous on Hygd's breast.

Thus Beowulf bore himself with valour; *Beowulf's exemplary*
life is extolled
he was formidable in battle yet behaved with honour
and took no advantage; never cut down
2180   a comrade who was drunk, kept his temper
and, warrior that he was, watched and controlled
his God-sent strength and his outstanding
natural powers. He had been poorly regarded
for a long time, was taken by the Geats
for less than he was worth: and their lord too
had never much esteemed him in the mead-hall.
They firmly believed that he lacked force,
that the prince was a weakling; but presently
every affront to his deserving was reversed.

2190   The battle-famed king, bulwark of his earls, *Hygelac presents*
Beowulf with a sword
and great tracts of
land
ordered a gold-chased heirloom of Hrethel's
to be brought in; it was the best example
of a gem-studded sword in the Geat treasury.
This he laid on Beowulf's lap
and then rewarded him with land as well,
seven thousand hides, and a hall and a throne.
Both owned land by birth in that country,
ancestral grounds; but the greater right
and sway were inherited by the higher born.

2200   A lot was to happen in later days *Time passes. Beowulf*
rules the Geats for fifty
years
in the fury of battle. Hygelac fell
and the shelter of Heardred's shield proved useless

As a loyal kinsman and thane, Beowulf delivers to his king the treasures he was given in Denmark. His uncle,
King Hygelac, then rewards him with a large estate and with the best sword in his possession. It would be hard
to find a more precious sword dating from the Germanic period than this ring-hilted one from Snartemo, in
Vest-Agder, Norway, with its decorative goldwork. Sixth century.

against the fierce aggression of the Shylfings:
ruthless swordsmen, seasoned campaigners,
they came against him and his conquering nation,
and with cruel force cut him down
so that afterwards
                        the wide kingdom
reverted to Beowulf. He ruled it well
for fifty winters, grew old and wise

2210   as warden of the land
                        until one began
to dominate the dark, a dragon on the prowl

A dragon awakes. An accidental theft provokes his wrath

from the steep vaults of a stone-roofed barrow
where he guarded a hoard; there was a hidden passage,
unknown to men, but someone managed
to enter by it and interfere
with the heathen trove. He had handled and removed
a gem-studded goblet; it gained him nothing,
though with a thief's wiles he had outwitted
the sleeping dragon; that drove him into rage,

2220   as the people of that country would soon discover.

The intruder who broached the dragon's treasure
and moved him to wrath had never meant to.
It was desperation on the part of a slave
fleeing the heavy hand of some master,
guilt-ridden and on the run,
going to ground. But he soon began
to shake with terror; . . . . . . in shock
the wretch . . . .
. . . . panicked and ran

2230   away with the precious . . . .
metalwork. There were many other
heirlooms heaped inside the earth-house,

The dragon dwells in "a stone-roofed barrow" to which a hidden passage gives entry. The poet is probably calling to mind a megalithic chambered tomb of a type well known in northwest Europe. Such tombs pertain to the Neolithic period, and hence they were highly archaic even in the Beowulf *poet's day. Though idealized in a rustic manner, this nineteenth-century engraving of a chambered tomb from Zealand is architecturally exact.*

Long ago, a hoard was
hidden in the earth-
house by the last
survivor of a forgotten
race

because long ago, with deliberate care,
somebody now forgotten
had buried the riches of a high-born race
in this ancient cache. Death had come
and taken them all in times gone by
and the only one left to tell their tale,
the last of their line, could look forward to nothing
2240   but the same fate for himself: he foresaw that his joy
in the treasure would be brief.
                        A newly constructed
barrow stood waiting, on a wide headland
close to the waves, its entryway secured.
Into it the keeper of the hoard had carried
all the goods and golden ware
worth preserving. His words were few:
"Now, earth, hold what earls once held
and heroes can no more; it was mined from you first
by honourable men. My own people
2250   have been ruined in war; one by one
they went down to death, looked their last
on sweet life in the hall. I am left with nobody
to bear a sword or burnish plated goblets,
put a sheen on the cup. The companies have departed.
The hard helmet, hasped with gold,
will be stripped of its hoops; and the helmet-shiner
who should polish the metal of the war-mask sleeps;
the coat of mail that came through all fights,
through shield-collapse and cut of sword,
2260   decays with the warrior. Nor may webbed mail
range far and wide on the warlord's back
beside his mustered troops. No trembling harp,
no tuned timber, no tumbling hawk
swerving through the hall, no swift horse

The thief takes a single cup from the hoard. The poet calls it a sinc-fæt, literally a "precious vessel" (2231), a nonspecific term. With some poetic freedom, Heaney calls it "a gem-studded goblet" (2217). Since the cup would have been almost as archaic as the barrow, it can perhaps best be visualized as a simple gold object, like this striking cup found at Rillaton, Cornwall. Bronze Age.

pawing the courtyard. Pillage and slaughter
have emptied the earth of entire peoples."
And so he mourned as he moved about the world,
deserted and alone, lamenting his unhappiness
day and night, until death's flood
2270   brimmed up in his heart.
                              Then an old harrower of the dark

*The dragon nests in
the barrow and guards
the gold*

happened to find the hoard open,
the burning one who hunts out barrows,
the slick-skinned dragon, threatening the night sky
with streamers of fire. People on the farms
are in dread of him. He is driven to hunt out
hoards under ground, to guard heathen gold
through age-long vigils, though to little avail.
For three centuries, this scourge of the people
had stood guard on that stoutly protected
2280   underground treasury, until the intruder
unleashed its fury; he hurried to his lord
with the gold-plated cup and made his plea
to be reinstated. Then the vault was rifled,
the ring-hoard robbed, and the wretched man
had his request granted. His master gazed
on that find from the past for the first time.

When the dragon awoke, trouble flared again.

The dragon in turmoil

He rippled down the rock, writhing with anger
when he saw the footprints of the prowler who had stolen
2290   too close to his dreaming head.
So may a man not marked by fate
easily escape exile and woe
by the grace of God.
                              The hoard-guardian
scorched the ground as he scoured and hunted

In one crucial regard, the action of the poem's final episode is difficult to visualize. Very few dragons are depicted in the visual arts of the Anglo-Saxon period, though snakelike and wolflike creatures abound. This gilded silver, rune-inscribed ornament was found in the River Thames near Westminster. The runes are perfectly legible but yield no meaningful message that can be discerned. Eighth century.

153

for the trespasser who had troubled his sleep.
Hot and savage, he kept circling and circling
the outside of the mound. No man appeared
in that desert waste, but he worked himself up
by imagining battle; then back in he'd go
2300   in search of the cup, only to discover
signs that someone had stumbled upon
the golden treasures. So the guardian of the mound,
the hoard-watcher, waited for the gloaming
with fierce impatience; his pent-up fury
at the loss of the vessel made him long to hit back
and lash out in flames. Then, to his delight,
the day waned and he could wait no longer
behind the wall, but hurtled forth
in a fiery blaze. The first to suffer
2310   were the people on the land, but before long
it was their treasure-giver who would come to grief.

The dragon began to belch out flames

The dragon wreaks havoc on the Geats

and burn bright homesteads; there was a hot glow
that scared everyone, for the vile sky-winger
would leave nothing alive in his wake.
Everywhere the havoc he wrought was in evidence.
Far and near, the Geat nation
bore the brunt of his brutal assaults
and virulent hate. Then back to the hoard
2320   he would dart before daybreak, to hide in his den.
He had swinged the land, swathed it in flame,
in fire and burning, and now he felt secure
in the vaults of his barrow; but his trust was unavailing.

Then Beowulf was given bad news,

Beowulf's ominous feelings about the dragon

a hard truth: his own home,

This gold artifact exemplifies the delight that Anglo-Saxon metalworkers took in the fantastic. A dragonlike figure is equipped with a forked tail, six stylized legs or infolded wings, and menacing teeth. The body is textured with interlace designs and studded with garnets, and a garnet marks its unfriendly-looking eye. This object was attached to the shield from Mound 1 at Sutton Hoo, East Anglia.

the best of buildings, had been burnt to a cinder,
the throne-room of the Geats. It threw the hero
into deep anguish and darkened his mood:
the wise man thought he must have thwarted

2330 ancient ordinance of the eternal Lord,
broken His commandment. His mind was in turmoil,
unaccustomed anxiety and gloom
confused his brain; the fire-dragon
had rased the coastal region and reduced
forts and earthworks to dust and ashes,
so the war-king planned and plotted his revenge.
The warriors' protector, prince of the hall-troop,
ordered a marvellous all-iron shield
from his smithy works. He well knew

2340 that linden boards would let him down
and timber burn. After many trials,
he was destined to face the end of his days
in this mortal world; as was the dragon,
for all his long leasehold on the treasure.

Yet the prince of the rings was too proud
to line up with a large army
against the sky-plague. He had scant regard
for the dragon as a threat, no dread at all
of its courage or strength, for he had kept going

2350 often in the past, through perils and ordeals
of every sort, after he had purged
Hrothgar's hall, triumphed in Heorot
and beaten Grendel. He outgrappled the monster
and his evil kin.
                    One of his cruellest
hand-to-hand encounters had happened
when Hygelac, king of the Geats, was killed

*Beowulf's pride and
prowess sustain him*

The Beowulf *dragon means to leave nothing alive in the land of the Geats, and the king's own hall is burned
to the ground. Experiments with fire conducted at the "Iron Age" village at Lejre, Denmark, have proven (to
no one's surprise) that the wooden and thatched houses of that period would have burned down quite well.*

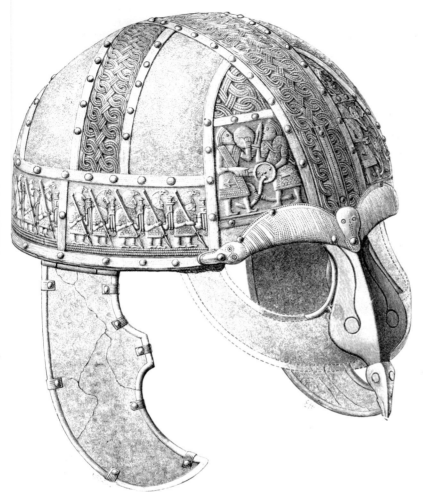

Fig. 1. $^1/_2$.

Fig. 3. $^1/_1$.

Fig. 4. $^1/_1$.

Fig. 7. $^1/_3$.

Fig. 2. $^1/_1$.

in Friesland: the people's friend and lord,
Hrethel's son, slaked a sword blade's
thirst for blood. But Beowulf's prodigious

2360 gifts as a swimmer guaranteed his safety:
he arrived at the shore, shouldering thirty
battle-dresses, the booty he had won.
There was little for the Hetware to be happy about
as they shielded their faces and fighting on the ground
began in earnest. With Beowulf against them,
few could hope to return home.

A flashback: Hygelac's death, Beowulf's rearguard action and escape across the sea

Across the wide sea, desolate and alone,
the son of Ecgtheow swam back to his people.
There Hygd offered him throne and authority

2370 as lord of the ring-hoard: with Hygelac dead,
she had no belief in her son's ability
to defend their homeland against foreign invaders.
Yet there was no way the weakened nation
could get Beowulf to give in and agree
to be elevated over Heardred as his lord
or to undertake the office of kingship.
But he did provide support for the prince,
honoured and minded him until he matured
as the ruler of Geatland.

Beowulf acts as counsellor to Hygelac's heir, Heardred

                         Then over sea-roads

2380 exiles arrived, sons of Ohthere.
They had rebelled against the best of all
the sea-kings in Sweden, the one who held sway
in the Shylfing nation, their renowned prince,
lord of the mead-hall. That marked the end
for Hygelac's son: his hospitality
was mortally rewarded with wounds from a sword.
Heardred lay slaughtered and Onela returned

Heardred is implicated in Swedish feuds and slain

By interweaving the theme of Geatish-Swedish hostilities into the dragon episode, the poet sets the story of Beowulf's death against the background of the rise and fall of dynasties. From an English perspective, the kings of Sweden would have represented raw pagan power. This iron helmet with bronze plates from Vendel grave 14 is adorned with motifs of a fantastic and probably mythological kind. Seventh century.

to the land of Sweden, leaving Beowulf
to ascend the throne, to sit in majesty
2390   and rule over the Geats. He was a good king.

In days to come, he contrived to avenge
the fall of his prince; he befriended Eadgils
when Eadgils was friendless, aiding his cause
with weapons and warriors over the wide sea,
sending him men. The feud was settled
on a comfortless campaign when he killed Onela.

*Beowulf inherits the
kingship, settles the
feuding*

And so the son of Ecgtheow had survived
every extreme, excelling himself
in daring and in danger, until the day arrived
2400   when he had to come face to face with the dragon.
The lord of the Geats took eleven comrades
and went in a rage to reconnoitre.
By then he had discovered the cause of the affliction
being visited on the people. The precious cup
had come to him from the hand of the finder,
the one who had started all this strife
and was now added as a thirteenth to their number.
They press-ganged and compelled this poor creature
to be their guide. Against his will
2410   he led them to the earth-vault he alone knew,
an underground barrow near the sea-billows
and heaving waves, heaped inside
with exquisite metalwork. The one who stood guard
was dangerous and watchful, warden of that trove
buried under earth: no easy bargain
would be made in that place by any man.

*The day of reckoning:
Beowulf and his troop
reconnoitre*

The veteran king sat down on the cliff-top.

The seat of power of the Ynglings, the legendary kings of Sweden, was Old Uppsala in Uppland. Here three great funeral mounds of about the sixth century A.D. can still be seen. Though their original purpose is unknown, attempts have been made to relate these mounds to the Swedish kings named by the Beowulf *poet. This lithograph by Carl-Johann Billmark dating from 1857–1859 accents the romantic atmosphere of the place.*

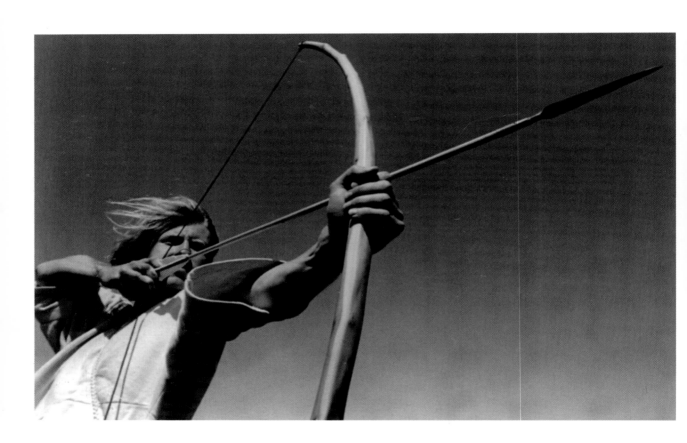

He wished good luck to the Geats who had shared
his hearth and his gold. He was sad at heart,
2420 unsettled yet ready, sensing his death.
His fate hovered near, unknowable but certain:
it would soon claim his coffered soul,
part life from limb. Before long
the prince's spirit would spin free from his body.

*Beowulf's
forebodings*

Beowulf, son of Ecgtheow, spoke:
"Many a skirmish I survived when I was young
and many times of war: I remember them well.
At seven, I was fostered out by my father,
left in the charge of my people's lord.
2430 King Hrethel kept me and took care of me,
was open-handed, behaved like a kinsman.
While I was his ward, he treated me no worse
as a wean about the place than one of his own boys,
Herebeald and Haethcyn, or my own Hygelac.
For the eldest, Herebeald, an unexpected
deathbed was laid out, through a brother's doing,
when Haethcyn bent his horn-tipped bow
and loosed the arrow that destroyed his life.
He shot wide and buried a shaft
2440 in the flesh and blood of his own brother.
That offence was beyond redress, a wrongfooting
of the heart's affections; for who could avenge
the prince's life or pay his death-price?
It was like the misery felt by an old man
who has lived to see his son's body
swing on the gallows. He begins to keen
and weep for his boy, watching the raven
gloat where he hangs: he can be of no help.
The wisdom of age is worthless to him.

*He recalls his early
days as a ward at King
Hrethel's court*

*An accidental killing
and its sad
consequences for
Hrethel*

*Hrethel's loss reflected
in "The Father's
Lament"*

Beowulf recalls the tragic incident when his uncle Herebeald, heir to the Geatish throne, was killed by a stray arrow shot by Herebeald's younger brother Haethcyn. When wielded by competent archers, the bows and arrows of this period were lethal weapons. This photo is a study in concentration and tensile strength: this archer should not miss his mark.

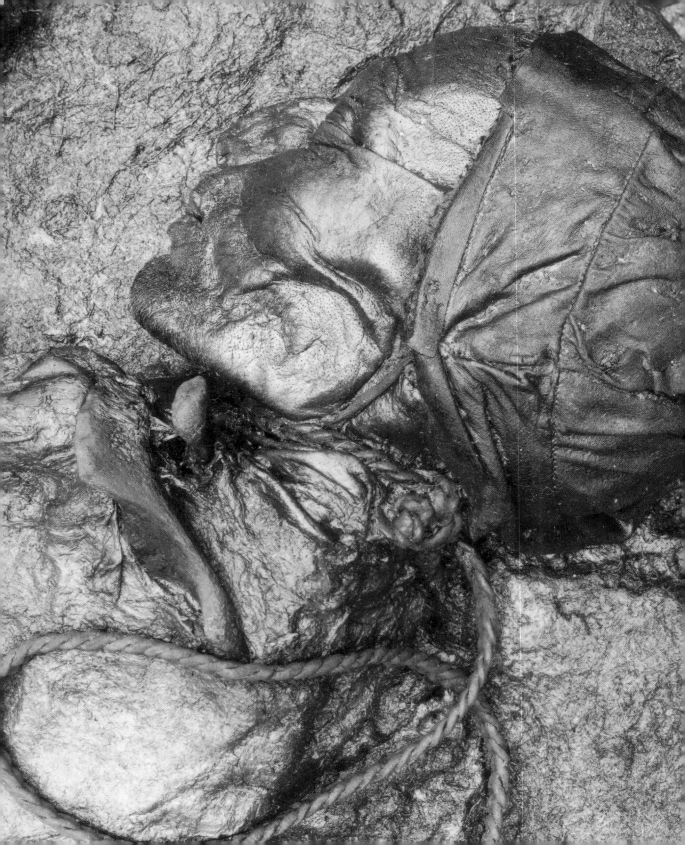

2450 Morning after morning, he wakes to remember
that his child is gone; he has no interest
in living on until another heir
is born in the hall, now that his first-born
has entered death's dominion forever.
He gazes sorrowfully at his son's dwelling,
the banquet hall bereft of all delight,
the windswept hearthstone; the horsemen are sleeping,
the warriors under ground; what was is no more.
No tunes from the harp, no cheer raised in the yard.
2460 Alone with his longing, he lies down on his bed
and sings a lament; everything seems too large,
the steadings and the fields.

                        Such was the feeling
of loss endured by the lord of the Geats
after Herebeald's death. He was helplessly placed
to set to rights the wrong committed,
could not punish the killer in accordance with the law
of the blood-feud, although he felt no love for him.
Heartsore, wearied, he turned away
from life's joys, chose God's light
2470 and departed, leaving buildings and lands
to his sons, as a man of substance will.

"Then over the wide sea Swedes and Geats
battled and feuded and fought without quarter.
Hostilities broke out when Hrethel died.
Ongentheow's sons were unrelenting,
refusing to make peace, campaigning violently
from coast to coast, constantly setting up
terrible ambushes around Hreasnahill.
My own kith and kin avenged
2480 these evil events, as everybody knows,

*Beowulf continues his
account of wars
between the Geats and
the Swedes*

---

*"Tollund man," the well preserved body of a man from Tollund, Jutland. The grief of King Hrethel for the dead
Herebeald is likened to that of an old man for a son who is hung on a gallows. Capital punishment was evi-
dently taken for granted during the Germanic Iron Age as a response to serious crimes. This man was throt-
tled and his throat cut before his body was left in a bog.*

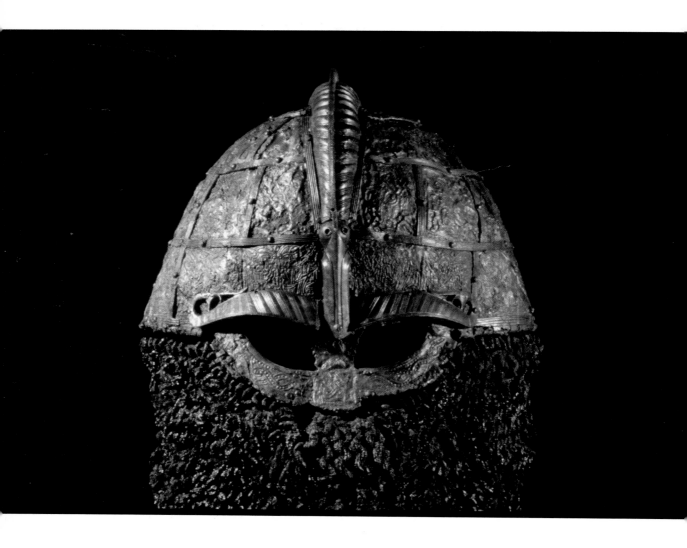

but the price was high: one of them paid
with his life. Haethcyn, lord of the Geats,
met his fate there and fell in the battle.
Then, as I have heard, Hygelac's sword
was raised in the morning against Ongentheow,
his brother's killer. When Eofor cleft
the old Swede's helmet, halved it open,
he fell, death-pale: his feud-calloused hand
could not stave off the fatal stroke.

*The Swedish king,
Ongentheow, dies at
the hands of Eofor, one
of Hygelac's thanes*

2490   "The treasures that Hygelac lavished on me
I paid for when I fought, as fortune allowed me,
with my glittering sword. He gave me land
and the security land brings, so he had no call
to go looking for some lesser champion,
some mercenary from among the Gifthas
or the Spear-Danes or the men of Sweden.
I marched ahead of him, always there
at the front of the line; and I shall fight like that
for as long as I live, as long as this sword
2500   shall last, which has stood me in good stead
late and soon, ever since I killed
Dayraven the Frank in front of the two armies.
He brought back no looted breastplate
to the Frisian king, but fell in battle,
their standard-bearer, high-born and brave.
No sword blade sent him to his death,
my bare hands stilled his heartbeats
and wrecked the bone-house. Now blade and hand,
sword and sword-stroke, will assay the hoard."

*Beowulf recalls his
proud days in
Hygelac's retinue*

2510   Beowulf spoke, made a formal boast
for the last time: "I risked my life

Beowulf's last boast

King Haethcyn of the Geats met his death in combat against King Ongentheow of the Swedes (corresponding
to Old Norse "Angantyr"). That death was then avenged. This helmet from grave 8 at Valsgärde, Uppland,
leaves no doubt in one's mind why a helm was called a "war mask." The ridge (Old English wala) stands out,
and the helmet is hung with chain mail. Seventh century.

often when I was young. Now I am old,
but as king of the people I shall pursue this fight
for the glory of winning, if the evil one will only
abandon his earth-fort and face me in the open."

Then he addressed each dear companion
one final time, those fighters in their helmets,
resolute and high-born: "I would rather not
use a weapon if I knew another way
2520   to grapple with the dragon and make good my boast
as I did against Grendel in days gone by.
But I shall be meeting molten venom
in the fire he breathes, so I go forth
in mail-shirt and shield. I won't shift a foot
when I meet the cave-guard: what occurs on the wall
between the two of us will turn out as fate,
overseer of men, decides. I am resolved.
I scorn further words against this sky-borne foe.

"Men at arms, remain here on the barrow,
2530   safe in your armour, to see which one of us
is better in the end at bearing wounds
in a deadly fray. This fight is not yours,
nor is it up to any man except me
to measure his strength against the monster
or to prove his worth. I shall win the gold
by my courage, or else mortal combat,
doom of battle, will bear your lord away."

Then he drew himself up beside his shield.
The fabled warrior in his warshirt and helmet
2540   trusted in his own strength entirely
and went under the crag. No coward path.

*Beowulf approaches the dragon's barrow alone, aware that his men are no match for such a fearsome adversary.
One of the more impressive of the* jættestuer, *or "giant's chambers," of southern Scandinavia is this Neolithic
chambered tomb that stands in a field near the village of Øm, Zealand, not far from Lejre.*

Hard by the rock-face that hale veteran,
a good man who had gone repeatedly
into combat and danger and come through,
saw a stone arch and a gushing stream
that burst from the barrow, blazing and wafting
a deadly heat. It would be hard to survive
unscathed near the hoard, to hold firm
against the dragon in those flaming depths.

2550   Then he gave a shout. The lord of the Geats
unburdened his breast and broke out
in a storm of anger. Under grey stone
his voice challenged and resounded clearly.
Hate was ignited. The hoard-guard recognized
a human voice, the time was over
for peace and parleying. Pouring forth
in a hot battle-fume, the breath of the monster
burst from the rock. There was a rumble under ground.
Down there in the barrow, Beowulf the warrior

2560   lifted his shield: the outlandish thing
writhed and convulsed and viciously
turned on the king, whose keen-edged sword,
an heirloom inherited by ancient right,
was already in his hand. Roused to a fury,
each antagonist struck terror in the other.
Unyielding, the lord of his people loomed
by his tall shield, sure of his ground,
while the serpent looped and unleashed itself.
Swaddled in flames, it came gliding and flexing

2570   and racing towards its fate. Yet his shield defended
the renowned leader's life and limb
for a shorter time than he meant it to:
that final day was the first time
when Beowulf fought and fate denied him

Dragon's-eye view looking out from Øm Jættestue. The Beowulf *dragon impatiently bides its time until nightfall, then flies forth like an Iron Age weapon of mass destruction. Later, the hero deliberately provokes it to emerge again from its dark chamber. There would be room enough within this ancient tomb for any fifty-foot-long dragon to lie coiled up.*

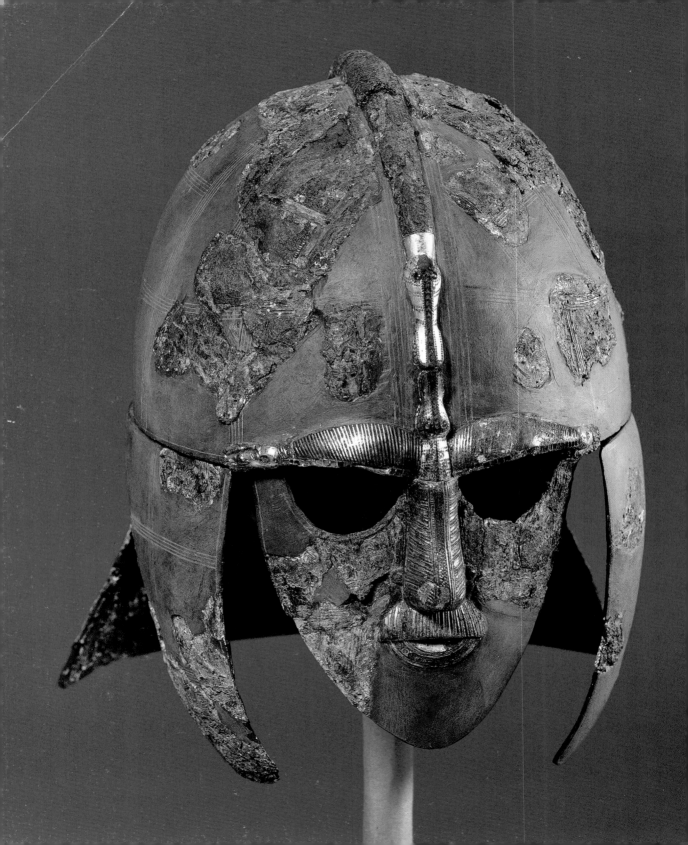

glory in battle. So the king of the Geats
raised his hand and struck hard
at the enamelled scales, but scarcely cut through:
the blade flashed and slashed yet the blow
was far less powerful than the hard-pressed king
2580   had need of at that moment. The mound-keeper
went into a spasm and spouted deadly flames:
when he felt the stroke, battle-fire
billowed and spewed. Beowulf was foiled

of a glorious victory. The glittering sword,
infallible before that day,
failed when he unsheathed it, as it never should have.
For the son of Ecgtheow, it was no easy thing
to have to give ground like that and go
unwillingly to inhabit another home
2590   in a place beyond; so every man must yield
the leasehold of his days.

                 Before long
the fierce contenders clashed again.
The hoard-guard took heart, inhaled and swelled up
and got a new wind; he who had once ruled
was furled in fire and had to face the worst.
No help or backing was to be had then

from his high-born comrades; that hand-picked troop
broke ranks and ran for their lives
to the safety of the wood. But within one heart
2600   sorrow welled up: in a man of worth
the claims of kinship cannot be denied.

His name was Wiglaf, a son of Weohstan's,
a well-regarded Shylfing warrior
related to Aelfhere. When he saw his lord

Helmet from Sutton Hoo, Suffolk. The hero Beowulf is never described in physical detail and remains fairly inscrutable. Since 1939, however, when the treasures buried at Sutton Hoo were unearthed, many persons have been tempted to associate the poem with objects found at that site. This helmet, for some present-day readers, may be as close to the man "Beowulf" as one can get. Seventh century.

tormented by the heat of his scalding helmet,
he remembered the bountiful gifts bestowed on him,
how well he lived among the Waegmundings,
the freehold he inherited from his father before him.
He could not hold back: one hand brandished
2610   the yellow-timbered shield, the other drew his sword—
an ancient blade that was said to have belonged
to Eanmund, the son of Ohthere, the one
Weohstan had slain when he was an exile without friends.

The deeds of Wiglaf's father, Weohstan, recalled

He carried the arms to the victim's kinfolk,
the burnished helmet, the webbed chain-mail
and that relic of the giants. But Onela returned
the weapons to him, rewarded Weohstan
with Eanmund's war-gear. He ignored the blood-feud,
the fact that Eanmund was his brother's son.

2620   Weohstan kept that war-gear for a lifetime,
the sword and the mail-shirt, until it was the son's turn
to follow his father and perform his part.
Then, in old age, at the end of his days
among the Weather-Geats, he bequeathed to Wiglaf
innumerable weapons.
               And now the youth
was to enter the line of battle with his lord,
his first time to be tested as a fighter.
His spirit did not break and the ancestral blade
would keep its edge, as the dragon discovered
2630   as soon as they came together in the combat.

Sad at heart, addressing his companions,
Wiglaf spoke wise and fluent words:
"I remember that time when mead was flowing,
how we pledged loyalty to our lord in the hall,

Wiglaf's speech to the shirkers

Beowulf's sword, previously infallible, fails to cut through the dragon's hide. Later on it breaks in two when brought down against the dragon's skull. If one associates the Sutton Hoo helmet with the hero himself, then it is natural to visualize him wielding a sword like this, which is also from Mound 1 at Sutton Hoo. The decorative pommel of this blade is of gold with inset garnets. Seventh century.

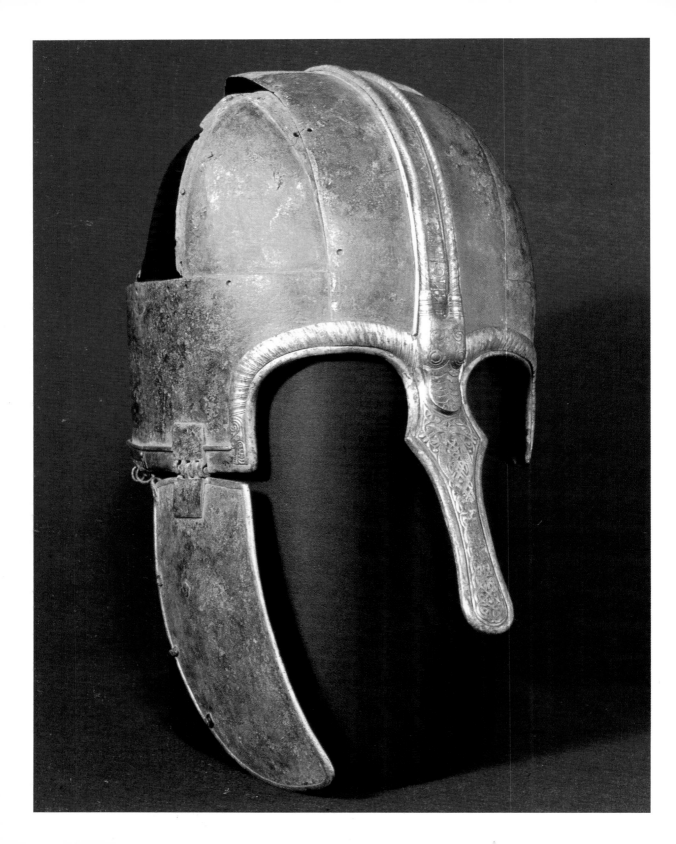

promised our ring-giver we would be worth our price,
make good the gift of the war-gear,
those swords and helmets, as and when
his need required it. He picked us out
from the army deliberately, honoured us and judged us
2640   fit for this action, made me these lavish gifts—
and all because he considered us the best
of his arms-bearing thanes. And now, although
he wanted this challenge to be one he'd face
by himself alone—the shepherd of our land,
a man unequalled in the quest for glory
and a name for daring—now the day has come
when this lord we serve needs sound men
to give him their support. Let us go to him,
help our leader through the hot flame
2650   and dread of the fire. As God is my witness,
I would rather my body were robed in the same
burning blaze as my gold-giver's body
than go back home bearing arms.
That is unthinkable, unless we have first
slain the foe and defended the life
of the prince of the Weather-Geats. I well know
the things he has done for us deserve better.
Should he alone be left exposed
to fall in battle? We must bond together,
2660   shield and helmet, mail-shirt and sword."
Then he waded the dangerous reek and went
under arms to his lord, saying only:
"Go on, dear Beowulf, do everything
you said you would when you were still young
and vowed you would never let your name and fame
be dimmed while you lived. Your deeds are famous,
so stay resolute, my lord, defend your life now

*Wiglaf goes to
Beowulf's aid*

---

*When Beowulf's men run for the woods, only his kinsman Wiglaf stands firm. He too deserves a helmet, and
this one, found recently at Coppergate, York, would serve him well. This view shows the details of its design,
including its cheek-guards, crest, eyebrow ornaments (see page 188 center), and handsomely decorated nasal.
Ca. seventh century.*

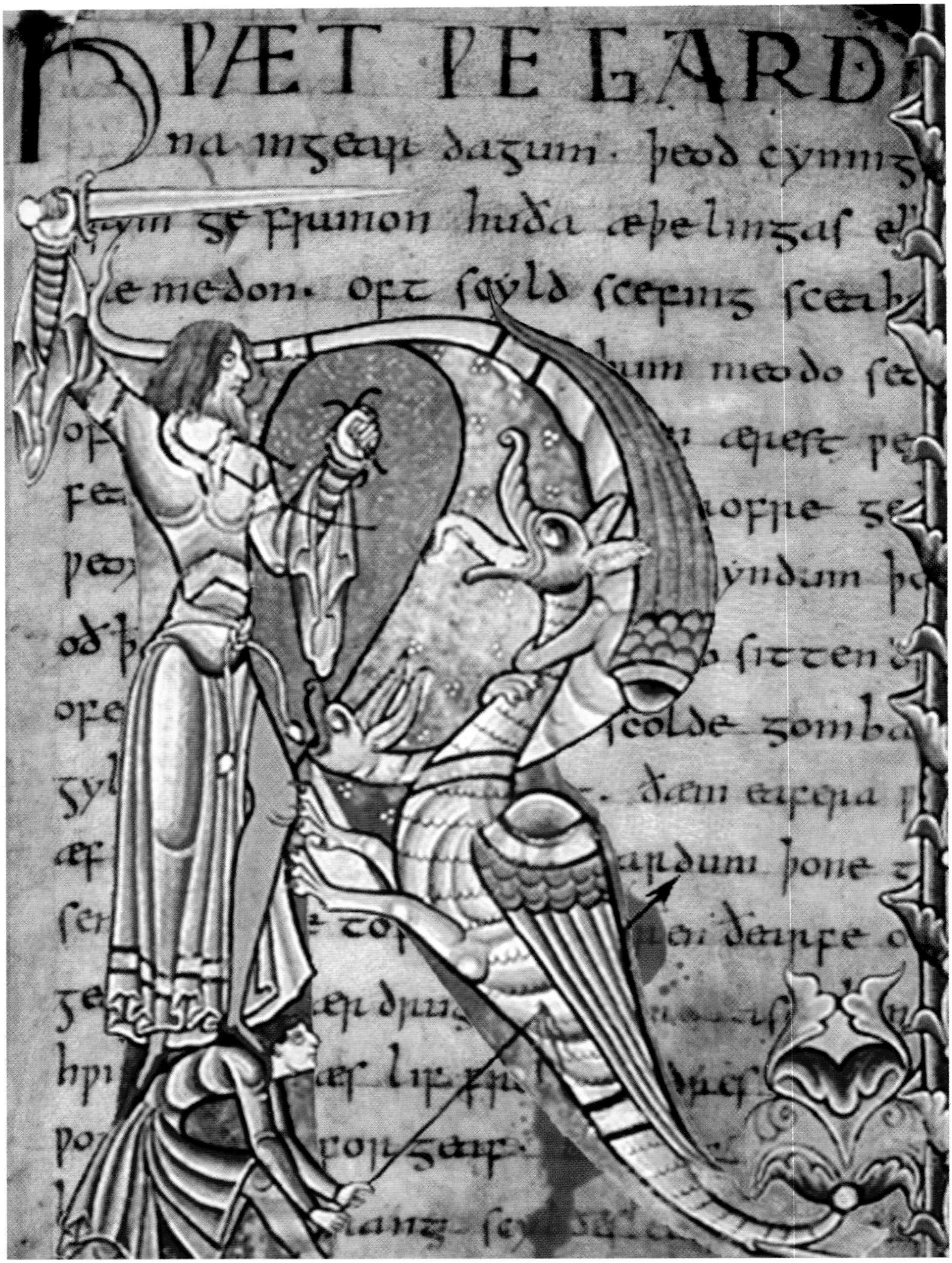
HƿÆT ƿE GARD

with the whole of your strength. I shall stand by you."

After those words, a wildness rose
2670   in the dragon again and drove it to attack,
heaving up fire, hunting for enemies,
the humans it loathed. Flames lapped the shield,
charred it to the boss, and the body armour
on the young warrior was useless to him.
But Wiglaf did well under the wide rim
Beowulf shared with him once his own had shattered
in sparks and ashes.
                Inspired again
by the thought of glory, the war-king threw
his whole strength behind a sword-stroke
2680   and connected with the skull. And Naegling snapped.
Beowulf's ancient iron-grey sword
let him down in the fight. It was never his fortune
to be helped in combat by the cutting edge
of weapons made of iron. When he wielded a sword,
no matter how blooded and hard-edged the blade
his hand was too strong, the stroke he dealt
(I have heard) would ruin it. He could reap no advantage.

Then the bane of that people, the fire-breathing dragon,
was mad to attack for a third time.
2690   When a chance came, he caught the hero
in a rush of flame and clamped sharp fangs
into his neck. Beowulf's body
ran wet with his life-blood: it came welling out.

Next thing, they say, the noble son of Weohstan
saw the king in danger at his side
and displayed his inborn bravery and strength.

The dragon attacks again

Another setback

The dragon's third onslaught. He draws blood

Wiglaf gets past the flames and strikes

With its portrayal of two warriors fighting a dragon—an older man fighting from above and a younger man from below—this illustration from a thirteenth-century French manuscript reminds one of the action of Beowulf. *Collage by Benjamin Slade, juxtaposing an image from Dijon Municipal Library MS 168, fol. 4b, against the first page of the* Beowulf *manuscript (British Library Cotton Vitellius A.xv, fol. 129a).*

He left the head alone, but his fighting hand
was burned when he came to his kinsman's aid.
He lunged at the enemy lower down
2700   so that his decorated sword sank into its belly
and the flames grew weaker.

                         Once again the king
gathered his strength and drew a stabbing knife
he carried on his belt, sharpened for battle.
He stuck it deep into the dragon's flank.
Beowulf dealt it a deadly wound.
They had killed the enemy, courage quelled his life;
that pair of kinsmen, partners in nobility,
had destroyed the foe. So every man should act,
be at hand when needed; but now, for the king,
2710   this would be the last of his many labours
and triumphs in the world.

                       Then the wound
dealt by the ground-burner earlier began
to scald and swell; Beowulf discovered
deadly poison suppurating inside him,
surges of nausea, and so, in his wisdom,
the prince realized his state and struggled
towards a seat on the rampart. He steadied his gaze
on those gigantic stones, saw how the earthwork
was braced with arches built over columns.
2720   And now that thane unequalled for goodness
with his own hands washed his lord's wounds,
swabbed the weary prince with water,
bathed him clean, unbuckled his helmet.

Beowulf spoke: in spite of his wounds,
mortal wounds, he still spoke
for he well knew his days in the world

*Beowulf delivers the
fatal wound*

*Beowulf senses that he
is near death*

---

*"The king / gathered his strength and drew a stabbing knife / he carried on his belt," and with this weapon he
deals the dragon its death-wound. This long knife, or* scramasax, *found in the River Thames near Battersea,
London, is a striking example of such a blade. An inlaid silver-gilt runic inscription preserves the owner's
name, "Beagnoth," together with a complete futhorc (runic alphabet). Ca. ninth century.*   181

had been lived out to the end: his allotted time
was drawing to a close, death was very near.

He thinks back on his life

"Now is the time when I would have wanted
2730   to bestow this armour on my own son,
had it been my fortune to have fathered an heir
and live on in his flesh. For fifty years
I ruled this nation. No king
of any neighbouring clan would dare
face me with troops, none had the power
to intimidate me. I took what came,
cared for and stood by things in my keeping,
never fomented quarrels, never
swore to a lie. All this consoles me,
2740   doomed as I am and sickening for death;
because of my right ways, the Ruler of mankind
need never blame me when the breath leaves my body
for murder of kinsmen. Go now quickly,

He bids Wiglaf to inspect the hoard and return with a portion of the treasure

dearest Wiglaf, under the grey stone
where the dragon is laid out, lost to his treasure;
hurry to feast your eyes on the hoard.
Away you go: I want to examine
that ancient gold, gaze my fill
on those garnered jewels; my going will be easier
2750   for having seen the treasure, a less troubled letting-go
of the life and lordship I have long maintained."

And so, I have heard, the son of Weohstan
quickly obeyed the command of his languishing

Wiglaf enters the dragon's barrow

war-weary lord; he went in his chain-mail
under the rock-piled roof of the barrow,
exulting in his triumph, and saw beyond the seat
a treasure-trove of astonishing richness,

Thinking that he has done his people a great service by winning the dragon's treasure, Beowulf wishes to see some of it before he dies. When Wiglaf enters the barrow, he discovers "a treasure-trove of astonishing richness." Objects made of gold would not have been subject to corruption. This is a hoard of chased and embossed gold bowls from Midskov, on the island of Funen, Denmark. Bronze Age.

183

wall-hangings that were a wonder to behold,
glittering gold spread across the ground,
2760 the old dawn-scorching serpent's den
packed with goblets and vessels from the past,
tarnished and corroding. Rusty helmets
all eaten away. Armbands everywhere,
artfully wrought. How easily treasure
buried in the ground, gold hidden
however skilfully, can escape from any man!

And he saw too a standard, entirely of gold,
hanging high over the hoard,
a masterpiece of filigree; it glowed with light
2770 so he could make out the ground at his feet
and inspect the valuables. Of the dragon there was no
remaining sign: the sword had despatched him.
Then, the story goes, a certain man
plundered the hoard in that immemorial howe,
filled his arms with flagons and plates,
anything he wanted; and took the standard also,
most brilliant of banners.
                              Already the blade
of the old king's sharp killing-sword
had done its worst: the one who had for long
2780 minded the hoard, hovering over gold,
unleashing fire, surging forth
midnight after midnight, had been mown down.

Wiglaf went quickly, keen to get back,
excited by the treasure. Anxiety weighed
on his brave heart—he was hoping he would find
the leader of the Geats alive where he had left him
helpless, earlier, on the open ground.

He returns with treasure

The dragon's hoard contains a miscellany of objects, including cups and vessels, helmets, swords, dishes, decorative armbands, wall hangings, and a shining standard. This miscellany of pagan grave-goods from Leuna, Saxony, is representative of the variety of items that were sometimes deposited with the dead. Third century.

So he came to the place, carrying the treasure,
and found his lord bleeding profusely,
2790   his life at an end; again he began
to swab his body. The beginnings of an utterance
broke out from the king's breast-cage.
The old lord gazed sadly at the gold.

"To the everlasting Lord of All,
to the King of Glory, I give thanks
that I behold this treasure here in front of me,
that I have been allowed to leave my people
so well endowed on the day I die.
Now that I have bartered my last breath
2800   to own this fortune, it is up to you
to look after their needs. I can hold out no longer.
Order my troop to construct a barrow
on a headland on the coast, after my pyre has cooled.
It will loom on the horizon at Hronesness
and be a reminder among my people—
so that in coming times crews under sail
will call it Beowulf's Barrow, as they steer
ships across the wide and shrouded waters."

Beowulf gives thanks and orders the construction of a barrow to commemorate him

Then the king in his great-heartedness unclasped
2810   the collar of gold from his neck and gave it
to the young thane, telling him to use
it and the warshirt and the gilded helmet well.

Beowulf's last words

"You are the last of us, the only one left
of the Waegmundings. Fate swept us away,
sent my whole brave high-born clan
to their final doom. Now I must follow them."
That was the warrior's last word.

Beowulf orders his tomb: his body will be cremated, and his ashes are to be left in a barrow overlooking the sea. But where is that barrow located? "In Geatland" is perhaps the only safe answer. Wanting to pinpoint a more definite location, some readers of the poem have searched for a suitable landscape on the southwest coast of Sweden—in the barrow-rich region of Bohuslän, for example.

He had no more to confide. The furious heat
of the pyre would assail him. His soul fled from his breast
to its destined place among the steadfast ones.

It was hard then on the young hero,
having to watch the one he held so dear
there on the ground, going through
his death agony. The dragon from underearth,
his nightmarish destroyer, lay destroyed as well,
utterly without life. No longer would his snakefolds
ply themselves to safeguard hidden gold.
Hard-edged blades, hammered out
and keenly filed, had finished him
so that the sky-roamer lay there rigid,
brought low beside the treasure-lodge.

Never again would he glitter and glide
and show himself off in midnight air,
exulting in his riches: he fell to earth
through the battle-strength in Beowulf's arm.
There were few, indeed, as far as I have heard,
big and brave as they may have been,
few who would have held out if they had had to face
the outpourings of that poison-breather
or gone foraging on the ring-hall floor
and found the deep barrow-dweller
on guard and awake.
                    The treasure had been won,
bought and paid for by Beowulf's death.
Both had reached the end of the road
through the life they had been lent.

                    Before long

The dragon too has been destroyed

Top: Bronze fibula from Öland, Sweden, in the shape of a coiled wyrm, *or "serpent, dragon." Center: Detail of dragonlike ornament from the Coppergate helmet, York (see page 176). Bottom: Dragon-shaped design from the Sutton Hoo hoard. The* Beowulf *dragon is a "sky-roamer," a "barrow-dweller," a "poison-breather," a "vile sky-winger," and "an old harrower of the dark," among other colorful epithets used in this translation.*

the battle-dodgers abandoned the wood,
the ones who had let down their lord earlier,
the tail-turners, ten of them together.
When he needed them most, they had made off.

The battle-dodgers
come back

2850   Now they were ashamed and came behind shields,
in their battle-outfits, to where the old man lay.
They watched Wiglaf, sitting worn out,
a comrade shoulder to shoulder with his lord,
trying in vain to bring him round with water.
Much as he wanted to, there was no way
he could preserve his lord's life on earth
or alter in the least the Almighty's will.
What God judged right would rule what happened
to every man, as it does to this day.

2860   Then a stern rebuke was bound to come

Wiglaf rebukes them

from the young warrior to the ones who had been cowards.
Wiglaf, son of Weohstan, spoke
disdainfully and in disappointment:
"Anyone ready to admit the truth
will surely realize that the lord of men
who showered you with gifts and gave you the armour
you are standing in—when he would distribute
helmets and mail-shirts to men on the mead-benches,
a prince treating his thanes in hall
2870   to the best he could find, far or near—
was throwing weapons uselessly away.
It would be a sad waste when the war broke out.
Beowulf had little cause to brag
about his armed guard; yet God who ordains
who wins or loses allowed him to strike
with his own blade when bravery was needed.

The role of reciprocity in the tribal world of Beowulf *is a crucial one. The king is the helm of his people. He gives his retainers food, treasures, weapons—all that they need to live. In turn, those gifts are to be repaid through acts of courage and fidelity. This modern replica of the Sutton Hoo helmet serves as a reminder of this heroic ethos, which centers on the figure of a single charismatic leader.*

There was little I could do to protect his life
in the heat of the fray, yet I found new strength
welling up when I went to help him.
2880   Then my sword connected and the deadly assaults
of our foe grew weaker, the fire coursed
less strongly from his head. But when the worst happened
too few rallied around the prince.

"So it is goodbye now to all you know and love
on your home ground, the open-handedness,
the giving of war-swords. Every one of you

*He predicts that
enemies will now
attack the Geats*

with freeholds of land, our whole nation,
will be dispossessed, once princes from beyond
get tidings of how you turned and fled
2890   and disgraced yourselves. A warrior will sooner
die than live a life of shame."

Then he ordered the outcome of the fight to be reported
to those camped on the ridge, that crowd of retainers
who had sat all morning, sad at heart,
shield-bearers wondering about
the man they loved: would this day be his last
or would he return? He told the truth
and did not balk, the rider who bore
news to the cliff-top. He addressed them all:
2900   "Now the people's pride and love,

*A messenger tells the
people that Beowulf is
dead*

the lord of the Geats, is laid on his deathbed,
brought down by the dragon's attack.
Beside him lies the bane of his life,
dead from knife-wounds. There was no way
Beowulf could manage to get the better
of the monster with his sword. Wiglaf sits
at Beowulf's side, the son of Weohstan,

*In the long speech known as the "Messenger's Prophecy" (lines 2900–3027), dire warnings are given of future
catastrophes facing the Geats: war at the hands of Franks and Frisians, war at the hands of the Swedes, men
and women forced into exile. This woodcut illustration by Sigurd Vasegaard, showing a file of warriors on the
move in wintry surroundings, calls up a mood of a comparable kind.*

the living warrior watching by the dead,
keeping weary vigil, holding a wake

2910   for the loved and the loathed.

                                    Now war is looming

*He foresees wars with
the Franks and the
Frisians*

over our nation, soon it will be known
to Franks and Frisians, far and wide,
that the king is gone. Hostility has been great
among the Franks since Hygelac sailed forth
at the head of a war-fleet into Friesland:
there the Hetware harried and attacked
and overwhelmed him with great odds.
The leader in his war-gear was laid low,
fell amongst followers; that lord did not favour

2920   his company with spoils. The Merovingian king
has been an enemy to us ever since.

"Nor do I expect peace or pact-keeping
of any sort from the Swedes. Remember:
at Ravenswood, Ongentheow

*The Swedes too will
strike to avenge the
slaughter of
Ongentheow*

slaughtered Haethcyn, Hrethel's son,
when the Geat people in their arrogance
first attacked the fierce Shylfings.
The return blow was quickly struck
by Ohthere's father. Old and terrible,

2930   he felled the sea-king and saved his own
aged wife, the mother of Onela
and of Ohthere, bereft of her gold rings.
Then he kept hard on the heels of the foe
and drove them, leaderless, lucky to get away,
in a desperate rout into Ravenswood.

*Ongentheow's last
engagement at
Ravenswood: he
cornered a Geatish
force*

His army surrounded the weary remnant
where they nursed their wounds; all through the night
he howled threats at those huddled survivors,

194

promised to axe their bodies open
2940 when dawn broke, dangle them from gallows
to feed the birds. But at first light
when their spirits were lowest, relief arrived.
They heard the sound of Hygelac's horn,
his trumpet calling as he came to find them,
the hero in pursuit, at hand with troops.

"The bloody swathe that Swedes and Geats
cut through each other was everywhere.
No one could miss their murderous feuding.
Then the old man made his move,
2950 pulled back, barred his people in:
Ongentheow withdrew to higher ground.
Hygelac's pride and prowess as a fighter
were known to the earl; he had no confidence
that he could hold out against that horde of seamen,
defend wife and the ones he loved
from the shock of the attack. He retreated for shelter
behind the earthwall. Then Hygelac swooped
on the Swedes at bay, his banners swarmed
into their refuge, his Geat forces
2960 drove forward to destroy the camp.
There in his grey hairs, Ongentheow
was cornered, ringed around with swords.
And it came to pass that the king's fate
was in Eofor's hands, and in his alone.
Wulf, son of Wonred, went for him in anger,
split him open so that blood came spurting
from under his hair. The old hero
still did not flinch, but parried fast,
hit back with a harder stroke:
2970 the king turned and took him on.

Hygelac relieved the besieged Geats

Ongentheow withdrew

The Swedish king fought for his life. He survived a blow from Wulf, hit back, but was killed by Wulf's brother, Eofor

Then Wonred's son, the brave Wulf,
could land no blow against the aged lord.
Ongentheow divided his helmet
so that he buckled and bowed his bloodied head
and dropped to the ground. But his doom held off.
Though he was cut deep, he recovered again.

"With his brother down, the undaunted Eofor,
Hygelac's thane, hefted his sword
and smashed murderously at the massive helmet
2980   past the lifted shield. And the king collapsed,
The shepherd of people was sheared of life.

"Many then hurried to help Wulf,
bandaged and lifted him, now that they were left
masters of the blood-soaked battleground.
One warrior stripped the other,
looted Ongentheow's iron mail-coat,
his hard sword-hilt, his helmet too,
and carried the graith to King Hygelac;
he accepted the prize, promised fairly
2990   that reward would come, and kept his word.
For their bravery in action, when they arrived home
Eofor and Wulf were overloaded
by Hrethel's son, Hygelac the Geat,
with gifts of land and linked rings
that were worth a fortune. They had won glory,
so there was no gainsaying his generosity.
And he gave Eofor his only daughter
to bide at home with him, an honour and a bond.

"So this bad blood between us and the Swedes,
3000   this vicious feud, I am convinced,

*The victorious Geats
returned home*

The "Messenger's Prophecy" ends with a bleak allusion to the birds and beasts of battle (lines 3024–27) — a familiar theme in Old English poetry, but one that the poet has strategically withheld until this moment. This woodcut by Sigurd Vasegaard presents a stark view of the aftermath of war. While ravens wheel overhead, scavengers strip the bodies of the slain.

197

is bound to revive; they will cross our borders
and attack in force when they find out
that Beowulf is dead. In days gone by
when our warriors fell and we were undefended
he kept our coffers and our kingdom safe.
He worked for the people, but as well as that
he behaved like a hero.

*The messenger
predicts that the
Swedes will soon
retaliate*

                        We must hurry now
to take a last look at the king
and launch him, lord and lavisher of rings,

3010 on the funeral road. His royal pyre

*With Beowulf gone, a
tragic future awaits*

will melt no small amount of gold:
heaped there in a hoard, it was bought at heavy cost,
and that pile of rings he paid for at the end
with his own life will go up with the flame,
be furled in fire: treasure no follower
will wear in his memory, nor lovely woman
link and attach as a torque around her neck—
but often, repeatedly, in the path of exile
they shall walk bereft, bowed under woe,

3020 now that their leader's laugh is silenced,
high spirits quenched. Many a spear
dawn-cold to the touch will be taken down
and waved on high; the swept harp
won't waken warriors, but the raven winging
darkly over the doomed will have news,
tidings for the eagle of how he hoked and ate,
how the wolf and he made short work of the dead."

Such was the drift of the dire report
that gallant man delivered. He got little wrong

3030 in what he told and predicted.
                        The whole troop

Top: The god Othin was associated with divine inspiration, prophesy, poetry, battle frenzy, and the dead. This image of a mounted warrior, with a snake at his feet and two birds in flight, appears on a plate attached to a helmet from Vendel grave 1. It probably represents Othin on the field of war. Seventh century. Bottom: Stylized birds of prey, a pair of shield mounts found near Sturry, Kent. Ca. seventh century.

rose in tears, then took their way
to the uncanny scene under Earnaness.
There, on the sand, where his soul had left him,
they found him at rest, their ring-giver
from days gone by. The great man
had breathed his last. Beowulf the king
had indeed met with a marvellous death.

But what they saw first was far stranger:
the serpent on the ground, gruesome and vile,
3040   lying facing him. The fire-dragon
was scaresomely burnt, scorched all colours.
From head to tail, his entire length
was fifty feet. He had shimmered forth
on the night air once, then winged back
down to his den; but death owned him now,
he would never enter his earth-gallery again.
Beside him stood pitchers and piled-up dishes,
silent flagons, precious swords
eaten through with rust, ranged as they had been
3050   while they waited their thousand winters under ground.
That huge cache, gold inherited
from an ancient race, was under a spell—
which meant no one was ever permitted
to enter the ring-hall unless God Himself,
mankind's Keeper, True King of Triumphs,
allowed some person pleasing to Him—
and in His eyes worthy—to open the hoard.

What came about brought to nothing
the hopes of the one who had wrongly hidden
3060   riches under the rock-face. First the dragon slew
that man among men, who in turn made fierce amends

Again the poet dwells on the great heap of treasures that Beowulf has won for his people, but now it is seen in a darker light. Much of it is rusted through. None of it, we learn, will be of use to the living. These Bronze Age funeral goods from Seddin, in Brandenburg, northern Germany, would have struck anyone living in Anglo-Saxon England as pertaining to a past yet more remote than that of the hero's day. Eighth century B.C.

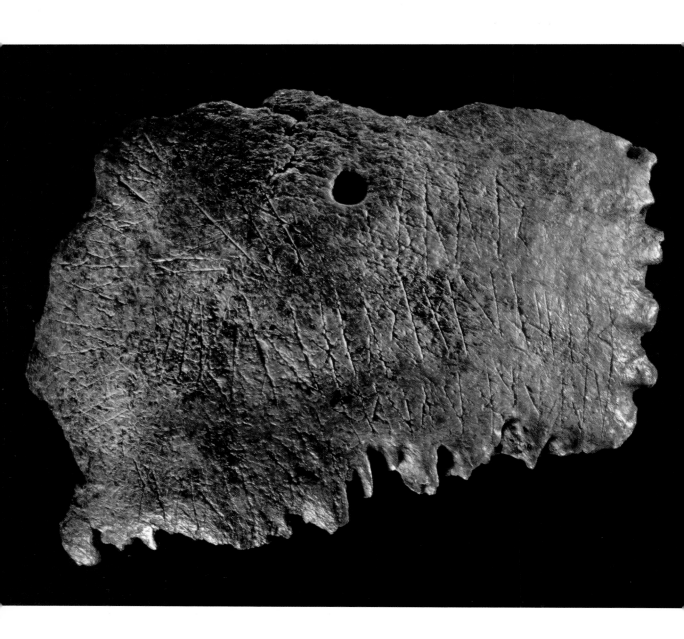

and settled the feud. Famous for his deeds
a warrior may be, but it remains a mystery
where his life will end, when he may no longer
dwell in the mead-hall among his own.
So it was with Beowulf, when he faced the cruelty
and cunning of the mound-guard. He himself was ignorant
of how his departure from the world would happen.
The high-born chiefs who had buried the treasure

3070   declared it until doomsday so accursed
that whoever robbed it would be guilty of wrong
and grimly punished for their transgression,
hasped in hell-bonds in heathen shrines.
Yet Beowulf's gaze at the gold treasure
when he first saw it had not been selfish.

Wiglaf, son of Weohstan, spoke:
"Often when one man follows his own will
many are hurt. This happened to us.
Nothing we advised could ever convince

3080   the prince we loved, our land's guardian,
not to vex the custodian of the gold,
let him lie where he was long accustomed,
lurk there under earth until the end of the world.
He held to his high destiny. The hoard is laid bare,
but at a grave cost; it was too cruel a fate
that forced the king to that encounter.
I have been inside and seen everything
amassed in the vault. I managed to enter
although no great welcome awaited me

3090   under the earthwall. I quickly gathered up
a huge pile of the priceless treasures
handpicked from the hoard and carried them here
where the king could see them. He was still himself,

Wiglaf ponders
Beowulf's fate

Only after the hero's death does the poet mention that the treasure is under a spell. A curse was once laid on it so that anyone who stole it would be "grimly punished," "hasped in hell-bonds in heathen shrines." Germanic paganism was not necessarily as gentle as some of its New Age counterparts. This human cranium from Ribe, southern Jutland, with its incised runes, may be only a surgeon's amulet, however.

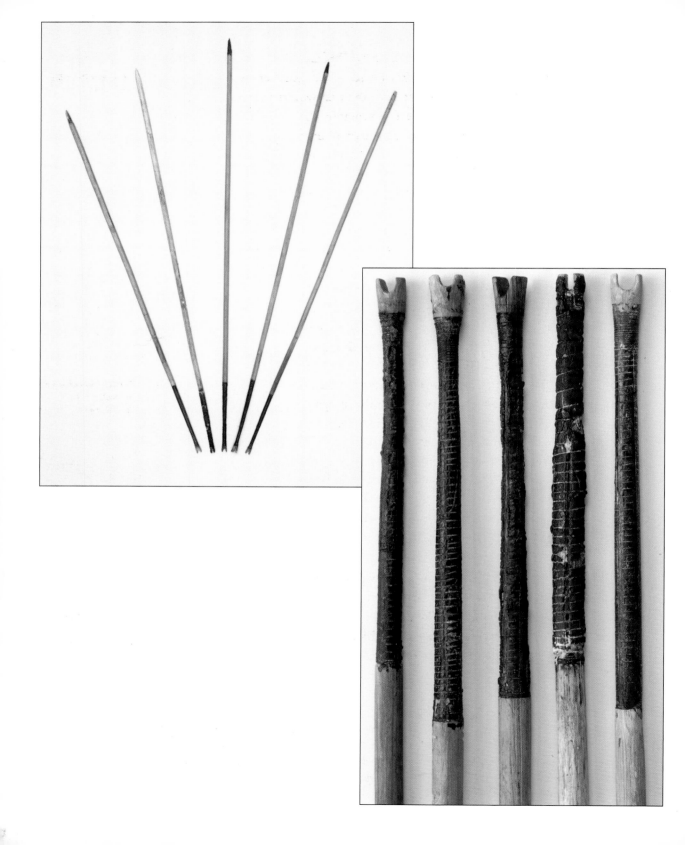

alive, aware, and in spite of his weakness
he had many requests. He wanted me to greet you
and order the building of a barrow that would crown
the site of his pyre, serve as his memorial,
in a commanding position, since of all men
to have lived and thrived and lorded it on earth

3100   his worth and due as a warrior were the greatest.
Now let us again go quickly
and feast our eyes on that amazing fortune
heaped under the wall. I will show the way
and take you close to those coffers packed with rings
and bars of gold. Let a bier be made
and got ready quickly when we come out
and then let us bring the body of our lord,
the man we loved, to where he will lodge
for a long time in the care of the Almighty."

He reports Beowulf's last wishes

3110   Then Weohstan's son, stalwart to the end,
had orders given to owners of dwellings,
many people of importance in the land,
to fetch wood from far and wide
for the good man's pyre.
                    "Now shall flame consume
our leader in battle, the blaze darken
round him who stood his ground in the steel-hail,
when the arrow-storm shot from bowstrings
pelted the shield-wall. The shaft hit home.
Feather-fledged, it finned the barb in flight."

Wiglaf gives orders for the building of a funeral pyre

3120   Next the wise son of Weohstan
called from among the king's thanes
a group of seven: he selected the best
and entered with them, the eighth of their number,

He goes with seven thanes to remove the treasure from the hoard

---

After the hero's death, warfare again threatens the Geatish people with an "arrow-storm shot from bow-strings," as in the past. These arrows were found in a bog at Nydam, Schleswig, where they formed part of an offering of weapons—spoils meant for a god, most likely. The notched end of each shaft is tarred and wound with thread where it was once fledged. Third century.

under the God-cursed roof; one raised
a lighted torch and led the way.
No lots were cast for who should loot the hoard
for it was obvious to them that every bit of it
lay unprotected within the vault,
there for the taking. It was no trouble
3130 to hurry to work and haul out
the priceless store. They pitched the dragon
over the clifftop, let tide's flow
and backwash take the treasure-minder.
Then coiled gold was loaded on a cart
in great abundance, and the grey-haired leader,
the prince on his bier, borne to Hronesness.

The Geat people built a pyre for Beowulf, *Beowulf's funeral*
stacked and decked it until it stood four-square,
hung with helmets, heavy war-shields
3140 and shining armour, just as he had ordered.
Then his warriors laid him in the middle of it,
mourning a lord far-famed and beloved.
On a height they kindled the hugest of all
funeral fires; fumes of woodsmoke
billowed darkly up, the blaze roared
and drowned out their weeping, wind died down
and flames wrought havoc in the hot bone-house,
burning it to the core. They were disconsolate
and wailed aloud for their lord's decease.
3150 A Geat woman too sang out in grief; *A Geat woman's dread*
with hair bound up, she unburdened herself
of her worst fears, a wild litany
of nightmare and lament: her nation invaded,
enemies on the rampage, bodies in piles,
slavery and abasement. Heaven swallowed the smoke.

At their king's request, his people build a great pyre for him. On it are set helmets, shields, and armor, together with "coiled gold . . . in great abundance" brought out from the dragon's chamber. This hoard of bronze rings from Smederup, Jutland, is suggestive of the superlative qualities that are attributed to practically everything mentioned in this poem. Early Iron Age.

Then the Geat people began to construct
a mound on a headland, high and imposing,
a marker that sailors could see from far away,
and in ten days they had done the work.

3160 It was their hero's memorial; what remained from the fire
they housed inside it, behind a wall
as worthy of him as their workmanship could make it.
And they buried torques in the barrow, and jewels
and a trove of such things as trespassing men
had once dared to drag from the hoard.
They let the ground keep that ancestral treasure,
gold under gravel, gone to earth,
as useless to men now as it ever was.
Then twelve warriors rode around the tomb,

3170 chieftain's sons, champions in battle,
all of them distraught, chanting in dirges,
mourning his loss as a man and a king.
They extolled his heroic nature and exploits
and gave thanks for his greatness; which was the proper thing,
for a man should praise a prince whom he holds dear
and cherish his memory when that moment comes
when he has to be convoyed from his bodily home.
So the Geat people, his hearth companions,
sorrowed for the lord who had been laid low.

3180 They said that of all the kings upon the earth
he was the man most gracious and fair-minded,
kindest to his people and keenest to win fame.

Beowulf's barrow overlooks the sea. Although this particular mound is not located on the coast, it is "high and imposing," as the poet declares Beowulf's barrow to be. Any mound like this concentrates one's attention. Gazing upon it, one may contemplate the difference that one heroic life can make in what is otherwise an unremarkable landscape.

Family Trees

Family trees of the Danish, Swedish, and Geatish dynasties.
Names given here are the ones used in this translation.

THE DANES or THE SHIELDINGS

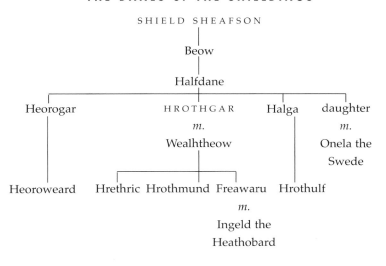

SHIELD SHEAFSON

Beow

Halfdane

Heorogar   HROTHGAR   Halga   daughter
                        m.   *m.*
                  Wealhtheow   Onela the
                                                        Swede

Heoroweard   Hrethric Hrothmund Freawaru   Hrothulf
                                          m.
                                    Ingeld the
                                    Heathobard

THE GEATS

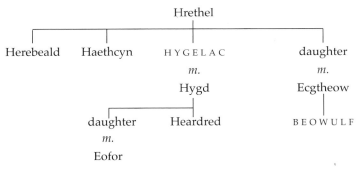

Hrethel

Herebeald   Haethcyn   HYGELAC   daughter
                              m.   *m.*
                              Hygd   Ecgtheow

              daughter   Heardred   BEOWULF
                m.
              Eofor

THE SWEDES

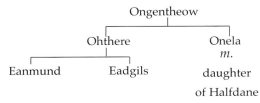

Ongentheow

          Ohthere   Onela
                                  m.
Eanmund   Eadgils   daughter
                            of Halfdane

AFTERWORD

Visualizing Beowulf

Death, divine power, horror, exultation, disgrace, personal devotion, fame—these are only a few of the elemental themes addressed in the *Beowulf* poet's story of high deeds set in an age of legendary splendor. How to visualize that narrative has always been a challenge for modern-day readers, who may well think of themselves as light-years removed in time, space, and temperament both from Anglo-Saxon England and from the more remote Migration Age when the poem is set.

The question of visualizing the poem's action would also have been a real one for people living in England during the period extending from the poet's own day (whenever that was, exactly) to about the year 1000, when the unique surviving text of the poem was written down.[1] Those people lived hundreds of years after the time when Beowulf and Hrothgar are imagined to have lived. They were separated from the poem's Scandinavian setting by hundreds of miles of open sea as well, at a time when spatial distance mattered far more than it does today. Toward the end of the first millennium A.D., the English inhabited a well-organized nation. They worshipped the God of the Old and New Testaments in churches built through an elaborate ecclesiastical hierarchy. They defended their land through a system of military obligation that was regulated by law and custom. They knew no more than we do now of ghoulish flesh-eating demons, of flying, fire-breathing dragons. They may never have seen with their own eyes objects like the high-end luxury goods of which the *Beowulf* poet speaks, even though today we may gaze on such things in museums thanks to the achievements of modern archaeology. The people of that time may have known little more than most people do today about great pagan cremation funerals, or about acts of huge and selfless heroism.

Moreover, it was surely part of the poet's design to let the action of the poem speak for itself. In order to listen well to a skilled storyteller,[2] one must focus on the inner realms of the imagination opened up by the flow of words. As we do so, we may be transported into territories only partially reminiscent of ordinary life. The lands to which entry is gained through storytelling can well be called "fabulous," for they are the creation of *fabulae* (Latin for "narratives"). In such realms, which are built of language rather than earth and stone, the laws that govern ordinary existence can be waived as easily as one opens or shuts a door. People become kings, beasts, and heroes. Nature is transfigured into surreal versions of itself. The world of human interaction is broken down into its primary constituent elements: "Death, divine power, horror, exultation, disgrace, personal devotion, fame," and other eternal themes. And when a narrator tells a story well, scenes of the utmost implausibility can be seen to cohere, in a configuration that may arouse sympathy to the point of joy and tears.

Nothing in this process demands that any one person's experience of a given narrative should match another's. Two people hearing the same story can "see" it in equally vivid terms, and yet their respective visualizations of it can be quite different. The existence of multiple illustrated versions of a particular story (whether one of the Grimms' tales or *Beowulf*), produced by different artists at one time or another, confirms that point.[3] Differences of visual interpretation are almost inevitable when a narrative crosses the threshold that separates ordinary life from otherworldly realms. What did it look like for the aged Beowulf to approach a dragon's barrow in the ancient land of the Geats? No one person's answer to this question can be much more authoritative than anyone else's, regardless of how much archaeology or early literature one has studied; for none of the elements of this scene is made of stuff more substantial than dreams.

The fundamental principle that has therefore guided the making of the present book is that *all individuals have the inalienable right to visualize the action of* Beowulf *in whatever manner they prefer.* There can be no question of "right" or "wrong" ways of imagining the poem. To put this same point another way, your dragon is just as good as my dragon, much as your understanding of the meaning of the poem itself has an inalienable rightness for you.

Granting that point, the question may still be posed: In what manner might the *Beowulf* poet and the members of the original audience have visualized the halls and barrows, ships and horses, jewels and tapestries, swords and helmets, and other material goods that figure so prominently in the poem? Here is where specialists in early medieval culture can perhaps be of use to present-day readers, given the giant strides in Iron Age and Viking Age archaeology, and its theoretical understanding, that have been taken during the past seventy-five years or so.[4]

The purpose of this illustrated edition of Seamus Heaney's translation of *Beowulf* is to enhance modern readers' experience of that poem—while not confining that experience in any way—by putting on display a gallery of images that have a meaningful relation to the objects and settings of which the poet speaks. The images are meant first and foremost for visual delight, so as to augment one's pleasure in reading the text. Some stunning examples of the skills of early medieval artists and artisans are therefore put on display. In some instances, in addition, an image will sharpen one's understanding of the things of which the poet speaks. When the poet mentions a "ring-hilted sword," for example, it is helpful to know that some swords of this era were indeed equipped with a metal ring attached to the hilt, set there perhaps chiefly for its symbolic value. To cite another example, when the poet uses the Old English term *wala* when speaking of a helmet's decoration (as he does at line 1031), it may help one's understanding of the poem to see concrete examples of the protective ridge that was denoted by that term.

Of course, many of the poet's themes and scenes could not possibly be illustrated except through an artist's fantasy. No attempt has here been made, for example, to illustrate Grendel's mother because there is nothing like her in nature. Similarly, it would be grotesque to try to identify a pictorial equivalent to Grendel's severed arm or decapitated torso. Moreover, there are times when efforts to illustrate the text must fail because even the poet may not have known exactly what he was speaking about, given the archaic words that were an inherited part of his vocabulary. When the poet specifies, for example, that *icge gold* is raised onto the funeral pyre of the dead hero Hnaef (1107), or that the aged Beowulf strikes the dragon with his *incge-lāf* (a sword term occurring in line 2577), one can only speculate as to exactly what kind of gold or weapon is meant, for both the adjective *icge* and the simplex *incge* are impenetrably obscure. The only answer one can give to this question is tautological: *icge gold* is the kind of gold that pagans used to put on funeral pyres, while an *incge-lāf* is the kind of sword one wants when fighting a dragon.

The images included here are meant to provide a visual counterpoint to the text, then, rather than to illustrate it in the usual sense. After a good deal of research and reflection, these particular images have been chosen from among a nearly infinite number of possibilities. Any other person who compiled a similar picture gallery might come up with different results that would be equally valid.

Many of these images are of artifacts now housed in the major archaeological collections of northern Europe. Some of these objects have suffered badly from the effects of time. Despite their damaged or fragmentary state, they provide an invaluable window on the Iron Age or Viking Age past. From the perspective of social history, of course, the view provided by that window is quite selective, for commonplace things are excluded. Farm implements, ordinary household items, and workaday clothes, for example, are not represented in the pages of this book, partly because of their perishable nature but chiefly because the *Beowulf* poet had no need or desire to speak of them. What he did tell of, again and again, were objects of great splendor, the sorts of things readily associated with a time and place "long ago and far away" when men, women, buildings, and even ordinary objects like mead-benches shone in a literally golden light.

PRINCIPLES GUIDING THE SELECTION OF IMAGES

In the section that follows this one, a brief bibliographical guide is offered to the images included in this book and the things they are meant to illustrate. The guide is organized topically. Images that illustrate a particular topic (e.g., the sword or the ship) are distributed here or there in the book depending on when such things are mentioned. The distribution of images is also influenced by aesthetics and by constraints of space, seeing that no more than one topic is displayed per page.

Before turning to that discussion, however, readers are entitled to a brief account of the criteria that guided the selection of images. The following paragraphs address that point.

1. *Of whose imagination are we thinking?* One question I have regularly asked myself while researching this book is, How might the *Beowulf* poet and the members of his audience have visualized this particular object or scene? Any response to that question must necessarily remain hypothetical, for no one of the Anglo-Saxon period left written comments on this poem. Moreover, it is helpful to think in terms of the poet's "audiences," rather than "audience," for at one time or another the work may have had multiple readers or listeners, both high and low in social status as well as both clerical and worldly in vocation. For these and other reasons, I have not pursued my own question with unrelenting rigor, but it has remained a starting point.

2. *Why accept anachronisms?* Some anachronism is inevitable, for suitable images are not always available from the historical period one would like to see represented. I have tried to keep such potential distractions to a minimum, however. Since the temporal setting of *Beowulf* is roughly the middle years of the first millennium, images are favored that relate to that period of prehistory. Nothing is represented that pertains to a period before the Roman Iron Age unless the poet himself asks the reader to call to mind a more antique era, as when he speaks of the dragon's barrow and its ancient hoard. Similarly, images pertaining to the period after the first millennium are generally avoided as being too late for our purposes. Some exceptions are made to these self-imposed guidelines. For example, when the poet tells of ships, he speaks of vessels bearing masts and sails. He is thus thinking in terms of ships of his own era, not of the simpler vessels that were in use ca. A.D. 500. The sea-voyages in *Beowulf* are therefore illustrated through images of Viking Age ships, even if of a date slightly later than that of the poem, that happen to be well documented, for vessels of this type are what the people of late Anglo-Saxon England would have known.

3. *Why is Denmark emphasized?* Since the setting of the main part of *Beowulf* is Denmark, and since many of the things that are named in the poem are of Danish origin or association (including the great hall Heorot and the gifts that are given out there), a deliberate attempt has been made to include images that pertain to that geographical area. In the latter part of the poem, however, the poet makes prominent mention of warfare involving the Swedes. Some images pertaining to Sweden therefore are featured at that point.[5] Throughout, as well, artifacts of Anglo-Saxon origin are put on display, for the English-speaking poet and his audience are likely sometimes to have thought in terms of things more or less familiar to them when visualizing this story set on the Continent at an earlier time. Images pertaining to Lejre, on the island of Zealand, Denmark, have a particular role to play because (as will be discussed in the next section) recent archaeological investigations have revealed that this was indeed, despite some former doubts, a major settlement at roughly the time when the action of *Beowulf* is set, and for many years thereafter. Although the poet never mentions Lejre by name, this is where the Shielding kings of *Beowulf* are reputed to have had their royal seat. The landscape and material culture of Lejre thus have a specific interest for readers of this Old English poem.

4. *Why introduce exotic artifacts?* Although most of the images included here relate to early medieval Britain and Scandinavia, items drawn from farther afield are included as well. Princess Freawaru (the daughter of Hrothgar, king of the Danes), for example, is imagined to be wearing a pair of Visigothic brooches from Spain (p. 136). This is pure fantasy on the editor's part, for the poet nowhere mentions Spain. My rationale in this instance is that these brooches are of a distinctly Germanic type. Moreover, they are representative of the luxury items that might well have come into the hands of such a fabulously wealthy family as the Shieldings are said to have been. Such people would have had high-level intertribal connections, some of them established through marriage. In a similar manner, when the poet speaks of Grendel's mother and the knife that she drives against the hero's chest, I invite readers to imagine her as armed with a military-style dagger, with silver decoration inlaid with niello on its hilt, that dates from the first century A.D. and was retrieved from the River Danube in the neighborhood of Belgrade (p. 104). This choice of a weapon is suggestive of the alien, exotic character of this creature and her abode. Toward the end of the poem, however, when the hero himself wields a long knife against the dragon, I invite readers to visualize an impressive weapon, inlaid with runes, that was found in the River Thames (p. 180).

5. *Why are artists' illustrations used so sparingly?* Since *Beowulf* depicts a preliterate tribal culture, the use of medieval manuscript illustrations could easily be thought to violate the poet's carefully managed decorum, and they are therefore generally avoided. Again, however, a few exceptions are made. One image showing a dragon fight (p. 178) could not be resisted even though it derives from France in the post-Conquest period. Two images depicting Grendel-like creatures are included (pp. 8, 46), for to my mind, there is no better way to reconstruct how the Anglo-Saxons conceived of humanlike monsters than to study their own artists' depictions of such things. Two manuscript illustrations depict emphatically Christian themes. One of these depicts the theme of Judgment, with devils and tormented souls in hell (p. 62), while the other depicts God ruling in majesty (p. 116). Readers may judge how apt they find these images to be. While Christian art may be thought out of place when used to illustrate a poem set in pagan times, one noteworthy feature of *Beowulf* is that Christian themes and sentiments abound in it. King Hrothgar, in particular, is characterized as a

pious monarch, almost a patriarchal figure, and he articulates a set of Christian values that many critics see as underpinning the entire poem. An Anglo-Saxon image of the deity therefore accompanies what is commonly called that king's "sermon."

As for modern illustrations of characters and scenes from *Beowulf*, many are available either in print or on the web, and some are highly expressive. They are avoided here, however, since the aim of this edition is to illustrate the poem chiefly through ancient artifacts. The one exception is a set of three woodblock prints by the Danish artist Sigurd Vasegaard (pp. 138, 192, 196). Originally made to accompany not *Beowulf* but rather a modern edition of Saxo's early-twelfth-century *History of the Danes* (Saxo Grammaticus 1970), these images help one visualize several of the poem's imagined scenes that, in their human drama, would otherwise be difficult or impossible to represent at all.

6. *What place do original photographs have?* Four photographs taken by the photographer Ole Malling at the Historical-Archaeological Research Centre, Lejre (pp. 56, 76, 156, 162), are included in part as a way of calling attention to the activities of the Centre, which each year introduces thousands of young people and adults to the cultural heritage of Scandinavia through living experiments with the past (Meldgaard and Rasmussen 1996; Niles 2007a: 461–67). A few photographs taken in the open air, chiefly by myself (and in one instance by my daughter), are included as a means of establishing the scene for the action of the poem, or else providing a visual analogue to it. A number of these photos, too, pertain to the lay of the land at Lejre, for in visiting that place I have been struck by how readily, at certain hours of the day, some features of that landscape could kindle the imagination of an impressionable storyteller or poet. Other photographs relate to the *Beowulf* poet's keen, though selective, interest in the natural world (pp. 36, 106, 108, 122, 124). These photos do not necessarily pertain to Scandinavia. One happens to have been taken in Maine, two in southern Wisconsin, one in the west of Ireland, and one in northwest Scotland. In making use of these latter photos, which were taken for reasons unconnected to the present project, I find myself grateful that the beauties of the physical world are not restricted to any one time and place. Sunlight in Scotland or North America in the year 2000 and sunlight in Denmark in the year 500 have an essential similitude, and the same is true of gannets, ice-locked shores, and other features of nature.

Two other points should be kept in mind. The first is that in the early medieval context, precious objects are not inert. They are an extension of the person who owns them, wears them, or made them (Leisi 1952–1953). An aura inheres in them that cannot be accounted for by their economic value alone. When the young warrior Beowulf walks into Hrothgar's court wearing a byrnie that the legendary smith Weland has made, his stature is thereby enhanced, for Weland was not just a master smith. He also has long been associated with elves, giants, and dwarves.[6] A byrnie of Weland's manufacture retains a quasi-numinous quality that lends a sheen to the man who wears it. Much the same is true of the magnificent gifts that Hrothgar and Wealhtheow, the king and queen of the Danes, present to the victorious young Beowulf (see especially p. 82), or the precious sword with which Hygelac, king of the Geats, rewards him on his return to his homeland (p. 146). Since these objects are conspicuous ones that have been owned by royalty, their presentation to the hero confirms that he too is endowed with the aura of kingship, even though a few years will elapse before he assumes the throne. In this edition, objects of unusual splendor are chosen to illustrate these scenes.

A second point worth emphasizing is that two different kinds of people inhabit the world of *Beowulf*. On the one hand, there is the royal line (the *cynecynn*, "royal race"). On the other, there is everyone else in society. In theory, only persons of royal blood are eligible to become king. Persons of such lineage are therefore literally a breed apart. In the poem, this category includes the Danish figures Hrothgar (with his queen Wealhtheow), Hrothulf, and Freawaru, as well as the Geatish figures Hrethel, Hygelac (with his queen Hygd), and Beowulf himself. These people should be visualized in terms that suit their special character. Anyone may enjoy fine possessions, but the precious objects owned by kings, queens, and princes are signs of royal status. When describing objects of this kind, the poet spares no superlatives. I have therefore thought it consistent with the poet's hyperbolic mode to display images of the richest kind when mention is made of gifts or entertainments in Hrothgar's or Hygelac's royal hall (pp. 24, 30, 38, 40, 64, 80, 82, 94, 134, 136, 140, 144, 146). If the objects depicted in this manner are thought to be a shade "too good to be true," then my work as editor will be in alignment with the narrative method of the *Beowulf* poet, who often stretches reality to its limits—and, it is hoped, with the style of the translator as well, Seamus Heaney, who never uses a cheap word when an extravagant one will do. What remains remarkable to contemplate is that all the ancient objects represented in this edition did actually circulate among real people.

BEOWULF AS A WINDOW ON IRON-AGE EUROPE

As has been said, users of this book are invited to enjoy its images for their own sake as a means of enhancing the experience of reading the poem. In addition, those readers who wish to know more about the material world evoked by the poet may welcome additional information about early European shipbuilding, jewelry, architecture, weapons manufacture, and the like. The rest of this Afterword is meant for them.

THE HALL AND ITS FURNISHINGS

> *And soon it stood there,*
> *finished and ready, in full view,*
> *the hall of halls.   (76–78)*

Halls are called to mind so many times in *Beowulf* as almost to serve as an emblem of social life in general. There is King Hygelac's hall; there is the aged King Beowulf's hall, which may or may not be the same one; there are the halls mentioned in the subordinate episodes involving Finn, King of the Frisians, and Ingeld, leader of the Heathobards; and of course there is King Hrothgar's great hall Heorot, "the hall of halls," the idealized type of them all.

The hall in *Beowulf* is a place dedicated to the valued pastimes of drinking, talking, and listening to songs and music. It is a ceremonial center—a peaceful sanctuary, for members of the warrior aristocracy—where gifts are distributed, and hence where honor is made visible. Here social relationships are established and confirmed. Heorot is unusual in having a name, for the only other named halls of Germanic antiquity pertain to mythology (as is true of Valhöll, the home of the gods). It towers high, wide-gabled, not far inland, and it is approached by a paved path (320). It can be seen from afar, especially since its roof is literally gilded.[7] It has a portico where spears and shields are stacked. Within its main assembly space, which has wooden flooring (1317), is a throne, perhaps set off in a special place (for Grendel cannot approach it). The men at the feast are seated on gilded benches (776). The interior floor plan is spacious enough not just for a large number of men to be seated comfortably, but also for a singer to perform, for cupbearers to circulate freely, and for horses to be displayed. Additional benches, ranged against the interior walls, are used as beds. Swords and helmets are hung on the walls at night.

The main entry is imagined to be large enough for a creature of Grendel's huge size to enter through. The door is secured with iron hinges and other iron reinforcements, and the whole hall is braced with iron bolts or nails as well (773–74; see *MScand*. 325–31, s.v. "ironwork"). Located somewhere close by the hall, apparently, is a block of stone or pedestal (Old English *stapol*, 926) on which, at one point, King Hrothgar stands while making a speech.[8] Also nearby the hall are the pagan shrines or temples (*hærg-trafu*, 175) where some of the Danes offer sacrifice. There is at least one secondary building to which King Hrothgar and Queen Wealhtheow retire to spend the night. We are perhaps meant to take for granted that the settlement includes additional buildings fulfilling various functions (a barn, kitchen, storehouses, workrooms, and the like), but of these the poet tells us nothing since his interest is entirely focused on the hall and, as its dismal counterpart, Grendel's infernal mere.

The hall, and its place in the literary world of *Beowulf*, has been well described; its possible place in the psychohistory of the Anglo-Saxons has been explored as well.[9] Whether halls reminiscent of the great one that is the setting for much of the first part of *Beowulf* were features of the cultural landscape of early Anglo-Saxon England, however, is hard to say. One sixth- and seventh-century hall complex has been excavated at Yeavering, Northumberland.[10] Here a substantial main building measuring 25 by 12 meters (about 82 by 39 feet) stood in proximity to a kitchen or butchering place that may have been the scene of sacrifices involving cattle. Not far away was a theater or assembly place. Another well-documented Anglo-Saxon settlement featuring relatively large buildings is the sixth- and seventh-century rural estate at Cowdery's Down, Hampshire; a third is King Alfred's ninth-century palace complex at Cheddar, Somerset.[11] Although these sites have been brought into relation to Heorot (Cramp 1993), none presents a particularly close parallel. The functions of large buildings like those at Cheddar, in the relatively complex Christian society of later Anglo-Saxon England, would have been different from the functions of a Migration Age hall but, one can assume, still analogous to them.

In Scandinavia, however, where the pagan religion of the North survived much longer than in Britain, there is clear evidence for an aristocratic "hall culture" that came into existence not long after the fall of imperial Rome and that was maintained in a number of locales until close to the year 1000, at which point it was replaced by new forms of social organization associated with the new religion of Christianity.[12] The settlement complex at Gudme, on the island of Funen, Denmark, is of keen interest in this regard.[13] At Gudme have been discovered the remains of a hall, dating from the fourth and fifth centuries, that measured about 47 meters (154 feet) in length, almost twice the length of the early Anglo-Saxon hall at Yeavering. Also discovered near Gudme and its associated port, Lundeborg, is the largest gold hoard known from Iron Age Denmark, the Broholm hoard (p. 30), in addition to a number of other precious objects (e.g., p. 70). Gudme is the earliest of the "central places" that, as is now known, served as pivotal points in the geography of southern Scandinavia during the late Germanic Iron Age and the Viking Age. These were sites that served not just political functions but also religious and economic ones.[14]

From the perspective of *Beowulf* studies, by far the most significant of the Scandinavian "central places" is Gammel Lejre, on the island of Zealand, Denmark, for it is at Lejre that the Shielding kings who play such a prominent role in that poem (Old English *Scyldingas*; Old Norse *Skjöldungar*) are said by numerous poets and chroniclers to have had their seat. Until recently, there existed no archaeological evidence to confirm that Lejre, which is now no more than a tiny village of a few houses, was ever the home of kings; but in 1986–1988 and again in 2004–2005, excavations undertaken just outside the old village of Lejre revealed the remains of a series of at least three halls that were among the most impressive buildings of their era (pp. 4, 48, 60, 84).[15] The earliest hall at Lejre was built about A.D. 550—that is, at about the same time when the action of *Beowulf* is set. A second hall, located about a half mile south of the first, was built about 680, while a third (a rebuilding of the second) was constructed about 890 and seems to have been used for another hundred years or so before being abandoned when, after the conversion of the Danish ruling class, a new capital was established at what is now the nearby city of Roskilde. Even if the Shielding kings themselves remain largely the stuff of dreams, a series of wealthy chieftains or kings are now known to have lived at Lejre over a period of nearly five hundred years.

Each of the Lejre halls was built on a plan somewhat like that of the well-known longhouses at the Viking Age fortress at Trelleborg, on the island of Zealand (pp. 130, 132; Andersen 1995). At 47 to 48.5 meters (154 to 159 feet) in length, each was a huge structure of the Gudme type, with its long walls bowed outward in the middle so as to yield a slightly convex shape. The roof was apparently somewhat convex in shape as well, slightly higher in the middle than at the gable ends. Pairs of large upright interior posts provided the main support for the roof, while external timbers, set in the ground outside the walls and slanting inward, provided bracing. While the earliest hall at Lejre measured only 7 or 8 meters (about 23 or 26 feet) in width, the later ones were 11.5 meters (38 feet) wide at the midpoint of the long walls and therefore encompassed an unusually large interior space. Each hall had three or four entrances. One of these, the one nearest the midpoint of one of the long walls, was larger than the others. Interior rooms were divided from one another by partitions, and a hearth located in the largest of these rooms (the "hall proper") is likely to have marked the chief focal point for social life. The size of the Lejre halls would have been intimidating to strangers, but a source of pride for any people who gathered there to celebrate themselves. Metal nails, bolts, and braces found in the vicinity (p. 52) are evidence for the timbers having been reinforced by ironwork.[16]

The halls were not used for cooking, for that would have been done in an outbuilding. At the later settlement complex at Lejre, additional buildings close by the hall seem to have served as a barn, storage units, houses for craft activities (including a smithy), and sleeping and living quarters. Interestingly, not far downhill from both the earlier hall site and the later one were found substantial deposits of animal bones in conjunction with a large heap of fire-heated stones that had been transported to that location, for some reason, year after year over a long period of time. While it is possible that the stones were used for a ritualistic method of food production, perhaps involving sacrifice, the exact purpose of the heap is unknown.

Since there is no archaeological evidence for furniture at Lejre, one can only speculate as to the possible presence there of benches, tables, and the like. A noteworthy bed of ninth-century date, however, was recovered from the ship burial at Oseberg, near Oslo Fjord (p. 120 top), and a few similar items are known in the archaeological record ($R-L^2$ 2: 316–20, s.vv. "Bett und Bettzeug"). When the king and queen of the Danes retire for the night to sleep in separate quarters, one is free to imagine them taking their rest on a handsomely carved bed like this. The thrones of this period, like the beds used by royalty, were doubtless much smaller than their modern equivalents but carefully wrought. Of interest in this regard is a small chair or stool recovered from a bog at Feddersen Wierde, near the mouth of the River Weser in lowland Germany (p. 10), carved in such a manner as to suggest a ceremonial function. With it was a footstool, bearing a runic inscription, on the bottom of which is incised the stylized image of a stag chased by hounds (p. 92 bottom). While this image of the stag may call "Heorot" to mind—an Old English name that, as a common noun, means "hart" or "stag"—it would be easy to overwork that connection.[17] The function of these two carved objects is unknown. Like other objects found at Feddersen Wierde (for which see Schön 1999; *R-L*[2] 8: 249–66), they may have served both as serviceable pieces of furniture and emblems of high rank.

THE SHIP

Over the waves, with the wind behind her
and foam at her neck, she flew like a bird   *(217–18)*

The passages that describe the hero's sea-voyage to Denmark and, later, his return trip to his homeland are often admired as among the beauties of the poem. When Beowulf's band of men set sail, however, they are engaged in an anachronistic activity. Northern European ships of the period when the poem is set, the fifth and sixth centuries A.D., were shallow-draft vessels that did not carry sail.[18] The art of building deep-keeled ships equipped with masts and sails came later. It was an art that the Vikings developed to perfection as a prelude to their voyages over almost all the known world, and beyond.[19] This is one instance, therefore, when the poet describes the Migration Age action of the poem in terms familiar to persons living at his own later date. Anyone who lived after the Vikings made their initial raids in the British Isles, beginning in A.D. 793, would naturally have thought of the hero as traversing the sea in a light warship of the kind first developed in Scandinavia, then imitated in other lands.

Because of the perishable nature of wood, relatively few ships dating from this period have survived even in part. For many years the outstanding ships that were recovered at Oseberg and Gokstad, near the mouth of Oslo Fjord, Norway, were taken to be nearly unique examples of royal shipbuilding from the Viking Age.[20] In Denmark, nothing like these vessels was found until 1935, when the remains of a light warship dating from the Viking Age were discovered in a funeral mound at Ladby, on the island of Funen. Almost nothing of the ship remained but its outline in the sandy earth and about two thousand rivets and spikes. Remarkable efforts at conservation, however, have resulted in the publication of two volumes describing the Ladby ship and its accompanying grave-goods (Thorvildsen 1957, Sørensen 2001). It is now known that the ship, which dates from the ninth or the first half of the tenth century, was 21.5 meters (about 70 feet) in length, with a decorative spiral-shaped prow and a spiked, dragonlike tail. It was equipped with fifteen or at most sixteen pairs of oars. A fine model of this vessel as it may once have looked is given pride of place on page 2.

Moreover, thanks to advances in underwater archaeology, a remarkable discovery was made in 1962 at Skuldelev, about halfway up Roskilde Fjord. There the remains of six ships of late Viking Age date were recovered where they had been scuttled, in a moment of crisis, as a means of protecting this part of Zealand against sea-borne attack (Crumlin-Pedersen 2002). An artist's representation of one of these vessels, Skuldelev 5, is featured on page 14. Its surviving timbers, like those of the other Skuldelev vessels, are on display in the Viking Ship Museum at Roskilde. A full-size replica, the "Helge Ask," can be seen docked at the museum if it is not being sailed up the fjord on a festive occasion (p. 128).

Like the Ladby ship, Skuldelev 5 was built rather late for our purposes (about A.D. 1040). Even though it was never a prince's vessel (for it was of workaday construction), it is a suitable choice to illustrate the sea-voyages in *Beowulf*. At a length of 17.5 meters (57 feet) and carrying a crew of up to thirty men, it may at first seem too large for the hero's use, for he sets out as one of a crew of fifteen. Later, however, we are told that he receives gifts in Denmark that include eight horses. Room has to be found in the ship for those horses too! Allowing each horse the space normally occupied by two men, and taking into account the loss of one of the retainers (the man named Handscio), the numbers come out just right.

As is typical of Viking Age warships, both the Ladby ship and Skuldelev 5 carried a single square sail that hung from a yardarm attached to the top of the mast. Each ship was clinker-built—that is, it was built of overlapping strakes secured with iron clinch nails, or "clinkers." Each was a versatile vessel that could have been either sailed or rowed. An outboard steering oar was secured at the rear starboard side. Skuldelev 5 might have had a detachable dragon's-head prow; it might also have been colorfully painted, as the Ladby ship is believed to have been.

A vessel like this could well have been a prince's most precious possession. Appropriately, the Danish coast-guard who gives Beowulf and his band of Geats permission to march inland has a watch set over Beowulf's ship. We are not told whether he does this out of goodness of heart or to inhibit treachery on the part of these armed strangers. The man who guards the ship is later presented with a gift of a handsome sword, a fit reward for his service.

WEAPONS AND ARMOR

When Beowulf and his men approach Heorot for the first time (301–31), the weapons they wear indicate their rank as members of the warrior aristocracy, for only men of rank would carry a full complement of arms. In a society where you are what you wear, these are persons whose honor one would insult at one's peril. Weapons had an intimate role in the gift economy of early Germanic societies, thereby cementing the reciprocal hierarchy of human relations that held a stable society together.[21]

The Coat of Mail

> . . . *the mesh of chain-mail*
> *on Beowulf's shoulder shielded his life,*
> *turned the edge and tip of the blade.*   *(1547–49)*

As a war-shirt that protected the whole torso against the storm of weapons, the byrnie (Old English *byrne,* "corslet, coat of mail") was a crucial element in an aristocratic warrior's defense of his body. In the elaborate arming scene that precedes the hero's fight in the depths of the mere, it is noteworthy that the byrnie is the first item mentioned (1443–47). In the hero's ensuing combat it proves indispensable, for without it—and without God's intervention too, we are told—serpents would have ripped his body apart or, if he had survived that initial onslaught, Grendel's mother would have driven her knife right into his chest.

Moreover, byrnies caught the eye. When Beowulf addresses King Hrothgar for the first time, his metal byrnie is said to give off light, just as the hall itself does, for both the roof and the byrnie are gilded (308, 551–52). Even without such gilding, any well-polished coat of mail would have been effulgent. A byrnie was audible as well. When Beowulf and his men land in Denmark, the jingling of their war-coats makes a musical accompaniment to their steps as they walk inland (see lines 226–27, 322–23).

With its many interlocking rings, a byrnie could readily serve as a symbol not just of its owner's rank, but also of the strength of the members of a war-band bound together by oaths of mutual fidelity. If acting as self-willed individuals, those same men could be scattered as easily as a handful of individual rings. In the heroic world of *Beowulf,* helms and byrnies that are left to rust on the ground untended are sources of grief, for they are signs of a dying civilization (see lines 2255–62).

Since iron generally corrodes if left in damp earth, few early byrnies survive in the archaeological record. Seeing that so much expense was involved in their manufacture, it is possible that relatively few were made. One byrnie that has survived almost intact was recovered from a bog at Vimose, on the island of Funen, where it was deposited in the early third century (p. 102; cf. $R-L^2$ 32: 401–14, s.v. "Vimose"). The date of this item is somewhat early for our poem, but byrnies did not change much from century to century. Like a vast number of other precious items of early Iron Age date that have been recovered from Danish bogs,[22] the Vimose byrnie appears to have been offered to a god or gods subsequent to some unknown group's victory in warfare. It consists of no fewer than twenty thousand iron rings individually joined together, with each ring painstakingly joined to four others.

Beowulf takes great pride in his byrnie, for (as he himself remarks) it was made by Weland, the legendary smith who in Old Norse tradition is known as king of the elves (p. 28; see *MEng.* 302–04, s.vv. "Franks Casket"). He wears it even while swimming on the open sea (550–53) or diving into the waters of Grendel's mere (1443 and following). Such acts reflect his superhuman capabilities, for a heavy iron byrnie like the one found at Vimose was scarcely meant for aquatic exploits.

The Sword

The iron blade with its ill-boding patterns
had been tempered in blood. (1459–60)

Swords of Iron Age and Viking Age date are fairly well documented in the archaeological record ($R-L^2$ 27: 523–97, s.v. "Schwert"; Peirce 2002). Those pertaining to England have been well described by Davidson (1962) with reference to archaeology, folklore, and legend. Swords would not, of course, have been "tempered in blood" other than metaphorically, when they drew blood in battle. The "ill-boding patterns" of such blades were real, however, for the elaborate process by which a double-bladed sword was forged by being hammered out of a bundle of straight steel and twisted iron rods resulted in each blade's having a distinctive wavy sheen—hence the name, "pattern-welded blade," by which such swords are known.[23] Reference to the variegated sheen of swords is frequent in *Beowulf*. Each pattern-welded blade had a unique visual appearance even if its shape was predictable (see p. 74 for Viking Age examples, and p. 78 for a modern one). It is therefore unsurprising for a Beowulfian sword to have an individual name, as we find with "Hrunting" (Unferth's sword) or "Naegling" (Beowulf's own, during the dragon fight).

Swords were precious items in the Iron Age gift economy. A noteworthy example is the outstanding sword with which Hygelac, king of the Geats, rewards Beowulf upon his return home. In this edition, this sword is represented by a remarkable gold-hilted blade from Snartemo, Norway (p. 146; see *R-L*[2] 29: 164–65; Rolfson and Stylegar 2003).

On more than a few occasions the poet refers to a sword's ornamented hilt.[24] On their blunt end, the forged blades of this period culminated in a tang, a narrow extension of the blade to which the hilt was attached. The hilt was rounded off by a pommel (p. 174). The hilt was often specially decorated, and its ornamentation could take the form of zoomorphic interlaced designs (p. 112), embossed gold plates (p. 146), or inset garnets or other precious stones (p. 174). Three times in *Beowulf* a sword is referred to by the phrase *hring-mæl* "ring-adorned [weapon]" (1521, 1564, 2037). Swords with metal rings attached to their hilts are in fact well known to archaeologists (Evison 1967; *R-L*[2] 25: 22–24, s.vv. "Ringschwerter"). This type of sword is exemplified here by a sword from Coombe, Kent (p. 100; Davidson and Webster 1967) as well as by the Snartemo sword. While some such rings might have held a chain or cord to secure the sword, others were not functional. In either event, a ring-hilted sword could well have symbolized the reciprocal social ties that bound the lord (or "ring-giver") and his retainer.

Swords of this period were formidable weapons when wielded by men trained in their use, to judge from anatomical injuries suffered by warriors of the Anglo-Saxon period (Wenham 1989). The blade was forged as a single piece that would have been as impressive for its flexibility as for its tensile strength and its keen edges. If swords tend to fail Beowulf, both when he is fighting in the depths of Grendel's mere and during the dragon episode, that motif is best taken as part of the poem's literary design rather than any failing on his part. In the earlier episode, he is in need of an extraordinary weapon if he is to save his life, and he receives it in the form of a sword literally made by giants. In the later one, his sword shatters when driven against the dragon's impenetrable hide, a sign that even though the hero's strength is undiminished, his end is near.

The Helmet

Boar-shapes flashed
above their cheek-guards, the brightly forged
work of goldsmiths . . .   (303–05)

Like other prized items of weaponry, helmets served as both functional defenses
and emblems of rank.[25] In *Beowulf* the helmet is referred to as a *grīm-helm,* or
"masked-helmet" (334), for it could hide enough of a person's features as to make
him almost unrecognizable as a human being (see p. 166 in particular). Like the
Roman parade helmets on which their design was partly based, Germanic helmets
were sometimes decorated in an elaborate manner with mythological motifs, as
with the helmet from tomb 14 at Vendel, Uppland (p. 158; see also pp. 190, 198);
dragonlike motifs, as with the Anglo-Saxon helmet from Coppergate, York (pp. 176,
188 center; Tweddle 1992; Webster and Backhouse 1991: 60–64); or zoomorphic
motifs of a fantastic kind, as with the helmet from Mound 1 at Sutton Hoo, which
is thought to have been of Swedish manufacture (pp. 172, 190). As the poet speci-
fies, helmets were often reinforced with a metal ridge running vertically over the
top, the *wala* (pp. 66, 166, 172, 190).[26] In addition to this defense, they sometimes
bore chain mail designed to protect the throat or the back of the neck (p. 166).
Moreover, when the *Beowulf* poet alludes to helmets adorned with "boar-shapes"
that are "the brightly forged work of goldsmiths," his reference has been confirmed
by archaeology. A freestanding iron figure of a boar, with silver-gilt studs and tusks
and with garnets forming the eyes, surmounts the celebrated Anglo-Saxon helmet
from Benty Grange, Derbyshire, for example (p. 20).[27] The wild boar was an emblem
of ferocity. Its association with the god Freyr (or Yngvi-Freyr), during pagan times,
must have added to its favorable associations. Indeed, helmets seem so often to
have been adorned with boarlike images that the words *swȳn* or *eofer,* each mean-
ing "boar," are used metaphorically in *Beowulf* to denote the helm (as at lines
1111–12).

The Seax, or Dagger

Once Wiglaf has weakened the dragon by striking it in its nether parts, the hero
revives from his swoon, draws the long knife hanging at his side, and uses it to cut
the *wyrm* in two. Although the single-bladed long knife (Old English *seax; R-L²* 26:
538–46, s.v. "sax") was apparently a commonplace weapon that a warrior might

have worn on practically any occasion, only once before this climactic scene does such a weapon figure in the poem. This is during the hero's second combat, when Grendel's mother drives her dagger against his chest. In the present edition, as has been mentioned, the she-demon has been armed with an archaic double-bladed dagger that would have been an exotic one from an Anglo-Saxon perspective (p. 104). The knife that the hero wields against the dragon, however, is represented by a handsome weapon of English provenance (p. 180). The runes inlaid in this latter blade, which is of unusual length and quality, lend it a superior dignity.

The Spear and Shield

Any warrior of the Germanic period would have owned a shield and spear. In graves of the pagan era, correspondingly, the presence of this pair of weapons has traditionally been construed as the "identification tag" of a person of male sex (Old English *wæpned-monn*, literally "weaponed person" or simply "male"), though if any person of female sex did happen to aspire to warrior status she would have carried these same weapons. Spears were normally made of ash, a wood favored for this purpose because of its straight grain and tensile strength. Shafts were sometimes decorated with markings or light incisions; examples are a set of handsome spears recovered from a bog at Kragehul, on the island of Funen, where they were deposited in the third century as part of a sacrificial offering (p. 22; *R-L²* 17: 276–81, s.v. "Kragehul"). Spearheads were generally made of iron and were forged in a variety of shapes and sizes depending on their intended use (for thrusting, hurling, or other purposes). They, too, on occasion, were given special decoration such as silver inlay (p. 16).

Shields were round in shape with a central iron boss designed to protect the hand (p. 26; *R-L²* 27: 81–106, s.v. "Schild"). They were fashioned from any of a number of hardwoods, among which linden wood (the wood of the lime tree) was favored on account of its resiliency and relatively light weight. The boards of a shield were sometimes covered with leather, its outer edge sometimes secured by a metal rim.

The Bow and Arrow

Bows have a long history in warfare and the hunt (Rausing 1967) but only an incidental role to play in the heroic world of *Beowulf*, where more prestigious weapons are foregrounded. At one point a serpent is shot with an arrow and drawn ashore

(1432–36). Of greater thematic significance is the later scene when the aged Beowulf, relating his family's tragic history, tells of the incident when his uncle Haethcyn accidentally shot and killed another uncle, Herebeald (2435–40). Bows were made of yew, a very dense hardwood, or of elm. When used by a skilled archer who knew how to direct his strength, a simple bow was capable of propelling a dart at a deadly velocity (p. 162). As for the shaft, it had to be made of a straight-grained wood such as ash. Sometimes the point was fire-hardened; sometimes an arrowhead was attached. The shaft was feathered using tar and waxed thread, as can clearly be seen with regard to five arrows recovered from a bog at Nydam, Schleswig (p. 204). Various kinds of arrowhead made of bone or iron were available, depending on the arrow's intended use.

TREASURES

Images of treasure abound in *Beowulf*. Nowhere, however, is a precious jewel or other precious object (or a group of such objects) depicted with such exactitude as to foreclose the possibility of imagining it in any of several ways. In an edition like the present one, therefore, any number of images of Iron Age treasures could have been chosen to illustrate the splendid things that are exchanged by members of the upper ranks of Beowulfian society, or that are worn or otherwise put on display on special occasions.

The Old English word *bēag* (plural *bēagas*) that occurs with some frequency with reference to things of value can denote anything from "ring" to "circlet" to "necklace" to "torque" to "bracelet" to "money" or "treasure." When the poet states that a woman is *bēag-hroden*, "ring-adorned," as Queen Wealhtheow is said to be (623), she could thus be visualized as wearing any of several kinds of personal adornments. Perhaps she is wearing a rune-inscribed diadem or band like one that was discovered at Strårup, Jutland (p. 80 top; Moltke 1985: 107–08; Jørgensen and Petersen 1998: 122–23). Perhaps she wears a gold bracteate, or die-stamped medallion with filagree decoration, of the kind that was produced in some numbers during the early Germanic Iron Age and that often featured a mythological scene and a runic inscription (p. 80 bottom; Axboe 2004). Perhaps she wears a beautiful necklace, torque, armband, or finger rings, or a combination of these things. Particularly since her name and family connections are suggestive of the British Isles,[28] I like to think of her as wearing the Desborough necklace (p. 38; Webster and Backhouse 1991: 28–29), but this is mere whimsy. This lovely example of seventh-century jewelry, found in a high-status Anglo-Saxon grave of the late pagan period, includes among its pendants a cross suggestive of a hybrid of pagan and Christian traditions.

The Queen's daughter Princess Freawaru, likewise, circulates through the hall *gold-hroden*, "adorned with gold" (2025), or in Heaney's phrase "in her gold-trimmed attire." Freawaru is betrothed to Ingeld, chief of the Heathobards, in a union that seems to offer only the prospect of bloodshed and tears. At the moment, however, she is still in her father's hall and is dressed in fine fashion. One can easily visualize her wearing some striking jewelry, as would befit a young woman of wealth and taste (p. 136), but one's imagination is left free in this regard.

As for the necklace or torque that Wealhtheow presents to Beowulf and that the hero later, in turn, presents to his queen Hygd (2172–76), the poet praises it as "the most resplendent / torque of gold I ever heard tell of / anywhere on earth or under heaven" (1194–96). Still, as with these other items, one is left free to imagine just what it looked like. The treasure chosen in this edition to answer to this passage is one of a set of three necklaces now in the Museum of National Antiquities, Stockholm, that are as impressive for their marvelous gold filigree and granulation as for their size. This one, from Färjestaden on the Baltic island of Öland, consists of five parallel cylindrical bands of intricately wrought gold (p. 82; see Montelius 1888: 128; *R-L*² 12: 335–43, s.v. "Goldhalskragen"). A person might well consider himself handsomely rewarded upon receiving a gift like this.

The nature and functions of treasure in early medieval society have been described by various scholars from a variety of perspectives.[29] What is emphatically clear from these publications is that members of the Iron Age aristocracy put a very high value on precious metalwork and jewelry, as indeed, people of wealth tend to do in all ages. Precious adornments give off light; they lend a star quality to those who wear them. Some such items are heirlooms that embody dynastic power and the stature that accrues to inherited wealth. When treasures are given to others, they embody both the magnanimity of the giver and the virtue and promise of the recipient. Everyone wants these things, and everyone who can afford to do so displays them on special occasions. Queen Wealhtheow fulfils the function of a peace-weaver in Danish society in part through the gifts she gives while circulating among the men and offering them supportive words. In this manner she does her best to secure her family's interests while dulling the men's murderous propensities.

When Wealhtheow and her daughter Freawaru offer the men drink, each of them does so in a manner respectful of individual status. In this refined setting, one can imagine alcoholic drinks being served in expensive glassware of the kind that was in circulation as luxury goods during this general period (R-L^2 12: 139–66, s.v. "Glas"; *Bl. Encl.* 205–06). Shown in this edition are a fine glass vessel found at Himlingøje, Zealand (p. 32), and a set of glass beakers from the pagan burial mound at Taplow, Buckinghamshire (p. 40). Equally well, one can visualize beverages being served in vessels made of horn, such as the fine gold-adorned ones, made from aurochs' horns, that were included among the funeral goods at Taplow (p. 134).[30]

The gifts that Hrothgar presents to each of Beowulf's men in Heorot in reward for their risking their lives are perhaps best envisioned as valuable items that, still, fall short of the splendor of the outstanding gifts the hero himself receives. A single gold or silver-gilt torque might have sufficed for each man (p. 68). As for the Geatish warrior named Handscio who is killed and eaten by Grendel, Hrothgar magnanimously pays his man-price (Old English *wergild*) straightway in gold (1052–54). Moreover, in the song about Finn and Hengest that is featured in the scene that immediately follows, King Finn is said to distribute treasures evenhandedly among his Frisian retainers and his Danish guests (1090–93). An image of a set of gold rings found at Lillesø, near the early Danish "central place" Gudme, is set on display here as an apt counterpart to either of these passages (p. 70; Jørgensen and Petersen 1998: 211–12). Other treasures (or prospective treasures) that receive prominent mention in the poem are the ones with which Hrothgar, in his youth, paid off a serious feud involving Beowulf's father, Ecgtheow, and the ones with which that same king promises he will reward the hero for the help he is offering in Denmark. The first of these treasures is envisioned here in terms of a magnificent hoard from Broholm, in the Gudme region (p. 30; Jørgensen and Petersen 1998: 208–10); the second is envisioned in terms of the Lejre hoard, a set of treasures found in 1850 somewhere in the area where the hall sites at Lejre were later discovered (p. 24). While a bit anachronistic to be introduced here (since it is of Viking Age date), the Lejre hoard calls to mind the wealth of Scandinavian kings of this general period.

At several other points in the narrative, special treasures are introduced. One of these is the gold cup that an unnamed thief takes from the dragon's barrow, violating a taboo in a manner that has grave consequences. One would think that a dragon could spare one cup; but perhaps this was an unusually valuable item that no miser would willingly part with. I have therefore chosen a particularly handsome cup as a counterpart to the Beowulfian one. This is a cup from Rillaton, Cornwall, that was found in a stone chamber underneath a barrow along with a skeleton, a dagger, and a few other grave goods (p. 150; British Museum 1953: 36). Made of pure beaten gold, it is the kind of treasure that Bronze Age warriors fought and died for, and one can easily imagine a dragon fuming over its loss.

Finally, the hero should be imagined to be in possession of at least one very fine item that he has chosen from Hrothgar's treasury himself, in accord with his statement that he was given leave to choose some things *on mīnne sylfes dōm*, "at my own will" (2147). If we wish to imagine Hrothgar in possession of treasures like an exquisite disc pendant, set with gold and garnets cloisonnés, that was found in a pagan burial at Faversham, Kent, and is owned by the British Museum together with other Kentish brooches of its type (p. 144; *R-L*² 8: 247–48, s.v. "Faversham"; Webster and Backhouse 1991: 26), then the hero might well have looked no farther than this.

MISCELLANEOUS POSSESSIONS

Several times the *Beowulf* poet draws attention to the presence and skills of harpists, who are represented as indispensable members of the Danish court (though, as it happens, no mention is made of their presence in Geatland). Early in the narrative, for example, the king's scop manages to enrage Grendel by singing of God's beautiful Creation (89–98). Later on, as Beowulf recounts the story of his reception in Heorot, he recalls that "some hero made the timbered harp / tremble with sweetness" (2107–08).

A fair number of harps or lyres occur in the archaeological record of early northern Europe (*R-L*² 14: 1–9, s.vv. "Harfe und Leier"; Bischop 2002). The most famous of them is the lyre from Mound 1 at Sutton Hoo, East Anglia, which has been painstakingly reconstructed by the staff of the British Museum from its remaining fragments (p. 6; B-Mitford 3: 611–731; cf. Boenig 1996). This was a six-stringed instrument with, it is thought, an oval shape. An instrument very much like this, remarkable for its decorative design, has been found at Trossingen, in northern Germany (p. 140; *R-L*² 31: 277–81). While only the tuning pegs, bridge, and two small gilt-bronze bird-headed escutcheons survive from the Sutton Hoo lyre, the actual wood from the Trossingen lyre is preserved. Inscribed on the body of this instrument is a frieze of two groups of warriors facing one another—a striking confirmation that Germanic lyres could indeed embody the ethos of the warrior class.

Fine horses and their trappings, too, were greatly prized in the aristocratic circles represented in *Beowulf*, as they have been among many of the peoples of Eurasia from prehistoric times to the present.[31] Among the treasures with which Hrothgar rewards Beowulf for having killed Grendel are eight horses with gold bridles. One of them carries the king's own war-saddle, which must be visualized as an impressive item (1034–38). In imagining these steeds, one should call to mind not the sleek Arabian racehorses that are now bought and sold for small fortunes, but rather the relatively small ponies still to be found in Iceland, where they have descended from Viking Age forebears (p. 56). Such horses, too, may have fetched a good price in their day.

A pair of Viking Age saddlebows from Funen, adorned at both ends with fantastic zoomorphic carvings, are introduced (even if somewhat anachronistically) as a counterpart to that point in the narrative when Hrothgar, seated on horseback, scouts out the terrain in the vicinity of Grendel's mere (p. 94; Pedersen 1997; *R-L²* 29: 201–03, s.v. "Søllested"). One can visualize both the king of the Danes and the riders mentioned elsewhere in *Beowulf* as mounted on steeds equipped with fittings like those recovered from bogs at Vimose, on the island of Funen, and Illerup Ådal, in north Jutland, where vast amounts of goods were deposited as thank offerings during the late Roman period. Typically these equestrian ornaments consist of an iron bit, some iron chain (which would have linked the bridle and the bit), two or more cheek-pieces, and a prominent nosepiece (p. 126).

Stylized horses are sometimes depicted in the metalwork of the Germanic period. Since the Danish coast-guard who asks the Geatish warriors to identify themselves upon their arrival in Denmark is mounted on horseback, a striking equestrian image from Veggerslev, Jutland, is introduced at that point in the narrative (p. 18).

When Heorot is decorated in preparation for the banquet that occupies much of the second day in Denmark, the poet calls attention to the tapestries or embroideries that adorn the walls:

> Gold thread shone
> in the wall-hangings, woven scenes
> that attracted and held the eye's attention.   *(993–95)*

The faded bits and pieces of tapestries or embroideries that survive from Iron-Age Europe scarcely allow one to visualize with much clarity the kind of textiles alluded to here, nor is the reader helped by the poet's disinterest in specifying just what woven scenes are depicted.[32] As a counterpart to this passage, therefore, a single gold-threaded braid from Snartemo, Norway, is presented here both in its original condition and in a more colorful modern reconstruction (p. 64; cf. Crowfoot and Hawkes 1967). Fashioned on a larger scale, a gold-threaded textile like this might well have caught and dazzled the eye.

Runes are mentioned only once in *Beowulf*, when Hrothgar gazes on the rune-inscribed hilt of the gigantic sword with which the hero has killed Grendel's mother and then decapitated Grendel himself (1694–98). By contrast, nine of the artifacts put on display in the present edition are adorned with runes. Several of these items confirm that swords and knives of this era were indeed sometimes inscribed with runes (as is discussed by Hawkes and Page 1967). Examples are the Chessel Down sword (p. 114), the Guilton pommel (p. 114, though the "runes" here are not true ones), and impressively, the Thames *scramasax* (p. 180, for which see Wilson 1964: 69–73, 144–46). Other rune-inscribed artifacts are the Sigurd runestone (p. 58), the Strårup ring (p. 80 top), the Roskilde bracteate (p. 80 bottom), the Feddersen Wierde footstool (p. 92), and a unique wolflike or dragonlike silver-gilt fitting from the River Thames (p. 152; Webster and Backhouse 1991: 225). None of these objects with the exception of the Sigurd runestone (for which see R-L^2 24: 124–28, s.v. "Ramsund") would seem to require the presence of runes in order for them to fulfill the practical or decorative function for which they were intended. However, whether constituting an intelligible message or not, runes may have been thought to enhance the value or efficacy of these things.[33]

As for other material objects, a few miscellaneous items round out the present edition. Among these is a collection of *goldgubber*, miniature gold plaques that were often deposited in or near the postholes of halls, perhaps as inducements to the fertility of a leading family (p. 42; see R-L^2 12: 318–23, s.v. "Goldblechfigürchen," and 13: 132–42, s.v. "Gubber"). Also on display are three ornaments depicting strange beasts (pp. 86, 198 bottom), examples of the fecund exuberance of the animal art of the Germanic period (Speake 1980; R-L^2 586–605, s.v. "Tierornamentik"). There is also a memento mori in the form of a skull, one cheek of which was pierced through by a lance head (p. 118). An image of "Tollund man," with the rope that throttled him, is included as well (p. 164). These images serve as reminders that violent deaths were part of the tenor of life, while capital punishment of the kind mentioned at one point by the *Beowulf* poet (2444–48, an allusion to death by hanging) seems also to have been a common practice.[34] A piece of a human cranium inscribed with runes (p. 202) may hint at pagan religious practices of an unpleasant kind, while a small gold image of an inscrutable human-like figure clothed only in a neckring (p. 12; *R-L²* 29: 111–12, s.v. "Slipshavn"; Jørgensen and Petersen 1998: 195–96) may take us as close to pagan idolatry, of the kind roundly condemned by the poet, as we are likely to get.[35]

SUPERNATURAL BEINGS

In addition to calling to mind the halls, ships, weapons, and other artifacts of a former civilization, the *Beowulf* poet had a special interest in depicting weird creatures of the natural world. What is remarkable is his ability to give these creatures such convincing solidity, as if they were just as real, in their horrific malignancy, as anything else described in the poem.

Grendel and His Mother

When Grendel is first introduced, he is presented as "a powerful demon, a prowler through the dark." Since his visits to Heorot are nocturnal and his habits solitary, the Danes never see him properly and have no way of visualizing him clearly. The audience is left in much the same situation. This is part of the poet's design. At the same time, the Anglo-Saxons and other peoples of their time did not think of cannibalistic giants as the stuff of dreams; they imagined them as inhabitants of the real world. They had their own names for them, such as *eoten* "giant, ogre, monster"— a name cognate with Old Icelandic *jötunn* "giant," though one cannot be sure just what kind of creature or creatures the Old English word denoted (see *R-L²* 24: 601–07, s.v. "Riesen").

Artists of the Anglo-Saxon period occasionally depicted monsters of this kind. Grendel is not just an ill-natured cannibalistic giant, however, like one that is depicted at one point by the illustrator of London, British Library Cotton Tiberius B.v (p. 8). Grendel represents evil incarnate. As one of the seed of Cain, he is literally cursed by God. His visceral response to anything good or happy is a satanic one: he wants to kill it. The epithets that are used of Grendel inform the audience of his devilish nature, even if his physical side remains paramount (Tolkien 1936: 278–80). The structural irony of the first part of the poem stems from the fact that the pagan Danes and Geats are ignorant of what kind of evil they confront. Even Beowulf can have no way of knowing what kind of enemy he faces, any more than he can be aware of his own role in what has been called a "Great Feud" going back to biblical times (Osborn 1978). Still he does the right thing instinctively, for he is the lucky one and his courage serves him well.

Depicting spiritual evil is a difficult task in the visual arts. It is one undertaken with success by that same Tiberius artist, however, on the page that concludes his illustrated version of *Wonders of the East* (p. 46). What he depicts at this point is a scene at hell mouth. A necromancer named Mambres, who is trying to summon his dead brother, has succeeded in calling up one of hell's diabolical inhabitants. What is interesting to observe is the manner in which this huge demon dominates the scene. His teeth are pointed as if they were all incisors. His fingers are tipped in claws, as Grendel's are (see lines 983–86). His eyes are painted a brilliant red, as if they were giving off flames. A reader of *Beowulf* may well be reminded of Grendel's eyes, from which shines "a baleful light, / flame more than light" (726–27). These two masters, the *Beowulf* poet and the Tiberius artist, seem to have been guided by a similar conception of spiritual evil made incarnate. Although many modern illustrators have tried their hand at portraying Grendel, it would be hard to find a closer equivalency than is offered here.

As for Grendel's mother, there is no clear way to visualize her on the basis of either the text of *Beowulf* or the illustrated manuscripts of the early Middle Ages. Even more than Grendel, she remains shrouded in mystery as a "swamp-thing from hell" (1518) that is part beast, part human being, and part she-devil.

The Dragon

What especially impresses one about the dragon that plays such a powerful role in the final episode of *Beowulf* is how individual its portrayal is. Unlike the more conventional dragons of folktales, romances, and hagiographical literature (Lionarons 1998, Rauer 2000), the *Beowulf* dragon is presented as "a figure of real oneiric power" (Heaney, p. xv above). Normally indifferent to humankind, it seethes with rage when its precinct is violated, even if what offends it is no greater crime than the theft of one cup from its hoard. Like Grendel, it bides its time until nightfall. It then issues forth spewing flames. It is a coiling *wyrm*, "serpent," on the ground, but it also takes to the midnight air as a horrific *lyft-floga*, "flying creature." Its teeth are sharp and venomous, and it is their poison that causes the hero's death (2713–15).

Once the dragon is stretched out inert, its length can be measured: it is fifty feet long (3042–43).

While dragonlike motifs are familiar enough in Germanic metalwork (see pp. 152, 188) as well as in the wood carvings and the runestones of the Viking Age (p. 58), no medieval artist succeeds in conjuring up a creature as awesome as the *Beowulf* dragon. The decorative dragon that is depicted on p. 178, reproduced from a medieval French illuminated manuscript copy of St. Gregory's commentary on Job, can scarcely substitute for the Anglo-Saxon poet's fearful night-flyer. Still, that illustration is worth including because of the parallel it presents to the climactic scene of *Beowulf*. A dignified older warrior is shown attacking a dragon frontally, while a younger warrior, crouching under the older man's shield, uses his spear (not a sword, as in *Beowulf*) to impale the dragon in a lower part of its body. Inspired by this parallel to the action of the poem, the maker of the computer-generated image included here has worked a page from the *Beowulf* manuscript into the background. More abstract and savage, and hence closer to the aesthetics of *Beowulf*, is a remarkable winged dragon from the face of the Sutton Hoo shield (p. 154; B-Mitford 2: 63–67).

Other Monsters

The Grendel-kin and the dragon may be the most prominent of the uncanny creatures represented in *Beowulf*, but they are by no means the only ones. Various creatures of the deep are said to have harried the young hero during his youthful swimming contest against Breca, only to leave their bodies lying at the shore (548–67). More immediately in terms of the poem's main plot, a number of serpents—"writhing sea-dragons / and monsters slouching on slopes" (1426–27)—are found in the neighborhood of Grendel's mere when the men approach that uncanny region. One serpent attempts to swim away but is shot with an arrow, speared, and hauled ashore. Creatures like these seem to have haunted the imagination of the early peoples of Europe. An impressive example of a wood carving of such a serpent was found in the River Schelde, Belgium (p. 34). A similar carving was discovered in the Oseberg funeral mound (p. 98). These may have been detachable ship's figureheads to be displayed aloft when the ship was on the high seas. The Oseberg object exemplifies the superlative skills of Viking Age woodcarvers, whose ebullient style of rendering zoomorphic figures has rarely been surpassed.[36]

THE LANDSCAPE OF BEOWULF

For the most part, the *Beowulf* poet shows only a cursory interest in nature. His interest is in the social world of human character and action. Tribes are separated by seas, but we are not told which seas these are. A few conventional geographical features are named, but that is all: seacoasts have cliffs, halls are built on eminences, and so forth. There is little here to attract a geologist's or landscape painter's interest. Standing out as exceptional, therefore, is the passage that describes Grendel's mere. To a lesser extent, the same is true of the dragon's barrow and the hero's own funeral monument.

The terrors of Grendel's mere are evoked first of all in a celebrated passage where King Hrothgar seems almost to dare the hero to venture his life in this half-known, hellish locale. Somewhat curiously, the place he describes is situated no more than a short distance from Heorot:

> *A few miles from here*
> *a frost-stiffened wood waits and keeps watch*
> *above a mere; the overhanging bank*
> *is a maze of tree-roots mirrored in its surface.*   (1362–65)

Since this place is described in ghastly terms (fire on the water, ice on the trees) that cannot fail to call to mind early medieval depictions of the hell or hell mouth, there would seem to be little point in illustrating it through scenes drawn from nature. Still, one curiosity of the landscape near Gammel Lejre, Zealand, where the great halls once stood, is that only a fifteen- or twenty-minute walk west of that village is a hummocky region known to geologists as a dead ice zone. Here, at the end of the last Ice Age, great masses of rubble were deposited at places where the ice sheets that once blanketed this region remained in place longer than elsewhere. Here stagnant pools and bogs alternate with hillocks in a helter-skelter fashion. Some of this region is wooded, and a good deal more of it may have been overgrown in former times. The mixture of woods, fields, and pools found here provides an attractive haven for wildlife. It may be a significant fact that in the eighteenth century, the estate to which much of this land pertains, Ledreborg Slot, was owned by the king's Master of the Hunt.[37]

It is for these reasons that some photographs taken in this dead ice region are provided here as a counterpoint to the poet's description of the landscape of

Grendel's mere (at pp. 44, 88, 90, 96, 110, and 142). Perhaps, long ago, some Danes out hunting in the region west of the Lejre settlement were impressed by the inhospitable nature of the landscape here and let their thoughts play over these differences, working their impressions into a story about the haunting of the Skjöldungs' hall by some troll-like creature or creatures of the wild. A local legend could thereby have arisen that eventually, with the passage of time and with Danish migration westward to the British Isles, gave rise to the elaborate, rhetorically heightened English poem we call *Beowulf*. This is a plausible line of speculation, at any rate, though it can be no more than that.

As for the dragon's barrow, it inevitably calls to mind, even if only generically, the megalithic chambered tombs of northern Europe. Some of these tombs would have been as impressive and mysterious to people living during the first millennium A.D. as they are to us today. They call to mind civilizations that existed in these regions in the distant past, leaving little more than these monuments to testify to their former greatness. Newgrange, not far from Dublin, is one of the most celebrated of these tombs of the Neolithic era; West Kennet long barrow, located near Avebury in the south of England, is another. Øm Jættestue, located only two miles southeast of Gammel Lejre, is a well preserved megalithic tomb somewhat smaller than these other more famous examples (pp. 168, 170; cf. p. 148; Johansen 2003). These monuments date from thousands of years before the main action of *Beowulf* is imagined to take place. It suits the antiquarian mood of the last part of the poem that a monument of this kind is introduced to the action, for the poet here is brooding on "the past in the past" and the mutability of earthly things.

When the dragon's lair is first introduced, it has the appearance of a stone-roofed barrow with a hidden passageway leading into its depths (2213–14). It is later described as "an underground barrow near the sea-billows / . . . heaped inside / with exquisite metalwork" (2411–13). Fronting it is a stone arch (2545) near which a stream gushes forth. When, later on, Wiglaf enters the barrow at the request of his dying lord, what he finds there is "a treasure-trove of astonishing richness" including goblets, vessels, helmets, and other objects. Some of these things are corroded; others are of refulgent gold (2757–64). In finding visual accompaniments to these scenes, I have chosen images relating to periods earlier than the action of the poem, though without any attempt at a precise chronology. One image is of a set of gold bowls of Bronze Age date from Midskov, Denmark (p. 182; Jørgensen and Petersen 1998: 102–03). Another shows a miscellany of grave-goods deposited at Leuna,

Saxony, during the Roman Iron Age (p. 184; Bekker 2001). Another shows an assortment of Bronze Age grave-goods from a high-status burial chamber and mound unearthed at Seddin, northern Germany (p. 200; $R\text{-}L^2$ 28: 1–14, s.v. "Seddin"); yet another, an early Iron Age hoard of one hundred sixty-five bronze rings found in a moor at Smederup, Jutland (p. 206; $R\text{-}L^2$ 29: 138–39, s.vv. "Smederup Moor"). There is little reason to make fine distinctions when choosing objects to serve as counterparts to the poet's account of the dragon's hoard, for what the poet presents are generalized images pertaining to an unspecified prior time.

The hero's funeral arrangements are described in a manner consistent with what is known of burial rites of the pagan period, though they read like a composite picture of several such ceremonies rather than an account of any single one.[38] First his body is cremated together with a great number of grave-goods. Then his barrow is built on a headland overlooking the sea:

> *Then the Geat people began to construct*
> *a mound on a headland, high and imposing,*
> *a marker that sailors could see from far away . . .*   *(3156–58)*

To this place, which the poet calls Hronesness ("Whale's Point"), are brought additional treasures lifted from the dragon's trove. Some present-day treasure-seekers equipped with metal detectors might give much to know just where this headland is located. The author is unlikely to have had any real-world place in mind, however. Of the two photographs exhibited here as counterparts to the poet's description of Beowulf's tomb, one was taken in Bohuslän, on the southwest coast of present-day Sweden, where the homeland of the western branch of the Gautar, or Geats, is traditionally located (p. 186; see Overing and Osborn 1994: 23–37). Not all scholars accept that the poet had this Swedish region in mind, however, for by the late ninth century, at least some Anglo-Saxons seem to have conceived of the Geats as a people who had once lived in Jutland, close by the ancestral home of the English (Niles 2007b: 130–36). Indeed, it is not clear that the Geats of Beowulf are anything other than a creation of the mythopoeic imagination. Included here as an "alternate take" of a Beowulfian-style barrow, therefore (p. 188), is an image of an ancient mound whose exact location does not matter. Known locally as "Skelhøj," or "Boundary Mound," it is the last mound left intact in Veksø parish in northern Zealand. It probably pertains to a much older culture than is portrayed in the poem. It is situated not on the coast but somewhat inland, in a gentle landscape amenable to agriculture. Beowulf's ashes will not be found there, scattered amidst some corroded treasures; but then again, neither will they be found in Bohuslän or anywhere else.

These, then, are somewhat more than one hundred images pertaining to what might broadly be called "the world of Beowulf." They are meant to stimulate a nuanced understanding of the sorts of objects and scenes that the poet and his audiences could have had in mind when telling or listening to the poem, though one can never be sure about such things. To repeat a point that deserves emphasis, the display of this particular set of images should by no means be thought to preclude alternative ways of visualizing the poem. It is hoped, all the same, that this counterpart to Heaney's outstanding verse translation will enhance readers' enjoyment of a work that both revels in hard, shining objects and asks of its audience a deep attentiveness to the promptings of their imagination.

NOTES

1. There is no need here to enter into the controversy as to when the original text of *Beowulf* was composed, let alone the question of what it means to speak of an "original" version of a poem of this character. The former consensus that the poem is of seventh- or eighth-century date has been challenged of late, but no new consensus has taken its place. The language of the poem is archaic, compared with that of other Old English poems, but archaism can be a feature of style as well as date. Many specialists now entertain the possibility that, leaving its ultimate origins aside, the poem was composed in its present form sometime after Viking raiders and settlers had come to Britain in some numbers. This would allow for its composition just about any time from the late ninth century up to the late tenth century (since the unique manuscript version of the poem, a copy, was written out around the year 1000). This was a period of national consolidation when Scandinavian cultural influences were being absorbed. Certainty in such matters, however, is beyond our present grasp. For a review of recent opinions, see Liuzza 1995; for a number of significant contributions to the debate, Chase 1981; for my own perspective, Niles 2007b: 13–58 passim.

2. When referring to *Beowulf* in its own time, it is wiser to speak of listeners than of readers, for a poem of this character, even if available for private reading, would have been most fully itself when voiced aloud. Even in the first decade of the twenty-first century, in an era when private reading is taken for granted, it is possible to experience *Beowulf* as a kind of performance art or

radio drama. Benjamin Bagby's celebrated concert performances of the poem in the original Old English language are an example of this renewed interest in the text as sound rather than script; Dick Ringler's recent translation of the poem (2006), recorded in a sound studio with multiple voices and audio effects, is another. Seamus Heaney's translation, too, was broadcast on BBC radio soon after appearing in print and subsequently has been heard widely on CD-ROM or cassette tape. Paradoxically, perhaps, narratives that are experienced through the ear can often be visualized precisely, though individually, by the mind's inner eye.

3. A number of illustrated versions of *Beowulf* are reviewed by Osborn 1997. In that same volume (Bjork and Niles 1997) can be found informed discussions of a wide range of critical approaches to the poem, with guides to relevant scholarship.

4. For Britain, see in particular the great catalogue of the Sutton Hoo ship burial and its artifacts (B-Mitford), supplemented by Farrell and Neuman de Vegvar 1992, Carver 1998, and Carver 2005; for Denmark, Jensen 2001–2004; for Germanic-speaking regions in general (including Anglo-Saxon England), numerous entries in R-L^2. The particular connections between *Beowulf* and archaeology have been traced by Cramp 1957, Hills 1997, and Webster 1998.

Since the division of prehistory into chronological periods varies somewhat from book to book, the terms adopted here should be defined. A distinction is made between the early Iron Age (500 B.C.–A.D. 530) and the late Iron Age (530–1050). The early Iron Age is subdivided into the pre-Roman period (500 B.C.–A.D. 160), the Roman period (160–375), and the early Germanic period (375–530). The late Iron Age is divided into the late Germanic period (530–800) and the Viking Age (800–1050). All these dates are no more than approximations. The Iron Age as a whole is distinguished from the Neolithic period (ca. 3900–1700 B.C.) and the Bronze Age (ca. 1700–500 B.C.), which in turn is subdivided into an early phase (1700–1200) and a late one (1200–500). The period A.D. 400–550 is also referred to as the Migration Age. While the *Beowulf* poet never dates the events described in his poem, other medieval sources speak of the death of Hygelac, King of the Geats, as occurring around the early 520s. By extension, the lifetime of Beowulf, that king's nephew, would seem to fall within the period from about 495 to 585—that is, in the later years of the Migration Age (for the most part), not long after the fifth-century period when lowland Britain was conquered by the Angles and Saxons. It is part of the poet's design, however, to leave the exact temporal setting of the action unspecified.

5. The practice followed in this book differs from what one sees in earlier pictorial compilations going back to Huyshe 1907 and Stjerna 1912—works published at a time when the poem's Swedish affinities were widely thought to deserve highlighting. The latter of these remains a valuable compendium today.

6. Davidson 1958; R-L^2 33: 604–22, s.v. "Wieland."

7. Line 716. Compare lines 926–27 of the Old English text: "*geseah stēapne hrōf / golde fāhne*," literally "he looked at the steep, gold-adorned roof."

8. Some translators (including Heaney) take this to be a flight of steps or a landing, but the noun *stapol* usually denotes a standing stone or megalith or something of that kind. It is hard to tell just what is meant.

9. For example Hume 1974; Shippey 1978: 21–24; Irving 1989: 133–67; on psychohistory, Earl 1994: 100–36. For a brief but systematic discussion of the hall Heorot, see *R-L²* 14: 392–94.

10. Hope-Taylor 1977; *Bl. Encl.* 497; *MEng.* 826–27. This is believed to be the place named by the Venerable Bede when, in book 2, ch. 13 of his *Ecclesiastical History of the English People* (completed in 731), he dramatizes the scene of the conversion of King Edwin of Northumbria.

11. For Cowdery's Down see Millett and James 1983, Arnold 1997: 37–54; for Cheddar see Rahtz 1979, *Bl. Encl.* 100–02.

12. See in particular Herschend 1993, Jørgensen 2001, and Hedeager 2002, and cf. *R-L²* 13: 414–25, s.v. "Halle."

13. Thrane 1993; Nielsen, Randsborg, and Thrane 1994; Hedeager 2001.

14. See Hårdh and Larsson 2002. Among early Scandinavian "central places" other than Gudme, noteworthy are Himlingøje, on the island of Zealand, Denmark, a site especially rich in luxury goods (Hansen 1995; p. 32); Uppåkra in Scania, in what is now southern Sweden but was once a Danish territory (Larsson 2001); Old Uppsala in Uppland, Sweden, the seat of power of the Swedish kings mentioned in *Beowulf* (p. 160; *R-L²* 10: 409–18, s.v. "Gamla Uppsala"); Borg in the far north of Norway, the site of the largest hall yet found from early Scandinavia (Munch, Johansen, and Roesdahl 2003); and Tissø on the island of Zealand, an important military complex and cult center of the early Viking Age (*R-L²* 30: 619–24). Worth noting as well in that connection is the early Viking Age settlement at Kaupang, in the region of Oslo Fjord, Norway (Skre 2007). Not far from Kaupang were discovered the Oseberg ship and the Gokstad ship, with their attendant grave-goods (pp. 98, 120).

15. There are two reports on the initial excavations (T. Christensen 1991a, 1991b). The latter of these studies, translated into English, is featured in Niles 2007a: 13–101, where it precedes a report on the most recent excavations (pp. 109–26). This collaborative volume includes several chapters on Lejre and its archaeology, legends, topography, and reputation in modern times. See also *R-L²* 18: 248–54, s.v. "Lejre."

16. See *MScand.* 325–41, s.v. "ironwork"; *R-L²* 27: 194–210, s.vv. "Schmied, Schmiedehandwerk, Schmiedewerkzeuge"; and Hinton 2003.

17. Worth noting, however, is that the stag was frequently associated with royalty and/or with mythological themes (see *R-L²* 14: 588–612). The presence of the freestanding image of a stag

surmounting the Sutton Hoo scepter, for example, is by no means fortuitous (p. 92; B-Mitford 2: 333–39).

18. The best-known example is the Nydam ship, a large vessel dating from A.D. 350–400 that is housed in the Schleswig-Holsteinisches Landesmuseum in Schleswig, Germany (Rieck 2003).

19. On this development see Brøgger and Shetelig 1951, A. Christensen 1972, Binns 1980, and *MScand.* 578–80, s.vv. "ships and shipbuilding"; also *R-L²* 3: 233–46, s.v. "Boot"; and *R-L²* 27: 13–20, s.vv. "Schiff und Schiffsarten."

20. These two ships, reconstructed in meticulous detail, are now housed in the Viking Ship Museum in Oslo (for which see Sjøvold 1979). The first of them dates from about 815/820, the second from about 890. The finds from the Oseberg ship burial have been given lavish publication in Brøgger et al. 1917–1927; cf. *R-L²* 22: 306–11, *MScand.* 457–59. For the Gokstad ship burial, see also *MScand.* 232.

21. Bazelmans 1999 offers an informed discussion of the ideology of weapons and armor in *Beowulf* and in the Germanic context more generally. For specific information on types and styles of Germanic weaponry, see *R-L²* 2: 361–482, s.v. "Bewaffnung"; *R-L²* 25: 429–49, s.v. "Rüstung"; and additional entries from *R-L²* cited below. For Anglo-Saxon weaponry see *Bl. Encl.* 45–47, s.vv. "arms and armour," and Hawkes 1989, Underwood 1999, and Pollington 2001; for Scandinavian weaponry, Shetelig and Falk 1937: 377–405 and *MScand.* 718–20, s.v. "weapons."

22. See, e.g., Engelhardt 1866; Jørgensen, Storgaard, and Thomsen 2003; *R-L²* 22: 107–27, s.vv. "Opfer und Opferfunde"; *R-L²* 33: 21–46, s.v. "Waffenopfer."

23. Hrisoulas 1994; see Engstrom, Lankton, and Lesher-Engstrom 1990, and *R-L²* 5: 191–213, s.v. "Damaszierung."

24. This is particularly true of the gigantic sword with which the hero first kills Grendel's mother and then beheads Grendel. It is called a *hæft-mēce*, "hilted blade" (1457) and also a *fetel-hilt*, an obscure word that might mean "hilt [or hilted blade] furnished with a ring or chain" (1563). It is not only a huge weapon but also, apparently, a semi-magical one, since all but the hilt melts away.

25. For information on helmets, see particularly B-Mitford 2: 138–231; *R-L²* 14: 317–38, s.v. "Helm."

26. "An embossed ridge, a band lapped with wire / arched over the helmet" (1029–30). On this aspect of the helmet's design, see B-Mitford 2: 152–59.

27. B-Mitford 1974: 23–52; *R-L²* 2: 237, s.v. "Benty Grange"; Webster and Backhouse 1991: 59–60.

28. As a common noun, the first element of her name, *wealh*, can denote a person or thing of British origin (cf. modern "Wales," "Welsh"). As for her family connections, she is said to be a Helming, and in the Old English poem known as *Widsith* a man named Helm is said (at line 29) to have ruled the Wulfings. This tribe, in turn, might have been thought to be ancestors of the Wuffings of East Anglia (Newton 1993: 122–28).

29. See Hårdh 1996; Tyler 2000; Coatsworth and Pinder 2002; and Hinton 2005: 7–170. For information on specific types of jewelry, pendants, and other adornments see *R-L²* 8: 411–607, s.vv. "Fibel und Fibeltracht"; 25: 3–12, s.vv. "Ring und Ringschmuck"; and 3: 337–401, s.vv. "Brakteaten, Brakteatenikonologie," among other entries. The guidebooks published by national and regional museums highlight specific objects in their collections, sometimes with fine photographs (e.g., Jensen 1993, Jørgensen and Petersen 1998, Andersson 2002).

30. For the Taplow site see *Bl. Encl.* 439–40. Similar horns were found at Sutton Hoo; see B-Mitford 3: 324–47. See further *R-L²* 31: 239–59, s.v. "Trinkhorn."

31. See *R-L²* 23: 24–96, s.vv. "Pferd," "Pferdegeschirr," and "Pferdegräber." Horses were sometimes either sacrificed as part of the grave-goods accompanying high-status burials or were accorded separate burials of their own—clear signs of the value put on them.

32. On prehistoric clothing and textiles from the Continent, see Munksgaard 1974. Those from Anglo-Saxon England are discussed by Netherton and Owen-Crocker 2005. See further *MEng.* 726–28, s.vv. "textiles and embroideries, Anglo-Saxon"; *MScand.* 96–100, s.v. "clothmaking" and 640–42, s.v. "textiles, furnishing"; and *R-L²* 12: 36–43, s.v. "Gewebe," and 12: 386–92, s.v. "Goldtextilien." Some embroideries from the Oseberg ship burial have survived, though in poor condition (Krafft 1956).

33. Runes in the Scandinavian context are well treated by Moltke 1985; in the English context, by Page 1999. See further the several entries relating to runes in vol. 25 of *R-L²*, plus *MScand.* 545–55.

34. On this topic see Glob 1969, Carver 1998, and cf. *R-L²* 20: 222–29, s.v. "Moorleichen."

35. See *R-L²* 13: 455–60, s.v. "Halsschmuck"; 12: 289–93, s.v. "Götterbilder"; and 15: 325–30, s.vv. "Idole und Idolatrie."

36. See also pp. 92, 120. For additional examples see *MScand.* 735–37, s.vv. "wood carving."

37. Information about the Ice Age landscape near Lejre is available in Niles 2007a: 178–80. For information about Ledreborg Estate, see www.ledreborgslot.dk/uk/.

38. See *R-L²* 10: 169–220, s.v. "Fürstengräber." For Anglo-Saxon sites see *Bl.Encl.* 376–78, s.vv. "princely burials"; for Scandinavian ones, *MScand.* 237–40, s.v. "graves." Davidson 1950 discusses the mounds in *Beowulf* with reference to folklore, literature, and archaeology.

ABBREVIATIONS

Five abbreviations are used in the Afterword. Each one refers to a work that is a mine of information about English, Germanic, and Scandinavian antiquities.

Bl. Encl.   *The Blackwell Encyclopaedia of Anglo-Saxon England*. 1999. Ed. Michael Lapidge et al. Oxford: Blackwell.

B-Mitford   Bruce-Mitford, Rupert. 1975–1983. *The Sutton Hoo Ship Burial*. 3 vols. in 4 pts. London: British Museum.

R-L²   *Reallexikon der germanischen Altertumskunde*. 1968–. Ed. Herbert Jankuhn et al. 2d ed. Many vols. Berlin: de Gruyter.

MEng.   *Medieval England: An Encyclopedia*. 1998. Ed. Paul E. Szarmach, M. Teresa Tavormina, and Joel T. Rosenthal. New York: Garland.

MScand.   *Medieval Scandinavia: An Encyclopedia*. 1993. Ed. Phillip Pulsiano with Kirsten Wolf. New York: Garland.

WORKS CITED

Andersen, Steen Wulff. 1996. *The Viking Fortress of Trelleborg*. Slagelse, Denmark: Trelleborg Museum.

Andersson, Kent, ed. 2002. *Guide: The Goldroom*. Stockholm: National Historical Museum.

Arnold, C. J. 1997. *An Archaeology of the Early Anglo-Saxon Kingdoms*. 2d ed. London: Routledge.

Axboe, Morten. 2004. *Die Goldbrakteaten der Völkerwanderungszeit: Herstellungsprobleme und Chronologie*. Berlin: De Gruyter.

Bazelmans, Jos. 1999. *By Weapons Made Worthy: Lords, Retainers, and Their Relationship in Beowulf*. Amsterdam: Amsterdam University Press.

Bekker, Matthias. 2001. "Luxus für das Jenseits." P. 112 in *Schönheit, Macht und Tod: 120 Funde aus 120 Jahren Landesmuseum für Vorgeschichte Halle*, ed. Harald Meller. Halle: Landesmuseum für Vorgeschichte.

Binns, Alan. 1980. *Viking Voyagers: Then and Now*. London: Heinemann.

Bischop, Dieter. 2002. "Das Leierfragment aus der kaiserzeitlichen Siedlung Bremen-Habenhausen." *Archäologisches Korrespondenzblatt* 32: 229–46.

Bjork, Robert E., and John D. Niles, eds. 1997. *A Beowulf Handbook*. Lincoln: University of Nebraska Press.

Boenig, Robert. 1996. "The Anglo-Saxon Harp." *Speculum* 71: 290–320.

British Museum. 1923. *A Guide to the Anglo-Saxon and Foreign Teutonic Antiquities*. Written by Reginald A. Smith. London: British Museum.

———. 1953. *Later Prehistoric Antiquities of the British Isles*. London: Trustees of the British Museum.

Bruce-Mitford, Rupert. 1974. *Aspects of Anglo-Saxon Archaeology*. London: Gollancz.

Brøgger, A. W., et al. 1917–1927. *Osebergfundet*. 3 vol. Oslo: Universitetets Oldsaksamling.

Brøgger, A. W., and Haakon Shetelig. 1951. *The Viking Ships: Their Ancestry and Evolution*. Trans. K. John. Oslo: Dreyer.

Carnap-Bornheim, Claus von, and Jørgen Ilkjær. 1990–1996. *Illerup Ådal*. 8 vol. Århus, Denmark: Aarhus University Press.

Carver, M. O. H. 1998. *Sutton Hoo: Burial Ground of Kings?* London: British Museum Press.

———. 2005. *Sutton Hoo: A Seventh-Century Princely Burial Ground and Its Context*. London: British Museum Press.

Chase, Colin, ed. 1981. *The Dating of Beowulf*. Toronto: University of Toronto Press. Reprinted in 1997 with an afterword by Nicholas Howe.

Christensen, Arne Emil. 1972. "Scandinavian Ships from Earliest Times to the Vikings." Pp. 159–80 in *A History of Seafaring, Based on Underwater Archaeology*, ed. George F. Bass. New York: Walker.

Christensen, Tom. 1991a. "Lejre beyond Legend—The Archaeological Evidence." *Journal of Danish Archaeology* 10: 163–85.

———. 1991b. *Lejre—Syn og Sagn*. Roskilde, Denmark: Roskilde Museum.

Coatsworth, Elizabeth, and Michael Pinder. 2002. *The Art of the Anglo-Saxon Goldsmith*. Woodbridge, Suffolk: Boydell.

Cramp, Rosemary. 1957. "*Beowulf* and Archaeology." *Medieval Archaeology* 1: 57–77.

———. 1993. "The Hall in *Beowulf* and in Archaeology." Pp. 331–46 in *Heroic Poetry in the Anglo-Saxon Period*, ed. Helen Damico and John Leyerle. Kalamazoo, Mich.: Medieval Institute Publications.

Crowfoot, Elizabeth, and Sonia Chadwick Hawkes. 1967. "Early Anglo-Saxon Gold Braids." *Medieval Archaeology* 11 (1967): 42–85.

Crumlin-Pedersen, Ole. 2002. *The Skuldelev Ships I: Topography, Archaeology, History, Conservation and Display*. Ships and Boats of the North 4.1. Roskilde, Denmark: Viking Ship Museum.

Davidson, Hilda Roderick Ellis. 1950. "The Hill of the Dragon: Anglo-Saxon Burial Mounds in Literature and Archaeology." *Folklore* [London] 61: 169–85.

———. 1958. "Weland the Smith." *Folklore* [London] 69: 145–59.

———. 1962. *The Sword in Anglo-Saxon England: Its Archaeology and Literature*. Oxford: Clarendon.

Davidson, Hilda Roderick Ellis, and Leslie Webster. 1967. "The Anglo-Saxon Burial at Coombe (Woodnesborough), Kent." *Medieval Archaeology* 11: 1–41, with plates I–VIII.

Earl, James W. 1994. *Thinking about Beowulf*. Stanford, Calif.: Stanford University Press.

Engelhardt, Conrad. 1866. *Denmark in the Early Iron Age*. London: Williams and Norgate.

———. 1867. *Om Vimose-Fundet*. Copenhagen: Thieles bogtrykkeri.

Engstrom, Robert, Scott Michael Lankton, and Audrey Lesher-Engstrom. 1990. *A Modern Replication Based on the Pattern-Welded Sword of Sutton Hoo*. Kalamazoo, Mich.: Medieval Institute Publications.

Evison, Vera I. 1967. "The Dover Ring-Sword and Other Sword-Rings and Beads." *Archaeologia* 101: 63–118.

Farrell, Robert T., and Carol Neuman de Vegvar. 1992. *Sutton Hoo: Fifty Years After*. Oxford, Ohio: Miami University Department of Art.

Glob, P. V. 1969. *The Bog People: Iron-Age Man Preserved*. Trans. Rupert Bruce-Mitford. Ithaca, N. Y.: Cornell University Press.

Hansen, Ulla Lund. 1995. *Himlingøje—Seeland—Europa*. Copenhagen: Royal Society of Northern Antiquaries.

Hawkes, Sonia Chadwick, ed. 1989. *Weapons and Warfare in Anglo-Saxon England*. Oxford: Oxford University Committee for Archaeology.

Hawkes, Sonia Chadwick, and R. I. Page. 1967. "Swords and Runes in South-East England." *Antiquaries Journal* 47: 1–26.

Hedeager, Lotte. 2001. "Asgard Reconstructed? Gudme—a 'Central Place' in the North." Pp. 467–507 in *Topographies of Power in the Early Middle Ages*, ed. Mayke De Jong and Frans Theuws. Leiden: Brill.

———. 2002. "Scandinavian 'Central Places' in a Cosmological Setting." Pp. 3–18 in Hårdh and Larsson, *Central Places*.

Herschend, Frands. 1993. "The Origin of the Hall in Southern Scandinavia." *Tor* 25: 175–99.

Hildebrand, Emil. 1873. *Teckningar ur svenska statens historiska museum.* Stockholm: Statens Historiska Museum.

Hills, Catherine M. 1997. "*Beowulf* and Archaeology." Pp. 291–310 in Bjork and Niles, *Handbook.*

Hinton, David A. 2003. "Anglo-Saxon Smiths and Myths." Pp. 261–82 in *Textual and Material Culture in Anglo-Saxon England*, ed. Donald Scragg. Cambridge: D. S. Brewer.

———. 2005. *Gold and Gilt, Pots and Pins: Possessions and People in Medieval Britain.* Oxford: Oxford University Press.

Hoernes, Moritz. 1892. *Die Urgeschichte des Menschen.* Vienna: A. Hartleben.

Hope-Taylor, Brian. 1977. *Yeavering: An Anglo-Saxon Centre of Early Northumbria.* London: Her Majesty's Stationery Office.

Hrisoulas, Jim. 1994. *The Pattern-Welded Blade: Artistry in Iron.* Boulder, Colo.: Paladin Press.

Hume, Kathryn. 1974. "The Concept of the Hall in Old English Poetry." *Anglo-Saxon England* 3: 63–74.

Huyshe, Wentworth, trans. 1907. *Beowulf: An Old English Epic.* London: Routledge.

Hårdh, Birgitta. 1996. *Silver in the Viking Age: A Regional-Economic Study.* Acta archaeologica Lundensia, series in 8°, no. 25. Stockholm: Almqvist and Wiksell.

Hårdh, Birgitta, and Lars Larsson, eds. 2002. *Central Places in the Migration and the Merovingian Periods.* Uppåkrastudier 6. Stockholm: Almqvist and Wiksell.

Irving, Edward B., Jr. 1989. *Rereading Beowulf.* Philadelphia: University of Pennsylvania Press.

Jensen, Jørgen. 1993. *Prehistory of Denmark.* Copenhagen: National Museum of Denmark.

———, 2001–2004. *Danmarks Oldtid.* Vol. 1, *Stenalder* (2001); vol. 2, *Bronzealder* (2002); vol. 3, *Ældre Jernalder* (2003); vol. 4: *Yngre Jernalder og Vikingetid* (2004). Copenhagen: Gyldendal.

Johansen, B-Joe. 2003. *Øm jættestue: en stenaldergrav in Danmark.* Lejre, Denmark: Little Creek Publishing.

Jørgensen, Lars. 2001. "From Tribute to the Estate System, 3rd–12th Century." Pp. 73–82 in *Kingdoms and Regionality: Transactions from the 49th Sachsensymposium 1998 in Uppsala.* Stockholm: Archaeological Research Laboratory.

Jørgensen, Lars, and Peter Vang Petersen. 1998. *Guld, magt, og tro: Danske guldskatte fra oldtid og middelalder.* Copenhagen: National Museum.

Jørgensen, Lars, Birger Storgaard, and Lone Gebauer Thomsen, eds. 2003. *The Spoils of Victory: The North in the Shadow of the Roman Empire.* Copenhagen: National Museum of Denmark.

Kemble, John M. 1863. *Horae Ferales; or, Studies in the Archaeology of the Northern Nations.* Ed. R. G. Latham and A. W. Franks. London: Lovell Reeve and Co.

Krafft, Sofie. 1956. *Pictorial Weavings from the Viking Age.* Oslo: Dreyer.

Larsson, Lars. 2001. "Uppåkra, an Iron Age Site with a Long Duration: Internal and External Perspectives." Pp. 51–61 in *Kingdoms and Regionality: Transactions from the 49th Sachsensymposium 1998 in Uppsala.* Stockholm: Archaeological Research Laboratory.

Leisi, Ernst. 1952–1953. "Gold und Manneswert im *Beowulf.*" *Anglia* 71: 259–73.

Lionarons, Joyce Tally. 1998. *The Medieval Dragon: The Nature of the Beast in Germanic Literature.* Enfield Lock, Middlesex: Hisarlik.

Liuzza, Roy Michael. 1995. "On the Dating of *Beowulf.*" Pp. 281–302 in *Beowulf: Basic Readings*, ed. Peter S. Baker. New York: Garland.

Lorange, Anders Lund. 1889. *Den yngre jernalders svaerd.* Bergen, Norway: Bergen Museum.

Meldgaard, Morten, and Marianne Rasmussen. 1996. *Arkæologiske eksperimenter i Lejre*. Lejre, Denmark: Rhodos.

Millet, M., and S. James. 1983. "Excavations at Cowdery's Down, Basingstoke, Hampshire 1978–81." *Archaeological Journal* 140: 151–279.

Moltke, Erik. 1985. *Runes and Their Origin: Denmark and Elsewhere*. Trans. Peter G. Foote. Copenhagen: National Museum of Denmark.

Montelius, Oscar. 1888. *The Civilization of Sweden in Heathen Times*. London: Macmillan.

Munch, Gerd Stamsø, Olav Sverre Johansen, and Else Roesdahl, eds. 2003. *Borg in Lofoten: A Chieftain's Farm in North Norway*. Trondheim, Norway: Tapir Academic Press.

Munksgaard, Elizabeth. 1974. *Oldtidsdragter*. Copenhagen: National Museum of Denmark.

Netherton, Robin, and Gale R. Owen-Crocker. 2005. *Medieval Clothing and Textiles*. Vol. 1. Woodbridge, Suffolk: Boydell.

Newton, Sam. 1993. *The Origins of Beowulf and the Pre-Viking Kingdom of East Anglia*. Cambridge, U.K.: D. S. Brewer.

Nielsen, P. O., K. Randsborg, and H. Thrane, eds. 1994. *The Archaeology of Gudme and Lundeborg*. Copenhagen: Akademiskforlag.

Niles, John D. 2007a. *Beowulf and Lejre*. Featuring contributions by Tom Christensen and Marijane Osborn. Tempe: Arizona Center for Medieval and Renaissance Studies.

———. 2007b. *Old English Heroic Poetry and the Social Life of Texts*. Turnhout, Belgium: Brepols.

Osborn, Marijane. 1978. "The Great Feud: Scriptural History and Strife in *Beowulf*." *PMLA* 93: 973–81.

———, 1997. "Translations, Versions, Illustrations." Pp. 341–72 in Bjork and Niles, *Handbook*.

Overing, Gillian R., and Marijane Osborn. 1994. *Landscape of Desire: Partial Stories of the Medieval Scandinavian World*. Minneapolis: University of Minnesota Press.

Page, R. I. 1999. *An Introduction to English Runes*. 2d ed. Woodbridge, Suffolk: Boydell.

Pedersen, Anne. 1997. "Søllested—nye oplysninger om et velkendt fund." Pp. 37–111 in *Aarbøger for Nordisk Oldkyndighed og Historie 1996*. Copenhagen: Det Kongelige Nordiske Oldskriftselskab.

Peirce, Ian. 2002. *Swords of the Viking Age*. Woodbridge, Suffolk: Boydell Press.

Pollington, Stephen. 2001. *The English Warrior from the Earliest Times till 1066*. 2nd ed. Hockwold-cum-Wilton, Norfolk: Anglo-Saxon Books.

Rahtz, Philip. 1979. *The Saxon and Medieval Palaces at Cheddar*. BAR British Series 65. Oxford: British Archaeological Reports.

Rauer, Christine. 2000. *Beowulf and the Dragon: Parallels and Analogues*. Cambridge: D. S. Brewer.

Rausing, Gad. 1967. *The Bow*. Acta archaeologica Lundensia, series in 8°, no. 6. Lund, Sweden: Gleerup.

Rieck, Flemming. 2003. "The Ships from Nydam Bog." Pp. 296–309 in Jørgensen et al., *The Spoils of Victory*.

Ringler, Dick. 2006. *Beowulf, The Complete Story: A Drama*. Produced by Norman Gilliland. Audio CD. Madison: NEMO Publications.

Rolfson, Perry, and Frans-Arne Stylegar, eds. 2003. *Snartemofunnene i nytt lyss*. Universitets kulturhistoriske museer skrifter 2. Oslo: University Museum of Cultural Heritage.

Saxo Grammaticus. 1970. *Danmarks Riges Krønike*. 3 vol. With woodcuts by Sigurd Vasegaard. Trans.

Jørgen Olrik. Copenhagen: Gyldendal.

Schön, Matthias D. 1999. *Feddersen Wierde, Fallward, Flögeln*. Bad Bederkesa, Germany: Museum Burg Bederkesa.

Shetelig, Haakon, and Hjalmar Falk. 1937. *Scandinavian Archaeology*. Trans. E. V. Gordon. Oxford: Clarendon.

Shippey, T. A. 1978. *Beowulf*. London: Edward Arnold.

Sjøvold, Thorleif. 1979. *The Viking Ships in Oslo*. Oslo: Universitetets Oldsaksamling.

Skre, Dagfinn, ed. 2007. *Kaupang in Skiringssal*. Oslo: University Museum of Cultural Heritage.

Speake, George. 1980. *Anglo-Saxon Animal Art and Its Germanic Background*. Oxford: Clarendon.

Stjerna, Knut. 1912. *Essays on Questions Connected with the Old English Poem of Beowulf*. Trans. and ed. John R. Clark Hall. Viking Club Extra Series, 3. Coventry: Viking Society for Northern Research.

Stolpe, Hjalmar, and T. J. Arne. 1927. *La Nécropole de Vendel*. Stockholm: B. Lagerstrom.

Sørensen, Anne C. 2001. *Ladby: A Danish Ship-Grave from the Viking Age*. Roskilde, Denmark: Viking Ship Museum.

Thorvildsen, Knud. 1957. *Ladby-Skibet*. Copenhagen: Lynge og Søn.

Thrane, Henrik. 1993. *Guld, guder og godtfolk: et magtcentrum fra jernaldereen ved Gudme og Lundeborg*. Copenhagen: National Museum of Denmark.

Tolkien, J. R. R. 1936. "*Beowulf*: The Monsters and the Critics." *Proceedings of the British Academy* 22: 245–95.

Tweddle, Dominic. 1992. *The Anglian Helmet from 16–22 Coppergate*. The Archaeology of York, vol. 17. London: Council for British Archaeology.

Tyler, Elizabeth M., ed. 2000. *Treasure in the Medieval West*. Woodbridge, Suffolk: York Medieval Press.

Underwood, Richard. 1999. *Anglo-Saxon Weapons and Warfare*. Stroud, Gloucestershire: Tempus.

Webster, Leslie. 1998. "Archaeology and *Beowulf*." Pp. 182–94 in *Beowulf: An Edition with Relevant Shorter Texts*, ed. Bruce Mitchell and Fred C. Robinson. Oxford: Blackwell.

Webster, Leslie, and Janet Backhouse, eds. 1991. *The Making of England: Anglo-Saxon Art and Culture AD 600–900*. London: British Museum.

Wenham, S. J. 1989. "Anatomical Interpretations of Anglo-Saxon Weapon Injuries." Pp. 123–39 in *Weapons and Warfare in Anglo-Saxon England*, ed. Sonia Chadwick Hawkes. Oxford: Oxford University Committee for Archaeology.

Wilson, David M. 1964. *Anglo-Saxon Ornamental Metalwork 700–1100 in the British Museum*. London: British Museum.

CREDITS FOR ILLUSTRATIONS

Page 2: Ladby ship, model by Vibeke Bischof, photo by Werner Karrasch, ©Viking Ship Museum, Denmark. **4:** Lejre hall site, photo by Flemming Rasmussen, © Roskilde Museum, Denmark. **6:** Sutton Hoo lyre replica, © British Museum, London, by permission of the Trustees of The British Museum. **8:** Cannibalistic giant, © British Library, London. **10:** Feddersen Wierde throne, © Museum Burg Bederkesa, Germany. **12:** Gold figurine, © National Museum of Denmark, Copenhagen. **14 top:** Skuldelev 5, watercolor by Flemming Bau, © Viking Ship Museum, Denmark. **14 bottom:** Architecture of a replica of Skuldelev 5, drawing by Søren Nielsen, © Viking Ship Museum, Denmark. **16:** Vimose spearhead, © National Museum of Denmark, Copenhagen. **18:** Veggerslev horse, © National Museum of Denmark, Copenhagen. **20:** Benty Grange boar, © Sheffield Museums and Galleries Trust, U.K. **22:** Kragehul spears, drawing by Conrad Engelhardt, © National Museum of Denmark, Copenhagen. **24:** Lejre hoard, photo by John Lee, © National Museum of Denmark, Copenhagen. **26:** Thorsbjerg shield, © National Museum of Denmark, Copenhagen. **28:** Franks casket, © British Museum, London, by permission of the Trustees of The British Museum. **30:** Broholm hoard, © National Museum of Denmark, Copenhagen. **32:** Himlingøje beaker, photo by L. Larsen, © National Museum of Denmark, Copenhagen. **34:** Sea-beast from River Schelde, © British Museum, London, by permission of the Trustees of The British Museum. **36:** Photo © Emily Niles. **38:** Desborough necklace, © British Museum, London, by permission of the Trustees of The British Museum. **40:** Taplow beakers, © British Museum, London, by permission of the Trustees of The British Museum. **42:** Lundeborg gold plaques, © National Museum of Denmark, Copenhagen. **42 inset:** Helgö gold plaque, photo by Gunnel Jansson, Museum of National Antiquities, Stockholm, Sweden. **44:** Photo © John D. Niles. **46:** Demon at hell mouth, © British Library, London. **48:** Architecture of the Lejre hall, drawings by Holger Schmidt, © National Museum of Denmark, Copenhagen.

Page 50: Smith's tools from Mästermyr, photo by Christer Åhlin, © Museum of National Antiquities, Stockholm, Sweden. **52:** Hardware, photo by Flemming Rasmussen, © Roskilde Museum, Denmark. **54:** Photo © John D. Niles. **56:** "Iron Age" riders, photo by Ole Malling, © Historical-Archaeological Research Centre, Lejre, Denmark. **58:** Sigurd runestone, photo by Bengt A. Lundberg, © National Heritage Board, Stockholm, Sweden. **60:** Computer drawing of Lejre hall, © Nicolai Garhøj Larsen and Eyecadger Media. **62:** Scene of judgment, © British Library, London. **64:** Snartemo braid, photo by Eirik Irgens, © Museum of Cultural Heritage, University of Oslo, Norway. **66:** Vendel 12 helmet, © Museum of National Antiquities, Stockholm, Sweden. **68:** Lejre torque, photo by Flemming Rasmussen, © Roskilde Museum, Denmark. **70:** Lillesø rings, © National Museum of Denmark, Copenhagen. **74:** Pattern-welded blades, from Lorange 1889, plate VI. **76:** "Iron Age" village, photo by Ole Malling, © Historical-Archaeological Research Centre, Lejre, Denmark. **78:** Pattern-welded blade, © British Museum, London, by permission of the Trustees of The British Museum. **80 top:** Strårup ring, © National Museum of Denmark, Copenhagen. **80 bottom:** Roskilde bracteate, © Roskilde Museum, Denmark. **82:** Öland necklace, © Museum of National Antiquities, Stockholm, Sweden. **84:** Iron Age hall at Lejre, computer graphic by Niels Valentin Dal, © Roskilde Museum. **86:** Galsted ornament, © National Museum of Denmark, Copenhagen. **88, 90:** Photos © John D. Niles. **92 left:** Sutton Hoo stag and scepter, © British Museum, London, by permission of the Trustees of The British Museum. **92 right:** Feddersen Wierde footstool, © Museum Burg Bederkesa, Germany. **94:** Søllested saddlebows, © National Museum of Denmark, Copenhagen. **96:** Photo © John D. Niles. **98:** Oseberg ship's figurehead, photo by Eirik Irgens, © Museum of Cultural Heritage, University of Oslo, Norway.

Page 100 left: Coombe sword, from Kemble 1863, p. 202 (detail). **100 right**: Hilt of Coombe sword, from Davidson and Webster 1967, p. 14, © Society for Medieval Archaeology, rpt. by permission of the Council of the Society for Medieval Archaeology. **102**: Vimose byrnie, © National Museum of Denmark, Copenhagen. **102 inset**: Drawing of Vimose mail, from Engelhardt 1867, plate 2 (detail). **104**: Belgrade dagger, © National Museum of Denmark, Copenhagen. **106**: Photo © Mike Bailey, Blue Rock Photography LLC. **108, 110**: Photos © John D. Niles. **112**: Ultuna hilt, from Hildebrand 1873, plate II. **114 left**: Chessel Down hilt, from Hawkes and Page 1967, p. 5 (detail), © Society of Antiquaries of London **114 top right**: Chessel Down scabbard mouthpiece, from Hawkes and Page 1967, p. 5 (detail), © Society of Antiquaries of London. **114 bottom right**: Guilton pommel, © British Museum, London, by permission of the Trustees of The British Museum. **116**: God in majesty, © Trinity College Library, Cambridge, U.K. **118**: Uglemosen skull, © National Museum of Denmark, Copenhagen. **120 top**: Replica of Oseberg bed, photo by Eirik Irgens, © Museum of Cultural Heritage, University of Oslo, Norway. **120 bottom**: Drawing of Gokstad headboard, from Brøgger et al. 1917, vol. 3, p. 215 (fig. 206, detail). **122, 124**: Photos © John D. Niles. **126 top**: Vimose equestrian trappings, © National Museum of Denmark, Copenhagen. **126 bottom**: Equestrian trappings from Illerup Ådal, Jutland, from Carnap-Bornheim and Ilkjær 1990–96, vol. 5, p. 266, fig. 198, © Aarhus University Press. **128**: The Helge Ask, photo by Werner Karrasch, © Viking Ship Museum, Denmark. **130**: Trelleborg hall, photo © Randolph Swearer. **132**: Trelleborg hall interior, photo © Randolph Swearer. **134**: Taplow horns, © British Museum, London, by permission of the Trustees of The British Museum. **136**: Eagle brooches, © Walters Art Museum, Baltimore. **138**: Woodcut by Sigurd Vasegaard, © Gyldendal Publishers. **140**: Trossingen lyre, photos by Manuela Schreiner, replica by Rainer Thurau, © Archäologisches Landesmuseum Baden-Württemberg, Germany. **142**: Photo © John D. Niles. **144**: Faversham brooch, © British Museum, London, by permission of the Trustees of The British Museum. **146**: Snartemo sword, photos by Eirik Irgens, © Museum of Cultural Heritage, University of Oslo, Norway. **148**: Chambered tomb, from Hoernes 1892, p. 302.

Page 150: Rillaton cup, © British Museum, London, by permission of the Trustees of The British Museum. **152** : Rune-inscribed ornament, © British Museum, London, by permission of the Trustees of The British Museum. **154**: Dragon ornament from Sutton Hoo shield, © British Museum, London, by permission of the Trustees of The British Museum. **156**: Thatched house aflame, photo by Ole Malling, © Historical-Archaeological Research Centre, Lejre. **158**: Vendel 14 helmet, from Stolpe and Arne 1927, plate XLI. **160**: Old Uppsala mounds, painting by C.J. Billmark, © Uppsala University Library. **162**: Archer, photo by Ole Malling, © Historical-Archaeological Research Centre, Lejre. **164**: Tollund man, photo by L. Larsen, © National Museum of Denmark, Copenhagen. **166**: Valsgärde 8 helmet, © Museum of National Antiquities, Stockholm, Sweden. **168**: Øm Jættestue, Photo © John D. Niles. **170**: Øm Jættestue interior, Photo © John D. Niles. **172**: Sutton Hoo helmet, © British Museum, London, by permission of the Trustees of The British Museum. **174**: Sutton Hoo hilt, © British Museum, London, by permission of the Trustees of The British Museum. **176**: Coppergate helmet, © York Archaeological Trust. **178**: Dragon fight, © Bibliothèque Municipale de Dijon, France; page from Beowulf MS, © British Library, London. **180**: Thames scramasax, © British Museum, London, by permission of the Trustees of The British Museum. **182**: Midskov hoard, © National Museum of Denmark, Copenhagen. **184**: Leuna grave goods, photo by Andrea Hörentrup, © Landesamt für Denkmalpflege und Archäologie Sachsen-Anhalt, Halle, Germany. **186**: Bohuslän outlook, photo © Randolph Swearer. **188 top**: Öland fibula, from Stjerna 1912, p. 161. **188 middle**: Dragon-head design from the Coppergate helmet, © York Archaeological Trust. **188 bottom:** Zoomorphic ornament, from B-Mitford vol. 3, part 1, p. 359 (fig. 261), © British Museum, London. **190**: Replica of Sutton Hoo helmet, © British Museum, London, by permission of the Trustees of The British Museum. **192, 196**: Woodcuts by Sigurd Vasegaard, © Gyldendal Publishers. **198 top**: Vendel 1 helmet plaque, from Montelius 1888, p. 140. **198 bottom**: Birdlike mounts, © British Museum, London, by permission of the Trustees of The British Museum.

Page 200: Seddin grave goods, photo by Klaus Göken, © Museum für Vor- und Frühgeschichte, Staatliche Museen zu Berlin, Germany. **202**: Rune-inscribed cranium, © National Museum of Denmark, Copenhagen. **204**: Nydam arrows, © National Museum of Denmark, Copenhagen. **206**: Smederup hoard, © National Museum of Denmark, Copenhagen. **208**: Skelhøj mound, Zealand, photo © John Jedbo.

ACKNOWLEDGEMENTS FOR ILLUSTRATIONS

This illustrated edition could not have been produced without the generous personal assistance of many individuals on both sides of the Atlantic. Among museum, library, and institute staff who have been helpful in my efforts to secure photographs, I wish particularly to thank the following: Morten Axboe, Lars Jørgensen, and Helga Schütze of the National Museum of Denmark, Copenhagen; Tom Christensen and Flemming Rasmussen of Roskilde Museum, Denmark; Mette Seir Nicolajsen of the Historical-Archaeological Research Centre, Lejre, Denmark; Ole Crumlin-Pedersen and Rikke Johansen of the Viking Ship Museum, Roskilde, Denmark; Laura Loiborg of Gyldendal Publishers, Copenhagen, Denmark; Ulla Eriksen of Silkeborg Museum, Denmark; Jens Kirkeby of the Institut for Antropologi, Arkæologi og Lingvistik, Højbjerg, Denmark; Siv Falk of the Museum of National Antiquities, Stockholm, Sweden; Rose-Marie Bjuhr of the National Heritage Board, Stockholm, Sweden; Bo Jænsson of Uppsala University Library, Sweden; Elizabeth Jansen Vogt of the Museum of Cultural Heritage, the University of Oslo, Norway; Dr. Matthias D. Schön of Museum Burg Bederkesa, Germany; Dr. Barbara Theune-Großkopf of the Archäologisches Landesmuseum Baden-Württemberg, Germany; Dr. Bettina Stoll-Tucker of the Landesamt für Denkmalpflege und Archäologie Sachsen-Anhalt, Halle, Germany; Dr. Heino Neumayer of the Museum für Vor- und Frühgeschichte, Staatliche Museen zu Berlin, Germany; Caroline Poulin of the Bibliothèque Municipale de Dijon, France; Angela Care Evans, Julie Mearns, and Jim Rossiter of the British Museum, London, U.K.; Martin Mintz and Christine Campbell of the British Library, London, U.K.; Joanna Ball of Trinity College Library, Cambridge, U.K.; Catherine Kendall of Sheffield Galleries & Museums Trust, Sheffield, U.K.; and Christine Kyriacou of the York Archaeological Trust, York, U.K. I am particularly indebted to Ole Malling for photos relating to the Lejre Historical-Archaeological Research Centre, to

Nicolai Garhøj Larsen for his computer graphic of the Lejre hall, to Randolph Swearer for three photos from his personal archive, to Benjamin Slade for an electronic collage from his website, to Mike Bailey for "Eye of the Sun," and to John Jedbo for the sunset photo on page 208. Additional courtesies were extended by John Hines, Marijane Osborn, and Dick Ringler. My greatest debt is to Amy Cherry, my editor at W. W. Norton, for her enthusiasm in sponsoring this project and her skilled help at every turn.

J.D.N.